Inside Greenwich Village

Inside
Greenwich Village

A NEW YORK CITY

NEIGHBORHOOD,

1898–1918

Gerald W. McFarland

University of Massachusetts Press

AMHERST

Copyright © 2001 by University of Massachusetts Press
All rights reserved
Printed in the United States of America
LC 00-054393
ISBN 1-55849-299-2
Designed by Jack Harrison
Set in Janson Text with Mistral display by Graphic Composition, Inc.
Printed and bound by Sheridan Books, Inc.

Library of Congress Cataloging-in-Publication Data

McFarland, Gerald W., 1938–
   Inside Greenwich Village : a New York City neighborhood, 1898–1918 / Gerald W.
McFarland.
       p. cm.
   Includes bibliographical references (p.) and index.
   ISBN 1-55849-299-2 (alk. paper)
   1. Greenwich Village (New York, N.Y.)—History—20th century.
   2. Greenwich Village (New York, N.Y.)—Social conditions—20th century.
   3. Greenwich Village (New York, N.Y.)—Ethnic relations.
   4. New York (N.Y.)—History—1898–1951.
   5. New York (N.Y.)—Social conditions—20th century.
   6. New York (N.Y.)—Ethnic relations.
   7. Minorities—New York (State)—New York—History—20th century.
   8. Social classes—New York (State)—New York—History—20th century.
I. Title.

F128.68.G8 M37 2001
305.8′009747′1—dc21
                                    00-054393

British Library Cataloguing in Publication data are available.

Title page: Washington Arch, ca. 1905. Milstein Division of United States History,
Local History and Genealogy, The New York Public Library, Astor, Lenox and Tilden
Foundations.

WITH APPRECIATION TO

Marguerite McFarland
Alice McFarland
L. E. Janzow
Jack Hillis
Adrienne Koch
Kenneth M. Stampp
Robert D. Cross
Eric L. McKitrick
Howard H. Quint
Dorothy Schalk
Shunryu Suzuki
Bruce Teague
Issho Fujita
Wilhelmina Van Ness
Dorothy J. McFarland

CONTENTS

ILLUSTRATIONS

FIGURES

MAPS

PREFACE

Most books about twentieth-century Greenwich Village history focus on the artists, writers, and cultural radicals whose activities brought the Village international fame as America's bohemia. Other residents of the Village, if mentioned at all, are discussed only in relation to the bohemian Villagers. This book reverses those priorities. Although the artists, writers, and radicals who lived in the Village between the turn of the century and World War I are described in some detail, the bulk of the text explores the lives of the nonbohemian Villagers.

I came to this contrarian focus out of a combination of curiosity and expediency. I have for some time now enjoyed researching topics that were well rooted in places that are, to some extent, still visible to the present-day visitor, and Greenwich Village suited my purposes because, for all the changes in its social geography, many streets, buildings, and institutions survive to the present. I was also drawn to the topic by the great diversity of the Village's population—a diversity largely invisible in studies that begin and end with the story of the tiny group of cultural radicals who lived in the neighborhood. I wondered how neighbors from such diverse classes and ethnic groups coexisted in a relatively small geographical area.

The practical or expedient aspect of my choice of topic arose from my hunch (which proved to be accurate) that the Village's long existence as an identifiable entity meant that I could find ample primary source material on its history. Indeed, a treasure trove of largely unexplored sources came to my attention: records of community groups (the Washington Square Association, Charity Organization Society, People's Institute), the papers of Village social settlements (Greenwich House and Richmond Hill House), church archives (mainly the Church of the Ascension, Our Lady of Pompei, and St. Joseph's), and materials on African American Villagers. I also did extensive research in the manuscript collections of well-known Villagers who were part of *The Masses*, Liberal Club, and Dodge Salon circles, and while giving those famous Villagers their due, I made it my goal to provide a more inclusive portrait of life inside Greenwich Village than had any previous history of the neighborhood in the early twentieth century.

I am grateful for the support I received from institutions and individuals. A Samuel F. Conti Faculty Fellowship Award from the University of Massachusetts Research Council gave me a year-long leave and got my project off to a good start in 1992–1993, and a research grant from the American Philosophical Society helped me in the project's final phase. I received invaluable suggestions from Lois Banner, James Boylan, Daniel Czitrom, Dorothy McFarland, Lois Rudnick, and Jack Tager, who read the entire manuscript, and Steven Watson, who read the later sections. The final product is immensely better for their advice to me. Kate Blackmer did splendid work in designing and producing maps for the book.

GERALD W. MCFARLAND
Leverett, Massachusetts

Inside Greenwich Village

The Latter Days of the Sixth Village

For MOST of its early history, Greenwich Village was physically separate from New York City, the metropolis that now surrounds and merges with it on all sides except on its western boundary, the Hudson River. During its long evolution from a separate settlement to a twentieth-century urban neighborhood, the Village went through a series of distinct phases. Each phase was so distinctive that the writer Floyd Dell, who lived in the neighborhood in the mid-1910s, identified seven historical Villages, each of which had been, like the "ancient cities which Schliemann dug up" at Troy, superimposed on its predecessors. The first four villages on Dell's list were those that had stood some distance north of the early city: the Indian settlement of Sappocanican, the Dutch farming district of Bossen Bouwerie, the English colonial village of Green Wich, and the American suburb of Greenwich, which in the early nineteenth century still had a buffer of open fields and scattered farms between itself and the rapidly advancing northern outskirts of the city's thickly settled parts.[1]

During the fifth of Dell's archaeological epochs, the Washington Square era, dense urban settlement reached the Village and, in a process that took several decades, roughly from the 1830s through the 1850s, began to surround it. Having lost its separate status, the Village became a West Side neighborhood bounded by the Hudson River, on the north by Fourteenth Street, on the east by University Place and West Broadway, and to the south below Houston Street by Charlton and Prince (map 1). In the pre–Civil War period the Washington Square section of the Village became a prime location for handsome houses occupied by some of the city's wealthiest families. The greater part of the Village, however, was home to thousands of working- and middle-class New Yorkers.[2]

The class and ethnic heterogeneity of Greenwich Village's population became even more pronounced during the sixth of Dell's Villages, which lasted from the 1860s to the early 1910s. Dell, an intellectual and a cultural radical, was interested primarily in his beloved Seventh Village, the bohemian enclave to which he moved in 1913 (the first full year of its preeminence), and he had almost nothing to say of its immediate predecessor. The Sixth Village era he dismissed in a single phrase as a time when the neighborhood was "left to decay into a picturesque twentieth-century slum."[3]

Subsequent historians have filled in the picture somewhat, and several have suggested, without much elaboration, that the nearly half-century of the Sixth Village's existence can be divided into two fairly distinct phases: an "American Ward" period from the 1860s to 1890 and a "Real Village" era (1890–1910). During the first phase Greenwich Village was called the "American Ward" because it had the highest percentage of native-born citizens of any ward in the city. Although factually accurate, this description implies much more ethnic homogeneity among Village residents than actually existed. Even in 1875, the midpoint of the American Ward era, approximately one-third of Villagers were foreign-born, and many others were second generation Americans, the children of immigrants from various western European countries.[4]

In the second half of the Sixth Village's existence, between 1890 and the early 1910s, the neighborhood's foreign-born population increased dramatically. Italian immigrants arrived by the thousands and crowded into the five- and six-story tenement buildings that were rapidly replacing the older one- and two-family homes south of Washington Square. Concurrent with the arrival of Italian immigrants was an invasion of the Village from the south and east by industrial and commercial establishments. Block after block that had once been exclusively residential was now occupied by factories that produced clothing, boxes, candy, and artificial flowers.

In the large body of literature available on Greenwich Village, almost no accounts have focused exclusively on the Sixth Village era. More often, the Sixth Village is mentioned only in relation to one of two other subjects, either the emergence of the bohemian Village or the history of some ethnic or class subgroup within the neighborhood. The first approach, by far the most popular, resembles Dell's in subordinating everything else to the story of how the Seventh Village came into being. Within this rise-of-bohemia

MAP 1. Greater Greenwich Village, 1900.

1. Patchin Place
2. Gay Street
3. Clinton Court
4. MacDougal Alley
5. Washington Mews
6. Washington Square West
7. Washington Square East
8. Minetta Lane
9. Minetta Street
10. Congress Street
11. Charles Lane
12. Weehawken Street

framework, little is said about the prebohemian Village except that it was a shabby, mixed-ethnic district whose quaint old houses, irregular street patterns, and cheap rental properties attracted artists and writers to the neighborhood. The strength of this approach is its tightly focused and dramatic story line; its weakness lies in its failure to provide a satisfactory description of the nonbohemian Villagers, who are treated as largely irrelevant to the history of cultural radicalism's rise and fall.[5]

A second source of information about the Sixth Village may be found in sociological studies that give extensive attention to the nonbohemian Villagers. Most such works are limited in scope, analyzing the history of a single ethnic or class subgroup within the Village. A more inclusive approach is evident in *Greenwich Village: Culture and Counterculture*, an anthology edited by Rick Beard and Leslie Cohen Berlowitz that contains essays on Villagers, bohemians and nonbohemians alike, from colonial times to the present. Although much useful information about the Sixth Village can be gleaned from this anthology, the fact remains that, like most histories of Greenwich Village, it does not attempt to outline in a systematic way the Sixth Village's central features. Only one book—Caroline Ware's justly acclaimed 1935 classic, *Greenwich Village, 1920–1930: A Comment on American Civilization in the Post-War Years*—takes as its sole focus a comprehensive description of Villagers from all classes and ethnic groups in the early twentieth century. Even Ware's book, however, falls short as a source on the Sixth Village era. As Ware's subtitle indicates, her principle concern was to analyze Village life in the 1920s. For that reason the pre–World War I Village figures mainly as a prelude to the Jazz Age Village, a topical focus that necessarily limits its usefulness as a portrait of the prewar Village.

The last years of the Sixth Village deserve more attention. The history of both the place and the time raises compelling questions. Here was a place where diverse class and ethnic groups lived in close proximity. How did these Villagers—working- and middle-class blacks, Italians, and Irish; middle-class social workers, artists, and writers; and upper-class Protestants—relate to one another in the neighborhood they shared? Moreover, what impact did the period (the so-called Progressive Era) and the extraordinary changes it brought in the American urban scene have on the neighborhood and its diverse inhabitants?

Nearly all scholars who have applied the two traditional approaches to the pre–World War I Village recognize that the neighborhood's population was very diverse. Most, however, devote little effort to investigating either how the neighborhood was changing just before the bohemian era began or how the Sixth Village's various ethnic and class subgroups related to one another. The rise-of-bohemia approach is particularly deficient in this respect, as its practitioners mention the existence of many class and ethnic groups within the Village without devoting significant attention to any group except the cultural radicals. This leaves it unclear what the vast majority of the Villagers were doing during a period of tumultuous change early in the twentieth century. Specialized studies of nonbohemian Villagers (most often of south Village Italians or of Washington Square North patricians) have filled in some gaps, though usually without any discussion of how members of each group related to neighbors from other ethnic and class backgrounds.

One partial exception is Ware's *Greenwich Village*. Although her focus is mainly on Village life in the 1920s, she ventures some provocative comparative statements about the distinctly different way Villagers of various types related to one another in the prewar and postwar periods. She asserts that the Jazz Age Village had, by 1930, "ceased to be a 'neighborhood' in anything but name." The prewar Sixth Village had been characterized by more community spirit and more social intimacy among Village residents.[6]

The stark contrast Ware draws between the Jazz Age Village and the prewar Sixth Village needs to be tested against the facts of neighborhood life before World War I. For a significant degree of social intimacy to have existed between neighbors as diverse as south Village blacks and Italians, west Village Irish, and north Village patricians (to name four of the most numerically prominent groups in the population of the turn-of-the-century Village), huge barriers posed by ethnic and class differences would have had to be overcome. Ware, who was deeply dismayed by what she viewed as the fragmenting impact of modern urban conditions on family and neighborhood cohesion, was impressed by the stories some old-timers among her informants told of earlier times when a spirit of easygoing neighborliness had existed in the Village. But what social realities underlay that remembered past?

An analysis of the Village's heterogeneous population, interesting in its own right, is also relevant to current debates about the strengths and weaknesses of America's multicultural society. The 1980s and 1990s witnessed a larger influx of immigrants to the United States than any time since the pre–World War I period, and many of the newcomers were nonwhites. Conservative social critics responded with cries of alarm, asserting that America's increasingly diverse population was likely to do irreparable harm to the nation's social fabric. Yet these jeremiads largely ignored the country's long experience as a multicultural society. The percentage of foreign-born residents in the United States was much higher just before World War I than in the 1990s, but the nation and its ethnically heterogeneous cities somehow survived and even flourished under those conditions in the early

1900s. As possibly the most socially heterogeneous neighborhood in a socially diverse metropolis, the Sixth Village is a veritable laboratory for investigating how a culturally diverse neighborhood functioned early in the
twentieth century.

The evolution of class and ethnic relations within the Sixth Village was
strongly influenced by progressivism, as the reformist spirit of the time was
called. Progressivism expressed itself in diverse and at times seemingly contradictory ways. Progressive reformers responded in conservative, coercive
ways to the moral issues raised by prostitution, Sunday consumption of alcoholic beverages, new and more sensual dance styles, and movies that had
sexually explicit or unpatriotic content. Typically, these attempts to shape
public morality were campaigns in which the mostly middle- and upper-
class (and often Protestant) reformers set out to impose social controls on
working-class Catholics and Jews, many of them recent immigrants, who
engaged in activities that the reformers regarded as vices.

Many progressives, however, including some of the same individuals who
supported anti-vice crusades, also believed that the new century brought
with it tremendous opportunities for social peace and economic prosperity
if only Americans would reach out to each other across class and ethnic
lines. In Greenwich Village this socially progressive credo led some middle-
and upper-class Villagers to devote themselves to trying to improve the lot
of their less privileged neighbors. Although the precise nature of these
cross-class initiatives differed from case to case, their extraordinary variety—social settlement reform, feminism, socialism, labor unionism, and
housing reform, among others—reflect the expansive spirit with which
many early twentieth-century Americans pursued the cause of social betterment.

Even those Villagers who did not consciously align themselves with specific reform causes—and there were many—could scarcely avoid the impact of broader social and economic changes that were transforming American life at the turn of the century. The Villagers of 1898 still lived in the
age of the horse, but by the mid-1910s automobiles were a commonplace
sight in the neighborhood's streets. Women's suffrage had received almost
no public attention from Villagers in late 1890s, but from 1910 onward
pro-suffrage paraders by the thousands regularly launched their votes-for-
women marches up Fifth Avenue from Washington Square. Few Villagers
concerned themselves much with U.S. foreign policy in 1900, despite a recent minor war with Spain, but American participation in World War I,
though of relatively brief duration (April 1917–November 1918), touched
Villagers much more deeply, with some playing notable roles in opposing
the war and a larger number supporting it.

Between 1898 and 1918, ragtime dances replaced the waltz in popularity, the first World Series and the first Rose Bowl game were played, a black boxer became the U.S. heavyweight champion, Stanford White was murdered by a jealous husband, the Titanic sank while the band played on, the Wright brothers launched their heavier-than-air machine at Kitty Hawk, Theodore Roosevelt used the presidency as a bully pulpit from which to name the muckrakers and then to condemn muckraking journalism, a new constitutional amendment authorized a federal income tax, the Socialist Party's candidate won nearly six percent of the vote in a presidential election, and Freudianism and Cubism arrived in America. The cumulative impact of these events on life inside Greenwich Village was nothing short of profound.

1

Neighbors and Strangers

In the summer of 1898 Neith Boyce, a young journalist who worked for the *New York Commercial Advertiser*, lived in a tiny room in the Judson Hotel, an economical boardinghouse on the south side of Greenwich Village's Washington Square (map 2). Coming home from work, Boyce would take the Sixth Avenue elevated train uptown to the Bleecker Street station and walk three blocks to her hotel. Once there, she often stopped in at the room of one of two other Judson residents who, like herself, were young women who had begun careers in the overwhelmingly male profession of newspaper journalism. Boyce and her friends—Marie Manning, author of the *New York Evening Journal*'s immensely popular Beatrice Fairfax advice column, and Olivia Dunbar of the *New York World*—would have a cigarette together (a symbol of their status as emancipated women) and laugh and talk about their day's work. Not infrequently that summer, these pleasant tête-à-têtes were cut short when Boyce excused herself to get ready to go out to dinner with her suitor, Hutchins Hapgood.

Hapgood, also a writer for the *Commercial Advertiser*, but older and better established in the profession than Boyce, had been courting her for almost six months. A self-described "intellectual and esthetic adventurer," Hapgood enjoyed introducing Boyce to his favorite haunts south and east of Washington Square: Yiddish theaters on the Lower East Side, puppet shows in Little Italy, and tough Bowery dives such as Chuck Connor's. Tonight, however, the next day in this hypothetical account being a workday, they content themselves with dinner at the Black Cat, a nearby Bleecker Street bohemian hangout.[1]

On leaving the restaurant after dinner, Boyce and Hapgood stroll through the immigrant and working-class parts of the Village near the restaurant. They are rewarded with sights and sounds that reflect the variety of ethnic communities to be found within a few minutes' walk from Washington Square. From their starting point at the Black Cat, they proceed west on Bleecker, a south Village street that even at this evening hour is crowded with vendors and pedestrians, most of them Italian immigrants. Three blocks west of the restaurant they cross MacDougal and begin to see increasing numbers of black Villagers, most of them African Americans but some West Indians too, who live on Minetta Street, Minetta Lane, or nearby. After another two blocks they reach Carmine Street, near the southern terminus of Sixth Avenue (it was extended farther south in the 1920s).

At this point they enter the edge of the west Village, an area occupied by various ethnic groups of European extraction but dominated by the Irish. Just ahead to their left is the east end of Leroy Street, whose Irish residents include representatives of every wave of immigration from the Emerald Isle to New York City over the past seventy years. Some are families whose older members came to the United States in the mid-nineteenth century and whose ownership of handsome row houses on a one-block section of Leroy, known as St. Luke's Place, offer clear testimony to their inhabitants' rise to substantial middle-class status. West of St. Luke's Place, however, are several blocks of tenement houses whose occupants are mainly working-class Irish, many of whom have only recently arrived in the States from their native land. But Boyce and Hapgood do not have time this evening to explore more of the Irish west Village; instead they turn right on Cornelia and then east on West Fourth Street, a route that sets them on their way back to the Judson. Their round-trip walk of barely ten blocks has taken them through a succession of ethnic enclaves representative of the Village's diverse population.

Neith Boyce and Hutch Hapgood were eager observers of the richly varied ethnic life of Lower Manhattan's immigrant districts, which include the south and west parts of the Village. Although their relatively high educational and occupational status meant that they had very little in common with working-class Villagers, the two journalists (Hapgood in particular) were deeply interested in the lives of Italian, Irish, and black Villagers whom they passed daily on the streets. Most working-class Villagers, however, did not share this cosmopolitan outlook toward neighbors outside their own respective ethnic group. Such contact did take place—on blocks

—Blackmer—

or in buildings that had residents from diverse ethnic backgrounds, in mixed-race saloons, in occasional attempts at political cooperation, and, most intimately, in mixed marriages—but it was the exception rather than the rule. Generally speaking, Italian, Irish, and black Villagers congregated in blocks and buildings where most residents were members of their particular ethnic group. Segregation along ethnic lines was also reflected in such important social relations as religious practice: Among Village Catholics, the west Village Irish attended Mass at St. Joseph's on Sixth Avenue, and the south Village Italians worshiped at Our Lady of Pompei on Bleecker. White Protestants belonged to white churches, and African American Protestants formed black Methodist and black Baptist congregations. And these lines of religious separation had parallels in every other sphere of daily life. Thus it was that at the turn of the twentieth century, members of the south and west Village's major ethnic groups were both neighbors and, for the most part, strangers.

The Heart of Little Africa

In 1898 the Village was home to one of the largest African American communities in the city. Blacks had lived in the Village ever since the Dutch colonial period, when former slaves first settled in the area. By the mid-1800s there were so many blacks in Greenwich Village that the section where they were concentrated was known as "Little Africa." Throughout much of the late nineteenth century, the total number of blacks in the Village changed little, but this relative numerical stability masked significant demographic shifts taking place the area. From the late 1860s on, many black Villagers moved out of the neighborhood to new residential districts that were becoming available farther uptown, mainly between Fourteenth and Thirty-seventh streets. But the number of African American Villagers was sustained by the arrival of black migrants from the former Confederate states, especially Virginia, and did not immediately show a sharp decline.[2]

Little Africa was only rarely mentioned in the popular literature of the late nineteenth century, and the few writers who did discuss it focused almost exclusively on the area's negative features, mainly squalor and criminality. The newspaperman and housing reformer Jacob Riis, who included a chapter titled "The Color Line in New York" in his best-selling book *How the Other Half Lives* (1890), regarded the Village's Little Africa as the social "bottom" of the narrow corridor on the West Side of Manhattan (the "top" was then at Thirty-second Street) where landlords were willing to rent to blacks. Riis described the dwellings that African Americans occupied on Thompson Street in the south Village as "vile rookeries" that inevitably debased their inhabitants.[3]

Riis was equally critical of an institution found throughout Little Africa's slums: the "black-and-tan saloon," a type of drinking establishment with a mixed-race clientele of poor whites, blacks, and tans (mulattoes). "The moral turpitude of Thompson Street," Riis declared, "has been notorious for years, and the mingling of the three elements does not seem to have wrought any change for the better." Riis saw the black-and-tan saloon as a gathering place for the "utterly depraved of both sexes, white and black," which attracted, as he put it, "all the lawbreakers and all the human wrecks within reach" (fig. 1). Although much of the rest of Riis's chapter on black New Yorkers was devoted to praising the virtues of African Americans in other parts of the city, he left the impression that debauchery was the rule rather than the exception among black Villagers.[4]

The young novelist and reporter Stephen Crane also visited Little Africa in the 1890s. Crane was on the lookout for colorful stories, and he found the neighborhood's unsavory reputation perfect for his purposes. He concentrated his attention on two narrow streets, Minetta Lane and Minetta Street, each of which was only a very short city block in length.

Crane exploited to the fullest the Minettas' notoriety as a dangerous and immoral locale. He wrote with relish about the black toughs—men and women known only by their nicknames, "No-Toe Charley," "Bloodthirsty," "Black-Cat," and "Apple Mag"—whose deeds had contributed to the Minettas' bad reputation. "Bloodthirsty" was a murderer, a large and "very hideous" man, "particularly eloquent when drunk," who wielded a wicked razor. "Black-Cat" was a "famous bandit." "Apple Mag" was a quarrelsome woman who reinforced her verbal assaults with "paving stones, carving knives and bricks." Other denizens of the Minettas such as Pop Babcock and Mammy Ross, old-timers whom Crane used as informants, lived a marginal existence. Mammy Ross passed her final days in a tiny kitchen at the end of a dark hallway in "an old and tottering frame house." Pop Babcock ran a squalid restaurant in a poorly lit room so small that its sparse furnishings— a cooking stove, a table, a bench, and two chairs—scarcely fit in the available space. On the occasion of Crane's visit there, three down-and-out loners were spending the night, one stretched out on the two chairs, a second asleep on the bench, and the third sprawled "on the floor behind the stove."[5]

Murders, knifings, muggings, and other violent acts were commonplace occurrences in the Minettas until the mid-1890s. At that point a reform administration came to power, and the new police commissioner, Theodore Roosevelt, replaced the police captain formerly in command of the local precinct with a hard-nosed law-and-order cop. A crackdown followed and the Minettas calmed down considerably, prompting one old-time Minetta Lane resident to tell Crane: "Why, disher' Lane ain't nohow like what it uster be—no indeed, it ain't. No, sir! My—my, dem times was diff'rent!" Though quieter in 1896 when Crane wrote his sketch, the Minettas were still an impoverished and unsavory place in which a modicum of order was maintained, according to Crane, only through police vigilance: "There is probably no street in New York where the police keep closer watch than they do in Minetta Lane" (fig. 2).[6]

The Riis–Crane portrait of Little Africa was colorful but incomplete. Poverty and wretchedness were abundantly present within Little Africa's borders, yet an exclusive emphasis on those features of the neighborhood produced a seriously distorted picture of life there. Riis, in particular, by focusing on the debauchery he associated with black-and-tan saloons, re-inforced a widespread prejudice of the time, which held that racial mixing always had a deleterious effect on both races and was a sign as well as a source of social decay. But there was more to Little Africa than saloons, or murder and mayhem in the Minettas. At the turn of the twentieth century, approximately twelve hundred blacks lived on west Village streets and alleys near and along lower Sixth Avenue, or on south Village streets in or adja-cent to the Minettas. This large aggregation of black Villagers included many sober and industrious individuals and families, and many of these individuals were associated with well established, prosperous African Amer-ican churches. Conspicuously absent from the Riis–Crane portrait of Little Africa, these individuals and institutions also displayed a stability and ambi-tion that ran counter to the era's popular prejudices about life inside a mixed-race neighborhood.

Had Riis wanted to tell a story about family stability among Little Afri-ca's inhabitants, he might have written about the Morgan J. Austins. This large family not only lived in Riis's black-and-tan district but was itself ra-cially mixed. The family's patriarch, Morgan J. Austin, was an African American born in Charleston, South Carolina, in 1851. The matriarch, An-nie Austin, was a native of Pennsylvania, born in 1865, the daughter of Irish immigrants. Her maiden name was Annie McCormick. Morgan and Annie were married in 1883, probably in New York, since all their children were born there. In 1900, after seventeen years of marriage, Annie had borne ten children, of whom eight, four boys and four girls, had survived and were living with their parents. The eldest was fifteen, the youngest barely eigh-teen months.[7]

In 1900 the Austins were renting an apartment at 101 MacDougal Street, a five-story tenement on the west side of the street midway between Bleecker Street and Minetta Lane. The census taker listed thirteen households at the address: eleven of them had from three to five members each, one household had six members, and the Austins had ten. Other than the Austins, only one was a black family. The rest were headed by Italians, a majority of whom had immigrated to the United States in the last five years.

The Morgan J. Austins appear to have had a higher family income than that of most (if not all) of the Italian Americans in the building. Most of the male heads of the Italian households were day laborers, the least skilled type of work available and consequently the least well paid. A contemporary social worker's survey of working-class incomes in Greenwich Village, Louise Bolard More's *Wage-Earners' Budgets* (1907), listed eight examples of families headed by "casual laborers," only one of whom earned more than $700 in the survey year, while the average income of the remaining seven was barely $450. By contrast, Morgan J. Austin was employed as a waiter, a service job that generally paid much better than unskilled day labor. More's survey listed three black waiters (one of whom, like Austin, had a white wife) who earned $734, $774, and $1,134 respectively.[8]

Although Morgan and Annie Austin had many mouths to feed, a large

1. Thompson Street black-and-tan saloon, photographed by Jacob Riis, ca. 1890. Museum of the City of New York, Jacob A. Riis Collection.

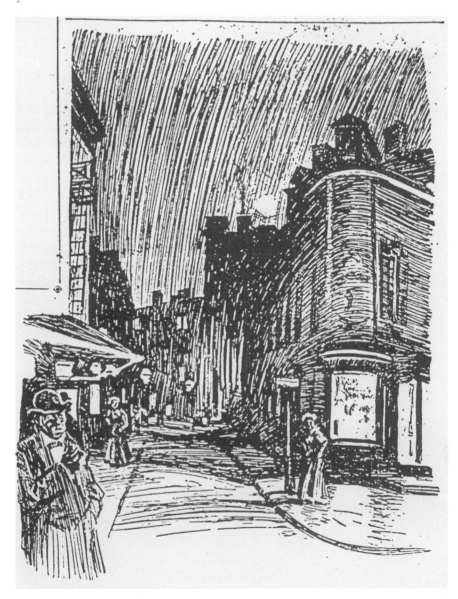

2. Stephen Crane's Minetta Lane at night. From *New York Herald*, December 20, 1896.

family was not necessarily a liability if some or all of the children were old enough to enter the work force. Such was the case with the Austins. In 1900 their oldest child, the fifteen-year-old boy, had already taken a job in a laundry and was thus making a small contribution to the family's income. Sometime during the next ten years the Austins moved to Minetta Lane.

In 1910 their household comprised seventeen individuals from four generations: Annie's mother, Annie and Morgan, all eight of their surviving children, two sons-in-law, three grandchildren, and a lodger. Not only had the
family stayed together, but its combined efforts could now mobilize a significant amount of earning power. In addition to Morgan Austin and the
young male lodger, four of Morgan and Annie's children and both the sons-
in-law were holding down jobs.[9]

Looking more generally at other Minetta Lane residents listed in the
census, even in 1900, ten years before the Austins show up at a Minetta
Lane address, the census takers' inquiries produced quite a different picture
from the one Crane had sketched only four years earlier. Gone in 1900—
either dead or moved away—were Pop Babcock and Mammy Ross. Murderers and bandits, of course, would not have identified themselves as such
and therefore are impossible to identify in the census, and Crane's homeless
loners, if they were still part of the scene, also were not enumerated. But
certain other features of life in the Minettas do come into bold relief in the
census records: the racially mixed character of the local populace, the family
ties that many residents maintained, and the common history that the area's
black population often shared as recent migrants from southern cities to
the North's greatest metropolis.

The attraction of cheap housing had brought a kaleidoscopic array of
ethnic groups into close proximity. This fact is readily apparent from a
quick look at who lived in the buildings on Minetta Lane's north side, eight
residences and a large livery stable. Most occupants of the residences were
either Italians or African Americans, but there were also whites from Germany, Russia, Belgium, and France, and blacks born in Africa, Bermuda,
and Barbados. Racial mixing was the order of the day in most of the buildings and some of the households. Of eight houses or tenements, all but
two—the tiny, two-story number 22, where a black couple lived, and number 16, home to a large Italian American family—had both black and white
occupants. Number 24, the tallest building on the block, was a five-story
tenement containing eleven households; nine were Italian and two were
African American families. Number 2 Minetta Lane, though only three stories tall and on a smaller lot than number 24, was divided into twelve apartments, four occupied by Italian immigrants, six by African Americans, and
two by mixed-race couples. Three other mixed-race couples lived on the
block: two in number 18 and one in number 26.[10]

Information collected by census takers indicated that the mixed-race and
black families of Minetta Lane laid claim to a significant degree of stability
in their marital relationships. Of seven Minetta Lane blacks who listed
Richmond, Virginia, as their birthplace, all reported that they were married

and living with their spouses in 1900. Except for Mary Clayton of 2 Minetta Lane, who had recently married for the second time, these individuals were partners in first marriages that had lasted for many years—no less than nine and as many as twenty-seven. Half of these couples had children living with them, a family configuration that was also found among most of their neighbors of all races in the Minettas. Even though family ties were no sure protection against poverty and despair, it seems fair to say that familial relationships were an important source of mutual aid on which many residents of Minetta Lane relied.[11]

Another fact that census data documents about Minetta Lane blacks in 1900 is that a majority of them were native southerners who had joined in a post–Civil War exodus of African Americans from the former Confederacy. As the seven Richmond, Virginia–born individuals mentioned above illustrate, many of these migrants were from urban rather than farm backgrounds. (At least fifteen more "Richmond Negroes," the label a contemporary scholar gave these blacks once they reached New York City, are listed in the 1900 census at addresses within one block of Minetta Lane.) Using the birthdates of the New York–born children of Minetta Lane's seven "Richmond Negroes" to estimate when their parents left Virginia, it appears that most of them emigrated to the North in the late 1860s or early 1870s, just after emancipation made it possible for former slaves to travel freely. Later in the nineteenth century and on into the twentieth, southern blacks by the tens of thousands followed in the footsteps of these early migrants, creating a mass movement called the Great Migration. Precisely what impact this shared experience had on relationships among Minetta Lane's Richmond-born blacks is not known. However, the large role that friendships and family connections played in the Great Migration is well documented. Undoubtedly, many of the twenty-two Richmond natives residing on or close to Minetta Lane in 1900 were aware of their neighbors' life histories and formed (or, more likely, preserved) bonds of friendship based on that shared past.[12]

Quite a lot is known about Richmond-born blacks in New York City before World War I because they were the subjects of research projects conducted by three Columbia University graduate students working under the direction of Professor Franklin H. Giddings, a distinguished sociologist. None of Giddings's protégés studied Greenwich Village's Richmond-born blacks, but their findings regarding African Americans living farther north on Manhattan's West Side mesh so well with what is known about Minetta Lane's residents that the data may be taken as representative of them as well. For example, Giddings's students reported that the vast majority of Richmond-born blacks worked at unskilled or semiskilled jobs, largely as a consequence of limited educational opportunities and occupational discrimination that excluded blacks from most highly paid work. Six of the former Richmond residents living on Minetta Lane in 1900 clearly conformed to this occupational profile: Annetta Jackson and Lizzie Doran were cooks, William Jackson a domestic servant, Lewis Hamlin a common laborer, Mary Clayton a laundress, and John Young an employee in a laundry. The only possible exception was George Brown, who was the proprietor of a restaurant in the basement of the same run-down, two-story house where Pop Babcock once cooked oysters for derelicts and drifters. Given what is known about Babcock's operation, Brown's entrepreneurial efforts may have given him only marginally higher occupational status than his working-class neighbors.[13]

With regard to the reasons why Richmond-born blacks had moved to New York City, the young Columbia sociologists found that the most frequently cited motivation was hope of economic betterment: the cost of living was higher in New York City, but wages were higher as well. The next most frequently mentioned reason for migrating was the wish to join relatives who had already settled in the city. (A number of informants said that family connections had become even more important to them in New York than they had been in Virginia.) A smaller, though significant, number of Richmond-born blacks indicated that they had been drawn to New York by the city's reputation as a glamorous and exciting place. Finally, several informants said they had left Virginia to escape constant reminders of the state's slave past and that, despite the many racial barriers they encountered in the North, they felt they had more personal freedom in New York than in the South.[14]

Both the positive and negative aspects of the Richmond blacks' experience in New York are evident in the fragmentary information available about Mary Clayton of number 2 Minetta Lane. Forty-eight years old in 1900, she had been born in the last years of the slave era, and during her childbearing years she had given birth to at least twelve children, only three of whom had survived childhood. Although all three were grown to adulthood by 1900 (the youngest boy was nineteen), they lived with Mary and her second husband, their stepfather, Griffen Clayton. Mary's eldest, a twenty-six-year-old daughter, Maria Gumby, had been married for six years and had a son who also lived with the Claytons, although the boy's father was not part of the household. Similarly, both of Mary's sons, William and Norman Blum, were listed as married, but their wives were not living with them. Whatever this may suggest about difficulties in the Clayton children's marriages, a look ahead to the 1910 census reveals that family ties were sustained across the generations; as of 1910 Mary and Griffen Clayton were still sharing their apartment with Mary's son William and two of her daughter's children, George and Deliah Gumby.[15]

The basic struggle to make ends meet probably played a large role in the decisions the Claytons made to live together. Griffen apparently had trouble finding a steady job. Unemployed in July 1900, he later found work as an express wagon driver, but he was frequently laid off when business was slow. Mary's earnings from taking in laundry helped a little, but laundresses typically earned no more than three dollars a week, a sum on which no family could survive for long. Mary's children had to help and did. In 1900, Maria was working as a chambermaid and William as a musician. The family members relied on each other, pooling their meager resources to obtain the bare necessities. For the Claytons, as for many other poor black Villagers, the family unit was the first line of defense to which they turned in order to make their way in a society that consigned most African Americans to marginal status economically.

For many Greenwich Village blacks a second institution, the African American church, served, as did the family, as a haven in a hostile world. Although there were other significant expressions of black cultural vitality in turn-of-the-century New York City—for example, the *New York Age* (a weekly newspaper), the black nightclubs and theaters of the San Juan Hill district in the West Fifties and Sixties, and a succession of popular black professional baseball teams—churches were the only large institutions inside Greenwich Village that blacks could truly call their own. These black congregations, several of which had upward of one thousand members, had come to the neighborhood in the mid–nineteenth century at a time when Greenwich Village had one of the largest populations of blacks in the city. But during the last decades of the century many members of these congregations left the Village for new homes above Fourteenth Street, and consequently in the 1890s two of Little Africa's black churches, Bethel A. M. E. (African Methodist Episcopal) Church and the Roman Catholic parish of St. Benedict the Moor, decided to abandon their south Village addresses and follow their parishioners to locations further north on Manhattan's West Side. However, two other prestigious black congregations, the Abyssinian Baptist Church and Zion A. M. E. Church, remained active in Greenwich Village at the beginning of the twentieth century. Their histories reveal that piety, respectability, economic and social achievement, and successful institution building were important features of African American life in turn-of-the-century Greenwich Village.[16]

The Abyssinian Baptist Church was located at 166 Waverly Place, two blocks west of Washington Square (fig. 3). This congregation's history dated back to 1808, when a handful of free blacks withdrew from the First

3. The Abyssinian Baptist Church on Waverly Place. Abyssinian Baptist Church.

Baptist Church of New York in protest against the practice of segregating blacks in what was called a "slave loft." Several of the protesters were Africans, natives of Ethiopia, then known as Abyssinia. By founding a new congregation and naming it the Abyssinian Baptist Church, these black men and women affirmed their African heritage and proudly called attention to the antiquity of Christian traditions in Abyssinia. Over the next few decades these black Baptists worshipped at a variety of sites in Lower Manhattan. Then in 1856, under a charismatic leader, Reverend William Spellman, the church bought the Waverly Place property. During Spellman's twenty-nine-year tenure the church prospered, gaining a reputation as one of the richest black churches in the city.[17]

In the 1880s the church experienced internal conflicts so severe that the trustees demanded Spellman's resignation. Forced out in 1885, he gathered a splinter group around himself that included some of the old congregation's wealthier members and established a new church on West Twenty-sixth Street that won recognition from the Southern New York Baptist Association as the legitimate claimant to the name Abyssinian Baptist Church. The Waverly Place church, led by a new minister, Reverend Robert D. Wynn, fought to preserve its title to the congregation's Greenwich Village property. Suits and countersuits eventually produced several court rulings in 1890 that favored Wynn and his followers, but many issues remained in dispute until Spellman, the secessionists' leader, died in the early 1890s and the Southern New York Baptist Association finally, in 1896, conceded that both the name "Abyssinian" and the church property belonged to the Waverly Place faction. In a curious twist, the victorious Reverend Wynn himself then became a source of disharmony by proposing that the church move from Waverly Place to Harlem, a suggestion vociferously opposed by many in his flock.

Despite these debilitating squabbles, the Abyssinian Baptist Church remained fundamentally strong. In 1900, the fifteenth year of Reverend Wynn's tenure, the congregation claimed to have more than one thousand members. Its choir was admired as one of the best in the city, and the congregation underwrote a wide variety of charitable activities, including aid to its indigent members and contributions to city missions and bible societies. As the new century began and the church's centennial year (1908) approached, the Abyssinian Baptists could point with pride to their accomplishments as institution builders.

Zion A. M. E. Church, the other great black church that remained in Greenwich Village as of 1900, had been organized in 1796 by a group of approximately twenty African American men and women who had broken with a white Methodist congregation because it discriminated against black worshipers. Zion's founders soon built a frame church on Orange (now Baxter) Street, and when this property was sold at a large profit in 1850, half the $90,000 sale price went to purchase a vacant Dutch Reformed Church at 351 Bleecker Street, on the corner of West Tenth. The rest of the money was invested in other city properties to provide income for the congregation's needs. Affectionately known as "Mother Zion," the church was the oldest congregation in the group that had joined together in the 1820s to form the African Methodist Episcopal Church. Such was the success of this denomination that in 1896, the centennial of Mother Zion's founding, it was proudly reported that the national A. M. E. Zion organization "has grown until it has church property valued at $3,687,351, including 1,615 church buildings, seven colleges, and ten other institutions."[18]

But institutional success was only one measure of Zion's significance for its members. Zion and the other black churches of Little Africa gave their members clear moral guidelines to follow, provided believers with a social community, and, most important of all, fed their souls.

After interviewing fifty blacks, William F. Ogburn, one of the Columbia University graduate students who researched the lives of black New Yorkers before World War I, concluded that they divided themselves into two main types based on lifestyle, with deeply committed churchgoers in one camp and totally unchurched blacks in the other. Although Ogburn's informants felt that most black New Yorkers fell somewhere between the extremes, they distinguished very clearly between the two types. Nonchurchgoers, they said, were associated with the pursuit of the "sporting" life and "fast pleasures," while churchgoers were described as being, on the whole, respectable, law-abiding people who shunned those pursuits.[19]

Gospel churches were the center of a religious black's social life and were open nearly every night for one activity or another. For example, at Zion's sister congregation, Bethel A. M. E. Church, Monday was concert night. Various club and class meetings were held on Tuesdays and Wednesdays. Thursday was reserved for "an entertainment" consisting of "literary activities, reciting, and singing." Church-sponsored evenings such as these were so popular among blacks that thirty of Ogburn's fifty informants said they had attended at least one such event in the recent past. Friday was the night for prayer meetings, and choir rehearsal was held on Saturday. Sunday was the busiest day, with activities in the morning, afternoon, and evening.[20]

On weekends black churchgoers donned their Sunday best. Although most were working-class people, even the poorest managed to scrimp and save enough to buy at least one fine quality outfit. By contrast with African Americans who pursued a faster lifestyle and who favored, according to one observer, flashy and even "fantastic and garish" attire, churchgoing black men wore conservative dark suits, "black derbies, black or dark brown or dark grey overcoats, and in many cases they carried canes." Black churchgoing women emulated the latest styles worn by white women, but they gave those fashions a distinctive African American touch. A *New York Times* reporter described the colorful crowd that packed Carnegie Hall the last night of Mother Zion's centennial celebration in 1896. "The boxes were as brilliant as upon the night of a Paderewski recital—perhaps more so," he wrote, observing that there "were more bright dresses in primary colors."[21]

The communal life of gospel churches was rooted in a deep spirituality, and religious services at Zion and its sister churches were occasions for fervent expressions of that spirituality. When, for instance, Reverend Martin R. Franklin, Zion's leader in the late 1890s and early 1900s, ministered to his flock from the pulpit, he expected his parishioners to answer him openly and often in the familiar pattern known as "call and response." If many minutes passed without his message eliciting a vocal response from those assembled, the good reverend would prompt the worshippers by asking whether they loved their Jesus. Voices would respond with a resounding "Yes, Lord!" or loud "Amen!" Further words of testimony and inspiration from Franklin would provoke shouts of "Hallelujah!" and "Praise be!" Cries of "Hallelujah!" "Glory to God!" and "Amen!" would follow his next impassioned utterance. Back and forth the exchange would go, building to a climax that would leave few unmoved and many with tears running down their cheeks.[22]

Every Sunday service at Mother Zion produced many expressions of intense religious feeling, and special occasions such as Mother Zion's one hundred and third anniversary celebration on Sunday, November 27, 1899, produced even more. Reverend Franklin and several guest ministers presided over a program of social and religious activities that began at 9 A.M. with a service of prayer and praise that the *New York Tribune* reporter called "a love feast." The regular morning worship service followed at eleven. At three in the afternoon a reunion of past Sunday School classes was addressed by one of the guest ministers, and that evening at six-thirty the Christian Endeavor Society held a special prayer meeting. Finally, at seven-thirty the regular evening service, as always the best attended of the day, featured a sermon by another visiting minister.[23]

Zion A. M. E.'s health as a congregation depended on the practical efforts of many devoted members, and no individual played that sort of role in the church over a longer period than James Chase, Zion's sexton. In 1900 Chase lived with his wife and their youngest daughter at 18 Jones Street, a small tenement five blocks from the church. As sexton, he was responsible for seeing that Zion's property and buildings were well maintained and for insuring that the church was open for all scheduled events and safely locked at the end of every day. Chase filled the role of sexton for almost thirty years, from the mid-1880s into the 1910s.

Although his long and devoted service to the church gave him a secure and honorable place in his world, Chase, like most members of Zion A. M. E. Church, was relatively poor. His economic status may be accurately assessed through research done by Louise Bolard More, a social worker who lived on Jones Street in 1903 and who used interviews with two hundred of the neighborhood's working-class families to develop a statistical profile of their incomes and expenses. Chase's salary of about nine dollars a week, $450 annually, placed him above the lowest-paid workers (who earned less than $250 annually), but still left him in the bottom 15 percent of More's informants. A family in this bracket, More reported, spent about half its income on food, a quarter on rent, and most of the rest for light, fuel, and insurance. Only a pittance would have been left for discretionary spending, and most of that would have been used for two priorities dictated by the family's commitment to respectability: home furnishings and a set of good Sunday clothes. However, according to William F. Ogburn, the Columbia University sociologist, only one room, the parlor, had to be, in his words, "profusely decorated." Indeed, Ogburn reported that no matter how plain the decor of other rooms in black New Yorkers' apartments might be, their parlors were furnished with the clutter of objects prescribed by the fashions of the day: "There are," Ogburn wrote, "coloured table covers and carpets, gilded mats and picture frames, and pictures that are rarely monotone. There is a great profusion of articles of decoration on the mantel, on the table, and on the walls."[24]

One object sure to be found in the Chase's parlor was the Bible, a visible symbol of the centrality of faith in the lives of these African American citizens. Chase would need all the security the rock of his faith could provide to meet challenges that he and his fellow African Americans would face in the years just after Mother Zion's 1896 centennial jubilee. Over the next decade the black community of Little Africa experienced many losses. The proportion of African Americans in the south Village dropped slowly as blacks left the Village for homes farther uptown and large numbers of Italian immigrants moved into newly built tenements on Thompson, Sullivan, Bleecker, and adjacent streets that had once been the heart of the Little Africa enclave.

It might seem that the Italians' arrival in and the blacks' departure from the south Village was a straightforward case of the Italians pushing blacks out. But the process was not that simple. Blacks were, indeed, leaving throughout the late nineteenth century, but the number of blacks in Little Africa's core area actually increased between 1870 and 1890 because departing African Americans were being replaced by newcomers from the South. And the bulk of the black departures was determined less by the growth of the neighborhood's Italian population than by individual and group aspirations among Little Africa's black residents. One knowledgeable contemporary observer in the early twentieth century summed up this process in one sentence: "The ambitious Negro has moved uptown." The cumulative effect of these departures, however, greatly weakened the Little Africa community, and, as noted earlier, the African American churches that had been the institutional bulwarks of black Village life soon followed their parishioners uptown. Bethel A. M. E. Church and St. Benedict the Moor (Roman Catholic) led the way in the 1890s. The Abyssinian Baptist Church and Zion A. M. E. joined the exodus in 1904 and 1905.[25]

As these major demographic and institutional changes were taking place,

Mary White Ovington, a white social worker whose commitment to black civil rights led her to play a crucial role in the establishment of the National Association for the Advancement of Colored People, was at work on a study of New York City's African Americans. The result was a book titled *Half a Man*, published in 1911, in which she devoted most of her text to conditions of black New Yorkers in the newer African American districts north of Fourteenth Street. What little she did say of Village blacks reflected the unfortunate side effects of the departure of many of the most ambitious residents from the neighborhood. The blacks who remained, she wrote, were "widowed and deserted women and degenerates" and "men and women who, unsuccessful in their struggle with city life, have been left behind in these old forgotten streets." But even though degeneracy, failure, and victimization were all evident in the lives of Little Africa's residents, it would be misleading to leave the impression that such phenomena summed up everything there is to know about black Villagers in the early years of the twentieth century. Between 1900 and 1918 there were in Little Africa also many stories of courage, hope, and social stability, as attested to by the family loyalty of the James Chases and Morgan J. Austins, the economic aspirations of Richmond-born blacks, and the dignity and piety of hundreds of churchgoing black Villagers.[26]

An Immigrant Church

From a trickle in the mid-1800s, the numbers of Italians reaching New York City swelled to a flood in the last two decades of the century. In 1880 there were only 44,230 foreign-born Italians in the United States. From 1881 to 1890, 307,309 more came; twice again as many (651,893) arrived in the 1890s, and the largest influx ever (2,135,877) came during the first decade of the twentieth century. Although some Italian immigrants eventually returned to Italy or moved on to other countries, many stayed, and most of those who stayed in the United States settled in East Coast cities, with New York City by far the most popular destination.[27]

The large influx of Italians immediately made itself felt in the Catholic church. As the largest non-English-speaking ethnic group in the church, Italian immigrants posed a significant challenge for an American hierarchy and clergy that was largely Irish. In New York City, first thousands and later tens of thousands of Italians took up residence in Lower Manhattan neighborhoods, and by the 1860s an Italian enclave had developed in the southernmost part of Greenwich Village between Canal and Houston streets. New York's diocesan leaders, lacking Italian-speaking priests to minister to this population in their native tongue, initially tried a hybrid solution: it combined their preferred form, a "territorial" parish led by English-speaking priests, usually Irish, with a "national" parish that provided non-English-speaking Catholics with a priest of the same nationality. St. Anthony of Padua on Sullivan Street was organized on this hybrid basis in the late 1860s under the leadership of Italian Franciscans. Initially, Irish Catholics outnumbered Italians in this ethnically mixed neighborhood, and Irish communicants were the main source of the parish's income. Even after their numbers surpassed those of the Irish in the 1890s, Italians were still forced to hold their Italian-language services in the church basement while Irish parishioners attended Mass in the main sanctuary upstairs. In practice, therefore, the solution of combining a territorial and a national parish tended to relegate Italians to second-class status.[28]

By the 1890s it was increasingly apparent to Catholic leaders in both Italy and the United States that new measures had to be taken to meet the needs of New York City's Italian Catholic immigrants. The plight of the Italian newcomers in the south Village was representative. In the closing decades of the nineteenth century, block after block along Bleecker and on adjacent streets between Thompson Street and Sixth Avenue had become filled with Italians as they spilled out of Italian neighborhoods just to the south (fig. 4). Yet despite their numbers, the south Village Italians had no parish they could truly call their own. At this juncture, Giovanni Battista Scalabrini, the Bishop of Piacenza, took a special interest in the fate of Italian emigrants and, with encouragement from the Vatican, founded a missionary order to minister to Italians abroad. In the early 1890s, several Scalabrinian Fathers were posted to New York City, and one of these, seeing what needed to be done among Italians in the south Village, appealed to Archbishop Michael A. Corrigan for help. Corrigan, deeply troubled by the widespread religious apathy displayed by nominally Catholic Italian immigrants, approved the founding of an Italian-language parish, Our Lady of Pompei, in 1892. Unlike St. Anthony of Padua a few blocks to the south, Our Lady of Pompei was an "ethnically homogeneous congregation" and as such grew swiftly, serving an Italian immigrant population of nearly ten thousand by the end of the century.[29]

In April 1895, the Italian Catholics of Our Lady of Pompei parish moved their services to a church building at 214 Sullivan Street in the block just south of West Third Street. This red brick structure had been purchased from Bethel Methodist Church, a congregation of "colored" (i.e., African American) Protestants who had owned the site since 1842. They, in turn, had bought the property from African American Baptists who had constructed the first church at that address in 1810.[30]

4. A Thompson Street scene, *Far from the Fresh Air Farm*, by William J. Glackens. From *Collier's*, July 8, 1911.

The Italian Catholics' tenure at 214 Sullivan was brief and marked by misfortune. In July of 1897 the small brick church was badly damaged by a gas explosion and fire, and less than a year later Our Lady of Pompei relocated again, this time to a Greek Revival church three blocks away at 210 Bleecker Street. The parish's new church was also a hand-me-down. It had originally been built for a congregation of white Unitarian Universalists and had been occupied more recently, from 1883 to 1898, by an African American Catholic parish named for Saint Benedict the Moor.[31]

On May 8, 1898, Our Lady of Pompei's parishioners formally completed the move from their former place of worship on Sullivan Street to their newly acquired church building on Bleecker Street. The weather that Sunday was dreadful, and the reporter who covered the dedication for one of New York's major Italian-language newspapers, *Il Progresso Italo-Americano*, described conditions as "eccezionalmente pervers[e] per la stagione" (exceptionally perverse for the season). High winds, driving rain, thunder and lightning, hail, and temperatures in the low- to mid-forties made the journey to the church a struggle. Outside the church, the Italian and American flags mounted on the building's face snapped like rifle shots as they were whipped about by gale force winds, but once participants got inside the church a spirit of camaraderie, pride, and delight prevailed.[32]

The day's festivities opened with a solemn high Mass. Despite the inclement weather, the sanctuary, which could accommodate upwards of eight hundred people, was full almost to capacity. Two guests of honor took the lead. Monsignor Giovanni P. Bandinelli, Provincial of the Passionist Fathers, was the principal celebrant, and Dr. Gherardo Ferrante, a member of Archbishop Corrigan's personal staff, gave the homily, the main point of which was that all present should view Catholicism and Italian patriotism as complementary forces for good in their community. After Mass, these worthies and other distinguished guests braved the elements to cross the street to the rectory for a banquet.

A round of speeches, all but one of them in Italian, followed dinner. The only address in English was made by a Catholic high school principal who spoke of the importance of developing good schools for Italian youngsters. Monsignor Bandinelli, speaking in Italian, professed that the happy occasion had left him with amiable feelings of being "above all Italian and Genovese." Dr. Ferrante followed and eloquently reiterated his homily's theme that the Italian heritage was a unique blend of national pride and Catholic piety. Father Francesco Zaboglio, the Scalabrinian missionary who was the parish's senior priest, rose to second this sentiment by invoking the phrase "L'Unione fa la Forza" (Unity makes Strength), adding, lest anyone mistake his meaning, that he was referring to the union of patriotism and religion.

Shortly before the gathering broke up, another priest proposed a toast to Pope Leo XIII, a gesture that was enthusiastically received.[33]

A number of details from the scene described above, when placed in historical context, serve to define major features of Greenwich Village's Italian community as the nineteenth century drew to a close: the use of both Italian and American flags in decorating the church, the emphasis placed by Dr. Ferrante on how Roman Catholicism and Italian nationalism complemented each other, the reference made by Monsignor Bandinelli to feeling Italian and Genovese, and the ties of Father Zaboglio to the Scalabrinian order.

To speak of Our Lady of Pompei's parishioners as Italians is accurate enough from a contemporary American perspective, but it probably does not reflect the way many recent immigrants from Italy thought of themselves in the 1890s. The political unification of Italy had been completed only recently (in 1870), and for many natives of Italy long-standing regional and local loyalties remained more important than a national identity. At the very least, many were sensitive to a distinction between northerners and southerners, with the former generally considered more modern and the latter often scorned as backward. This prejudice was one, along with many, that a contemporary social worker encountered among her working-class informants in Greenwich Village. "The Irish," she wrote, "hate the Italians ('Dagos') and negroes ('niggers'), and the North Italians despise the Sicilians." Large numbers of both groups came to New York City, with northerners dominating the first wave of Italian immigration and southerners prevailing by an overwhelming margin, almost six to one, by the 1890s.[34]

In practice, the north-south distinction, though strongly felt, was often not nearly as significant as the identification Italian immigrants felt with the province or village where they had been born. "The focal point of solidarity for the [Italian] immigrant," one scholar has written, "was the group of fellow townsmen. Immigrants who knew each other in the village often emigrated together and settled in the same neighborhood." As a result, on many streets in New York's Little Italy districts, natives of particular provinces, cities, or villages could be found clustered together, dominating the residential, social, and business life of the neighborhood. Before 1900, most Greenwich Village Italians were from a variety of northern provinces—Lombardy, Venice, Piedmont, Emilia, and Liguria—with natives of Genoa, a major seaport and the capital of Liguria, present in particularly large numbers (fig. 5).[35]

Genovese were also well represented among Our Lady of Pompei's parishioners. A survey of Pompei's early baptismal records found that many recipients' parents were from the Genoa area, specifically the nearby town

5. Carmine Street near Our Lady of Pompei in the Village's Italian district. Museum of the City of New York, Print Archives.

of Chiavari. An awareness of this large Genovese presence was reflected in Monsignor Bandinelli's comment at the church dedication in 1898 that the occasion left him feeling "above all Italian and Genovese," and in the practice, widespread in the early 1900s, of referring to Pompei as "the church of the Genovese." Still, the Genovese were not the only northern Italians in the parish. Father Pio Parolin, a priest who served the parish from 1904 to 1914, criticized the use of the term "la Chiesa dei Genovesi," insisting that Italians from many northern provinces, not just the Genoa area, worshipped at Our Lady of Pompei during his tenure there. Moreover, the number of southern Italians in the area grew rapidly from the late 1890s onward. In 1893 more than ninety percent of the couples who registered to marry at Pompei were northerners, but that percentage dropped to fifty-one by 1903 and to thirty-three by 1908.[36]

Practically speaking, it could not have been otherwise. A parish serving nearly ten thousand Italian immigrants in the heart of a diverse Italian enclave was simply too large to draw its constituency from only one Italian locale. South Village Italians continued to feel strongly about old regional and local ties, but the process of building an Italian-language parish led former strangers to cooperate in a common enterprise and prompted what one scholar has called a "breakthrough to a wider solidarity" based on being Italian, not just Genovese, Piedmontese, or Tuscan.[37]

Long-standing political prejudices would also have to give way if Our Lady of Pompei's parishioners were to embrace the message that Dr. Ferrante and Father Zaboglio proclaimed about the compatibility of Italian nationalism and Catholicism. During the Italian unification movement of the 1850s and sixties, bitter disputes arose between the Vatican hierarchy and Italian patriots. Zealous unifiers viewed the Vatican's commitment to preserving its temporal power over the Papal State as an obstacle to unification, and they were right. Popes, recognizing the threat to papal power inherent in the nationalist program of patriots such as Giuseppe Garibaldi (who lived briefly near the Village on Irving Place as a political exile in the early 1850s), used their armies and their diplomatic influence, often with considerable success, to impede unification. When the nationalists triumphed in 1870 and stripped the papacy of its temporal power, the rivals remained hostile toward each other: the unifiers were angry about the Church's role in retarding unification, and conservative Catholics were unforgiving toward the radicals for dismantling the Papal State and making Rome Italy's capital city.

But twenty-eight years later at Our Lady of Pompei, Dr. Ferrante and Father Zaboglio sought to transcend this decades-old quarrel by arguing that Catholicism and nationalism were twins that together defined Italian identity. At the same time parish leaders, by decorating the front of the church with Italian and American flags, affirmed a belief that Italians were a patriotic people, loyal both to their country of origin and to their new homeland. Thus, in the liberal spirit that prevailed among participants in the 1898 dedication ceremony, three sentiments that often seemed to be at odds with each other—devout Catholicism, Italian nationalism, and American patriotism—were, rhetorically at least, juxtaposed as entirely compatible.

During Our Lady of Pompei's early years a small group of lay leaders made a major contribution to the fledgling church's success. All of these men were middle-class individuals and most had come to the United States before the great surge of Italian immigration began in the 1890s. By 1898 they had become owners of small businesses that served the south Village Italian community: Angelo Cuneo ran a fruit stand, Michael Pepe was a real estate agent, Giuseppe Miele a tailor, Joseph Personeni a druggist, and Edward Bergonzi and Andrea Sabini grocers. These were the men who gave dollars when most parishioners could scarcely give pennies, and who formed the backbone of such key parish organizations as the St. Joseph's Society and the Parish Finance Committee. They also sponsored and even performed in parish fundraisers, such as a highly successful variety show in 1900 (fig. 6).[38]

Luigi V. Fugazy, one of the parish's first trustees and a major financial contributor, held a loftier position in New York's Italian community. An 1896 *New York Times* article on "Papa" Fugazy, as he was called, portrayed him as a father figure to thousands of Italian immigrants. As such, he was an example of a well-known social type in Italian communities, the padrone, an individual who played a paternal role in relation to others, giving them advice, assistance, and protection. In the United States, one popular image of the padrone—accurate in all too many cases—depicted him as exploiting his immigrant dependents, for whom he found jobs only to take nearly all their wages, with the result that the newcomers remained in an impoverished and servile condition.[39]

Fugazy used his considerable influence in much more benign ways. Born in San Stefano, a suburb of Genoa, he was a hero of the Italian unification movement. Emigrating to New York City in the late 1860s, he established himself as a banker and notary public. In 1900, Fugazy's offices were located at 147 Bleecker Street, the very heart of the south Village Italian neighborhood. Poor Italians came to those offices to deposit tiny sums that they feared might otherwise be lost to robbers or con artists. Italians of all classes availed themselves of his notary services, bringing wills, contracts, and mortgages for his endorsement. In the course of such transactions, Fugazy was always ready to be the good "Papa," offering his clients advice on all sorts of legal and personal matters, including how to steer safely through the alien territory of the American legal system. Fugazy was also admired for his charitable activities. He was the guiding light of more than one hundred mutual aid societies and the chief promoter of a citywide federation of these societies. He urged all the individual societies, most of which were organized around highly parochial village-based ties, to develop allegiances to a broader Italian American community by affiliating with the citywide organization. Finally, Fugazy served as a political power broker, representing the interests of New York's Italians to the Tammany Democratic machine, with which he had long-standing ties. Clearly, the scope of Fugazy's activities was too broad for him to devote a great deal of time specifically to Our Lady of Pompei; still, his friendship was eagerly sought and generously returned.[40]

Despite the impressive success of a Luigi Fugazy, Italians were still on the fringe of mainstream American society, which regarded the newcomers with either hostility or indifference. Although the elder Fugazy was the subject of an occasional article in the *New York Times*, even the most important occasions in the life of Our Lady of Pompei parish went unreported by

6. Funeral procession approaching Our Lady of Pompei. Center for Migration Studies of New York.

mainstream English-language newspapers. Pompei's dedication in 1898 was covered by a correspondent from an important Italian paper, Rome's *Tribuna*, and by representatives of New York City's Italian-language press, but the major New York dailies ignored the event and instead covered Archbishop Corrigan's presence that same Sunday at the dedication of a Staten Island church. When Bishop Scalabrini came to the United States in 1901, his arrival in New York was noted in the city's major English-language papers, but the rest of his activities while in the city, including two visits to Our Lady of Pompei, received almost no newspaper attention in the secular press.[41]

By the time Bishop Scalabrini journeyed to New York in 1901, Our Lady of Pompei had been under the leadership of Father Antonio Demo for slightly more than two years. Demo's predecessor, Father Zaboglio, had had to abandon the post because of the lasting effects of injuries he had sustained in the church fire of 1897. He and two other men had gone to the church basement to investigate a gas leak, lit a match, and caused an explosion that killed his companions and left him in poor health. After Zaboglio's resignation in mid-1899, Demo took over. Only twenty-nine at the time, Demo was a native of Vicenza province in northern Italy, an army veteran, and a Scalabrinian ordained by the order's bishop-founder in 1896 (fig. 7).[42]

The parish that Demo took over in 1899 and Scalabrini visited in 1901 was still in every sense an immigrant church that served the needs of the Italian immigrant enclave and had minimal contact with the surrounding host society. Before his appointment to Our Lady of Pompei, Father Demo had served a Scalabrinian mission in Boston for nearly two years without acquiring much facility in English. He hadn't needed it there, and initially he didn't need to be fluent in English in New York either. Italian was the common idiom used in the homes and shops of the south Village. Anacleto Sermolino, an Italian who arrived in the early 1890s, later recalled that after standing on the corner of Bleecker and Sullivan for the first time and seeing pushcarts loaded with Italian cheeses, pasta, and vegetables and hearing women shoppers conversing in Italian, he had told his wife: "This is not a strange land we have come to, but a little piece of Italy." Given this environment, Father Demo at first conducted the church's business in Italian. Only later, when his pastoral duties required him to deal more often with Pompei's English-speaking neighbors, did he learn to speak and write English well.[43]

Even in Pompei's first decade of 1892–1902, however, south Village Italians were never completely isolated from or unnoticed by English-speaking Americans and their institutions. The nearby Irish parish, St. Joseph's, let Pompei use its meeting hall for early musical events and fundraisers, and

7. Father Antonio Demo (*center*) and the priests of Our Lady of Pompei. Center for Migration Studies of New York.

Our Lady of Pompei also benefited enormously from the generosity of a wealthy heiress, Annie Leary. "Miss Leary," as she was popularly known, was in her early fifties in 1896 when she decided to become the struggling Italian parish's guardian angel. She paid all the parish's outstanding debts, funded repairs and improvements to its Sullivan Street building, and played a crucial role in reassuring Archbishop Corrigan that Pompei's purchase of its Bleecker Street church would work out financially. Father Zaboglio, Demo's immediate predecessor at Pompei, credited Annie Leary with nothing less than having enabled the parish to survive. "If it had not been for her," Zaboglio asserted, "our church of the Madonna of the Rosary of Pompei would have closed."[44]

St. Joseph's priests and Annie Leary were not the only non-Italians to respond to the presence of Italians in the south Village. In the 1890s a diverse group of literary and artistic types discovered the joys of "Spaghetti Hour" at Maria's, a MacDougal Street restaurant that offered generous portions at budget prices. In the same period the founders of Judson Church, a Baptist congregation that had established itself on Washington Square South in 1892, attempted to proselytize Italian Catholics by offering services in their native tongue. Toward the end of the 1890s the explosive growth of the south Village Italian enclave led the Charity Organization

Society, a body organized to coordinate the efforts of all the city's public and private charitable agencies, to set up a special committee to develop programs aimed specifically at local Italian-speaking people. Finally, in 1900 the University Settlement Society established a West Side Branch, later called Richmond Hill House, on King Street for the express purpose of providing social services to south Village Italians.[45]

Despite these varied forms of outreach, for most south Village Italians contact with their non-Italian neighbors at the beginning of the twentieth century remained quite limited. Once Our Lady of Pompei had a hall of its own that could house major parish events, it no longer turned to St. Joseph's to provide a site for those occasions. Miss Leary's attentiveness to Pompei's needs lessened noticeably after a tiff with Father Demo; the strong-willed heiress was used to doing things without consulting her beneficiaries, and the rather stiff-necked Italian priest objected that she was disregarding his prerogatives as Pompei's leader. Judson Church's effort to evangelize south Village Italians was a disappointment to its sponsors; like similar Protestant initiatives elsewhere in the city, Judson's program failed to attract even 2 percent of local Italian Catholics into the Protestant fold. The University Settlement Society's West Side Branch got off to a slow start and remained small, and the Charity Organization Society's committee on Italian immigrants, set up in 1899, had little practical effect locally until 1906, when the C.O.S.'s Greenwich district office finally hired an Italian stenographer to record interviews with Italian-speaking applicants. Spaghetti Hour at Maria's remained popular with English-speaking patrons for at least a decade, but the restaurant's non-Italian diners were themselves outside the American mainstream, artists and writers who liked red wine, pasta, and the restaurant's MacDougal Street locale precisely because the combination made for an exotic foreign ambience.[46]

The Green in Greenwich

As Italians moved into the Village in the late nineteenth century, the newcomers took up residence on blocks that had once been occupied by other ethnic groups, primarily blacks and the Irish. By 1898 Italians were the dominant presence in the Village south of Washington Square on Bleecker, Thompson, Sullivan, and adjacent streets, but in the Village west of Sixth Avenue, especially from Leroy north to West Fourteenth Street, Irish immigrants and their children and grandchildren still set the neighborhood's tone. Though the west Village's diverse population included many residents of German, French, English, Dutch, and African backgrounds, the Irish were the largest single subgroup in the area. As one social worker who knew the neighborhood well observed, "The population, while varied, was, when I came to [Jones Street] in 1902, mainly Irish-American, that is, of parentage born in Ireland with a plentiful sprinkling of relations and friends still coming from Ireland."[47]

The Irish had first come to the Village as domestic servants and construction workers in the 1820s and 1830s, during the early years of the Washington Square era. A Catholic parish, St. Joseph's, was founded in the west Village in 1829 to serve the spiritual needs of these working-class immigrants. By 1898 most of this first generation of Irish Villagers had died off or moved on; however, Irish migration to the Village had continued at a substantial rate from the 1830s through the rest of the century. The later waves of Irish migrants to the west Village fell into two broad generations: an older group that had left Ireland during the famine years of the 1840s and 1850s, and a group of newer Irish Villagers who began arriving in the neighborhood after the American Civil War.[48]

William H. Walker can serve as an example of the older generation of Irish Villagers. He was born in Ireland in 1850. Still just a boy when he immigrated to the United States, Billy Walker joined the household of an Irish friend in the west Village, became a communicant at St. Joseph's Church on Sixth Avenue, and earned his living as a carpenter. At Mass he met and fell in love with Ellen Roon, the pretty daughter of James Roon, owner of a Village saloon. Convinced that the formidable Mr. Roon would never give them permission to marry, the young couple contrived to be wed in a neighboring parish. They then set up housekeeping in an apartment on Leroy Street, two and a half blocks from the Hudson River docks. Ellen Walker was soon pregnant with a son whom the Walkers named William Junior. More pregnancies followed, but of the nine babies she bore (including two sets of twins), only four of Ellen's children—three boys and a girl—survived infancy.[49]

Billy Walker was ambitious and energetic, and like many members of the famine Irish generation, he achieved significant economic and social mobility. His carpentry work expanded into a construction business, and with profits from those endeavors, he opened a lumberyard. His business successes also enhanced the family's social status. In the late 1880s, he purchased a handsome row house at 6 St. Luke's Place. This was less than two blocks east on Leroy Street from the family's old apartment, but their new neighbors were nearly all members of the solid middle class—families headed by small businessmen, real estate agents, and a few professional men—and most were second-generation Americans of Irish or German descent. By contrast, the residents of the 100 block where the Walkers once lived were primarily working-class. In 1900, for instance, the old Walker residence, a four-story tenement at 110 Leroy, was occupied by four Irish American families, the heads of which were listed as a truckman, a truck driver, a blacksmith, and a clerk in a flour milling company.[50]

Many of the residents who lived on the three blocks of Leroy between St. Luke's Place and the waterfront were members of the newest generation of Irish Villagers, immigrants who had arrived in the United States since the early 1880s. Typically, the newcomers worked at unskilled or semi-skilled jobs. Women from this group were seamstresses, washerwomen, factory workers, and domestic servants employed by middle- and upper-class Villagers. As a north Village patrician whose family recruited its staff of servants from the ranks of the newest of the Irish newcomers observed: "There were plenty of Irish girls arriving by every boat and looking for a place to start; they had to be shown how to light the gas and use a coal stove, but they were good-natured and willing to learn." Like their female counterparts, men from this generation of recent Irish immigrants were employed in entry-level jobs. Manual labor was the rule, with numerous day laborers (one of the era's lowest-paying occupations), and others earning their way as factory workers, janitors, truck drivers, and the like. All of these were jobs that Irish newcomers might find in practically any part of the city. But among the Leroy Street Irish who lived nearest the waterfront, many also worked as longshoremen, an occupation more particular to the west Village. The nearby Hudson River docks were used by some of the era's leading passenger and shipping companies, and these firms employed hundreds of Irishmen and many Villagers of other national backgrounds as well.[51]

It might seem that the Walker family's move from 110 Leroy to 6 St. Luke's Place—that is, from a working-class tenement to a middle-class row house—signified a decisive separation between the upwardly mobile Walkers and their still struggling Irish neighbors. This, however, was not the case. Powerful cultural bonds connected all the west Village Irish, regardless of when they had arrived in the Village or the class status they had achieved once there. Three institutions were particularly instrumental in fostering ethnic solidarity among the west Village Irish: Irish county societies, the Catholic church, and the Tammany Hall Democratic party organization.

County societies—social and political clubs organized according to the Irish county of their members' origins—were a popular means of maintaining old country ties (fig. 8). Several Irish counties were particularly well represented in the west Village. Natives of County Antrim clustered in the neighborhood's northwestern corner around Jackson Square. Sons

8. Scenes from an Irish county society ball. From *New York World*, January 30, 1910.

and daughters of County Clare were even more numerous. One historian observed that "no neighborhood at the turn of the century was as closely identified with a specific county as was County Clare with the western section of Greenwich Village," and researchers for Caroline Ware's Greenwich Village study in the early 1930s found that one major west Village thoroughfare (probably Hudson Street) had been nicknamed "County Clare Street."[52]

Villagers from County Clare organized a variety of county societies in the decades immediately before the turn of the century, among them a County Clare Men's Association, which was active from the 1880s into the

1910s, and a shorter-lived County Clare Ladies' Association. In theory membership in these organizations was open to any man or woman with the appropriate old country background, but in practice their ranks were drawn mainly from among middle-class Irish Villagers who were businessmen, owners of homes, and parents able to pay to educate their children for the professions. Men of this sort served as officers of the County Clare Men's Association and organized, in 1909, the County Claremen's Evicted Tenants Protective and Industrial Association, a society for giving moral and economic aid to old country Irish tenants driven from their land by English landlords. The latter association's first meeting was held at Crotty's Hall, Peter J. Crotty's wholesale liquor establishment at 420 Hudson. Crotty was named a trustee of the new organization. Other Irish Villagers served as president of the older Clare Men's organization: Peter J. McInerney, the owner of a Hudson Street tavern, held the office from 1899 to 1908; his successor was William Crowley, a highly successful west Village businessman who was the proprietor of another Hudson Street saloon and the owner of a cigar manufacturing company whose most popular brand sold under the name Na Bocklish (Gaelic for "Don't mention it").[53]

The frequency with which the names of saloon owners appeared as leaders of the county societies was no accident. Saloons were one of the first businesses into which ambitious members of the older generation of Irish immigrants could move. This was no less true of Billy Walker's imposing father-in-law, James Roon, than it was of Peter J. Crotty and William Crowley. With credit from a brewer and only a small amount of capital, a man of modest means could open a saloon for business. Little wonder, then, that saloons occupied many streetcorners and mid-block storefronts throughout the west Village. Jones Street, though only one block long, had no less than five saloons on it at the beginning of the century.[54]

The west Village's Irish saloons served many functions in their patrons' lives. Laborers went to saloons to drink and socialize after work and on weekends. Politicians found them a convenient place to meet voters; as an old-time Village Democrat recalled, "In those days a great deal of canvassing was done in saloons." Saloons were also prime locales for affirming one's Irishness, whether that took the form of a county society meeting or the reportedly widespread practice of defending the neighborhood's Irish saloons as places "where only an Irishman was allowed in."[55]

The Catholic church was another important bulwark of Irish American solidarity. Throughout the nineteenth century, Irish immigrants were the targets of much verbal abuse and many physical assaults by anti-Catholic bigots. A nasty example of nativist mob violence took place in the Village on July 4, 1853. An Independence Day parade that was sponsored by the

Ancient Order of Hibernians and whose participants wore green scarves and badges was assaulted at Abingdon Square (in the northwestern corner of the Village) by a mob of red-shirted nativists who shouted, "Kill the Catholic sons of bitches!" Dozens of Hibernian marchers were injured, and their parade broken up.[56]

Incidents of this sort, together with widespread anti-Catholic feeling throughout the United States, led many Irish Catholics to develop a bunker mentality. They looked to the church to be a buffer between Irish Catholics and the Protestant host society in which they found themselves. This defensive outlook was shared by the conservative Irish clerics who led the New York diocese and who were sincerely convinced that American culture at large was inimical to Catholicism and Irishness. There was, however, an articulate minority of Catholic priests and lay people who challenged these attitudes and formulated what came to be called the liberal Catholic position. These liberals, some of them associated with St. Joseph's parish in Greenwich Village, rejected the conservatives' defensive posture and argued that the church should take positive steps to create "working alliances with non-Catholic elements" in the United States.[57]

St. Joseph's parish had a long and distinguished history. Founded in 1829, it is one of the oldest Catholic parishes still active in the city. Its present church building, which is the original structure dedicated in 1834, has a Greek revival exterior and an interior graced by a handsome fresco of the Transfiguration in the chancel. Several priests who later figured prominently in the local diocese—the conservative Father John McCloskey, who became the first American cardinal, and Father Edward McGlynn, one of McCloskey's most vociferous liberal critics—served the parish in its early years. From 1857 to 1880, St. Joseph's pastor was another liberal, Father Thomas Farrell, a native of Ireland who was ordained at St. John's College (later Fordham) in the Bronx in 1848. During the Civil War, when Irish prejudice against blacks erupted in violent attacks on African Americans during the New York City draft riot of 1863, Farrell was staunchly pro-black. He supported Lincoln's emancipation policy and urged that freed slaves be given political rights. He continued to befriend blacks all his life; his will included a $5,000 bequest for establishing a new parish to serve African American Catholics, and this legacy enabled the Church of St. Benedict the Moor to open its doors on Bleecker Street in 1883.

Farrell was also a strong admirer of America's democratic institutions, and he was forward-looking and optimistic about the ways in which the relationship between Irish Catholics and Protestant Americans might evolve. In the late 1860s he and a small circle of like-minded priests gathered regularly for discussion sessions at St. Joseph's. Though they differed on details, members of this group, which took "the Accademia" as its name, shared a liberal outlook. They believed that a new culture was in the process of emerging, born of the mix of old stock Protestant Americans and new immigrants, and they hoped to leaven that new culture by bringing to it the truths of the church. In addition, they felt that Catholics should open themselves to the democratic society around them and should foster their children's Americanization by sending them to public schools. With regard to the church itself, these liberals urged the modification or abandonment of such traditional Catholic practices as priestly celibacy and the Latin liturgy. Reforms of this sort, they argued, would make the church more effective among its own communicants and also weaken the grounds that Protestant critics had for charging that the church was undemocratic and reactionary and therefore un-American.[58]

Little is known about how much (if any) of Father Farrell's openness to American society at large figured in the thinking of St. Joseph's clerical and lay leaders in the years immediately after Farrell's death in 1880. However, Father Dennis O'Flynn, who was St. Joseph's pastor from 1892 to 1906, seems to have been relatively open to relationships with non-Catholic institutions in the neighborhood. A case in point was his response to the social workers who moved to the neighborhood in 1902 to take up residence in a Jones Street building less than two blocks from St. Joseph's Church. A Catholic clergyman had good reason to be suspicious of non-Catholic philanthropic and social agencies whose Protestant employees often displayed some degree of insensitivity to, if not outright hostility toward, the Catholic faith. Father O'Flynn, however, did not foreclose the possibility of friendly relations with St. Joseph's new neighbors, and once he was confident that the residents of the Jones Street settlement house had no covert religious agenda, he welcomed them as a benign influence in the west Village.[59]

Father O'Flynn was a native of Ireland who had received his education in Ireland, France, and Belgium. A big man physically, of whom it was reportedly said that "his heart was in proportion to the size of his body," he had become rector of St. Joseph's in 1892, after having served in several New York parishes and one in the Bahamas. All the available evidence about Father O'Flynn's nearly fifteen-year tenure at St. Joseph's indicates that the parish flourished under his leadership. He oversaw the construction of a new rectory on Waverly Place, just north of the church, and in September 1897, the sixth year of his pastorate, St. Joseph's opened a large parochial school at 109–111 Washington Place. This modern school building, capable of serving up to a thousand students, also became, from 1902 onward, home to a parish Boys' Club that featured training in a variety of athletic activities: wrestling, boxing, gymnastics, and bowling. Thus did the Irish-born rector of St. Joseph's contribute to the distinguished history of an institution in which west Village Irish Catholics could justly take pride.[60]

Along with Irish county societies and the Catholic church, the third pillar of Irish ethnic solidarity was the Democratic Party. In response to anti-Catholic and anti-immigrant prejudice that came at first mainly from Whigs and later from the Know-Nothings and Republicans, the mass of poor Irish who arrived in East Coast cities gravitated toward the Democratic Party. Democrats solidified that loyalty in the middle of the nineteenth century by giving immigrants material aid and opposing nativist and anti-Catholic programs. By the Civil War era, Irish were beginning to move up in the party's ranks, which in New York City meant taking leadership roles in Tammany Hall. Under John Kelly, the first Irish Catholic to serve as its Grand Sachem, Tammany in the 1870s and early 1880s became a highly organized urban political machine. After Kelly's death in 1886, another Irish boss, Richard Croker, took over as Grand Sachem and retained that position until 1902.

The organizational structure that Kelly put in place was highly effective; district leaders oversaw each election ward and precinct captains helped the ward boss keep the mass of ordinary voters in the fold. Kelly's system carried the Irish-led machine to victory after victory. Nevertheless, coalitions of Republicans, Independents, and disaffected Democrats occasionally managed to win control of the city's administration. Two such successes happened on Croker's watch. The first was the so-called Committee of Seventy campaign in 1894 that resulted in the election of a reform administration led by the Republican businessman William L. Strong. Tammany won the next round, the mayoral election in 1897, the first in which the five boroughs were unified as Greater New York City. But anti-Tammany forces made an immediate comeback in 1901, when a ticket sponsored by Citizens' Union, an independent municipal reform party, made Seth Low (president of Columbia University and former mayor of Brooklyn) Greater New York's mayor. Although the period of Croker's leadership had been marred by major scandals in city affairs, he was deposed as party chief in 1902 less because Tammany insiders were troubled by evidence of corrupt conduct on his part than because he had failed to lead the Democracy to victory in two out of the last three elections.[61]

Tammany's formula for success required contributions from many loyal partisans: enterprising ward leaders, attractive candidates, and loyal campaign workers. In the west Village in the early twentieth century the individual most responsible for building and maintaining the local Democratic organization was Charles Culkin, the Tammany district leader. Born in Greenwich Village in 1872, he was of Irish descent, the son of a wholesale liquor dealer who was a long-time Village resident. The elder Culkin died when Charles was only fifteen. Forced at an early age to begin managing the family business, the son proved equal to the task, but his first love was always politics. A diligent worker for Tammany's interests, Culkin was rewarded in 1897 when local party leaders named him their candidate for city alderman in a west Village district that nearly always went Democratic by a wide margin. Victorious in this, his first try for office, Culkin served three terms, resigning in 1905 to accept an appointment as Clerk of the Court of Special Sessions, a municipal post and patronage job that guaranteed him a tidy salary of $4,000 a year.[62]

Culkin's official positions as alderman and court clerk were, on the whole, less politically significant than his long service as the west Village Democratic Party's district leader, a party post with no official standing in American law that he assumed in 1902 when Richard Croker was ousted as Grand Sachem. Tammany's success in elections was in large part due to district leaders who labored literally day and night to win voter loyalty to the Democracy's cause. The classic method of achieving this result was to extend a helping hand to working-class constituents who needed assistance finding jobs, dealing with city agencies and the courts, or surviving personal disasters: a fire that destroyed a family's belongings, sickness that forced the chief breadwinner out of work, or a death in the family. "I found from experience," Culkin said, "that you cannot be too zealous in the interests of these poor people." Culkin was nothing if not zealous. He was reportedly "found almost daily at his headquarters" at the Jefferson Club office on West Twelfth Street, and in order to keep track of who lived in his district and what they might need from him, he kept a card file of information that he constantly updated. According to one admiring report, "at a glance he could tell an inquirer just where a Jim Smith or John Jones stood as to employment and if out of work the cause of it."[63]

As Tammany district leader, Culkin also made sure that west Village voters associated the Democratic organization with good times. He sent families food and presents at Christmas, provided free entertainments such as dances, picnics, and boat excursions, and paid to send local kids to summer camp. Many of the beneficiaries of this largesse were Irish Villagers, but one secret to Tammany success (and continued Irish control of most of the top spots in the organization) was that ethnicity was no bar to being a recipient of Tammany handouts. Villagers of every kind—Italian, African American, and the rest—were all potential voters, and by assiduous attention to the needs of all of his working-class neighbors, many of whom had little money for recreation and no cushion to fall back on when disaster struck, Culkin insured a good turnout for Tammany's candidates at election time.

As one old-time Tammany alderman put it, "Look out for the poor people of [your] district. That's all. Look out for 'em all the time—jobs, favors, rent, food, outings—anything they want, give it to 'em. Then in November you get the votes and get elected."[64]

It helped, of course, to have solid candidates such as the aforementioned Billy Walker of St. Luke's Place. Like nearly all Irish Villagers, Billy Walker was a staunch Democrat. He was active in both the district Jefferson Club and the Tammany Society, and when he ran for office, as he did quite often in the 1880s and nineties, he brought to the task a personable nature that appealed to Villagers of many types. Popular with middle-class Irish Villagers who, like himself, had gotten ahead in the world materially, he also was blessed with a nice common touch. Although he was a teetotaler, which might have set him apart from the average Irishmen who frequented west Village saloons, he handled this potentially damaging trait in a creative way. When, as was customary, he made campaign visits to local saloons, he simply told the bartender, "Give me a milk punch," which in reality was nothing but milk and seltzer water. He also had an open-minded temperament that led him to make many friends outside the Irish community, among others the head of a Greenwich Village settlement house (Mary Simkhovitch) and a Democrat of old Dutch stock, John R. Voorhis, who lived on Greenwich Street and who, like Walker, had been a carpenter, had held office under Tammany administrations, and was willing, on occasion, to split with the Tammany organization.[65]

Billy Walker won more campaigns than he lost. In the late 1880s he was elected to the Board of Aldermen and served four terms. In 1892 and 1893 he represented the district as its state assemblyman. The only hitch in this otherwise unbroken string of electoral victories came in 1894, when he announced that he was going to vote for William Strong, the Committee of Seventy's anti-Tammany mayoral candidate. This act of apostasy cost him in two ways: anti-Tammany candidates carried Walker's district, preventing him from being reelected to the State Assembly; then, as punishment for his having backed Strong, the Richard Croker–led Democratic machine denied Walker further public preferment. His political career remained in limbo until Croker was ousted and Croker's successor, Charles F. Murphy, in an effort to revitalize Tammany by reaching out to Democrats who had shown some independence of the machine, backed Walker's appointment as Superintendent of Public Buildings for the Borough of Manhattan.[66]

District leaders like Culkin and candidates like Walker all depended on loyal rank-and-file Democrats to perform a variety of chores at election time. Most such individuals remain forever anonymous; however, something is known about the campaign activities of Billy Walker's son Jimmy, whose career as the city's mayor in the late 1920s set biographers scrambling for information about his childhood. And, as they found, in the 1890s Jimmy Walker was simply an Irish American Villager distinguished from his young friends only by his relation to his father, the candidate.

Jimmy Walker received a thorough grounding in the practical art of ward-level electioneering during his father's many campaigns for office. At election time Jimmy, his brothers, and their best friends (two sets of Higgins brothers who lived down the block from the Walkers' home) supplemented their usual recreational activities—baseball and football, pranks and fisticuffs—with the varied entertainments that party battles offered. The boys gathered wood and combustibles and used them to start the bonfires that illuminated nighttime campaign rallies. On election day they loafed around local polling places, which at the turn of the century were located at such quintessentially male hangouts as barber shops and cigar stores, and listened as Tammany orators harangued voters going to cast their ballots. That evening, if things went as they usually did in the west Village, the boys joined in the revels as Tammany's partisans celebrated yet another victory for the district's Democrats.[67]

Like his father, Jimmy Walker was comfortable rubbing shoulders with ordinary Villagers, but Jimmy had developed this capacity in quite a different way. Billy Walker had been a poor boy when he immigrated to the United States, and had acquired a direct knowledge of the laboring man's life during his years as a carpenter. By contrast, his son had been fairly well-off as a youth and had acquired his common touch through participation in the urban mass entertainments of the time. As a boy, he played football in the fall, and in the spring and summer he joined other west Village men and boys every Saturday near the West Street docks for baseball games that determined who could claim bragging rights in the neighborhood. He was a fan of boxing, and as a young man in his twenties, he sometimes refereed fights at Peter J. Crotty's wholesale liquor house on Hudson Street, less than a block from the Walker residence.[68]

Jimmy was also fond of vaudeville shows and Broadway musicals, and for a time he had dreamed of pursuing a career as a songwriter. He had begun to write lyrics early in the 1900s and succeeded in getting a few of his songs published. His activity as a lyricist reached its peak in 1905 in a cooperative venture with Ernest R. Ball, a prolific composer whose gift for creating popular melodies is apparent in his Irish American ballads "When Irish Eyes Are Smiling" and "Mother Machree." A collaborative piece, "Will You Love Me in December as You Do in May," words by J. J. Walker, music by Ernest R. Ball, became a best-seller in 1905.

Jimmy Walker's playboy lifestyle in the 1920s and the fact that scandals forced him to resign as mayor have led most scholars to treat Walker's connections with pre–World War I popular entertainments as little more than examples of an early predisposition to frivolity. Yet Walker's wish to be a songwriter and his zest for cheap amusements, as mass market entertainments were called at the turn of the century, were entirely congruent with his west Village Irish milieu. Among Irish Democrats, egalitarian politics and popular culture went hand in hand. Tammany's political ethic of befriending the poor had its parallel in an affinity shared by both the Tammany leadership and its rank-and-file members for popular amusements. "Big Tim" Sullivan, the most powerful Tammany district leader of the century's first decade, owned several theaters, and he was renowned for the spirited annual balls and lavish summer excusions to which he treated his Lower East Side constituents. In the same years the *Tammany Times*, official mouthpiece for the Democratic machine, featured a section labeled "Amusements" with numerous advertisements for dances, theater productions, and vaudeville shows. Perhaps fittingly, the first-floor occupant of Tammany's main headquarters building on Fourteenth Street was Tony Pastor's variety show theater, one of the most boisterous and popular vaudeville establishments in the city. Through his love of commercial entertainments, Jimmy Walker identified himself with one of the most powerful cultural trends of his time.[69]

Anyone, even someone of Irish background, who challenged the political and cultural loyalties that united turn-of-the-century Irish neighborhoods was asking for trouble. This was a lesson that Henry H. Curran, a young lawyer, learned quite forcefully in 1903. Curran was an Independent Democrat who usually voted for Republicans in municipal elections, and he had volunteered to speak in support of reelecting Mayor Seth Low, the Citizens' Union (i.e., anti-Tammany) candidate who had been voted into office in 1901. It was to be Curran's first-ever campaign speech.

On the appointed night a horse-drawn wagon with three occupants—a driver, a man assigned to introduce Curran, and another man whose job was to start a bonfire to draw a crowd—picked Curran up and took him to the tough Lower West Side location near the riverfront where he was to speak. The fire-builder soon produced an impressive blaze and a small group of curious onlookers gathered. The man making the introduction did his job, ending with a rhetorical flourish in which he presented Curran as "that great Irish-American orator."[70]

No one in the mainly Irish crowd was fooled for a moment. Curran, regardless of his ethnic background, was a representative of the enemy camp, the good-government, kid-glove snobs who were going to vote for Seth Low. Curran had barely gotten to his feet and cleared his throat when the first projectile, a turnip, was hurled in his direction by someone just beyond the circle of light made by the fire. A cabbage, a rotten tomato, part of a cobblestone, and a dirt clod followed, several missiles passing close to Curran's head and one of them striking the fire-builder on the neck. Being a prudent fellow, Curran shouted to the driver, "Whip up, Bill!" and, spurred by the lash, the old horse broke into an awkward canter that carried the Low contingent safely out of range.[71]

Irish Democrats not only chased Curran off, but Tammany defeated Low and recaptured control of the city's administration in the 1903 election. From the perspective of most Irish Villagers it probably seemed that their hegemony in the neighborhood was still firmly in place. From alderman to congressman, with a single exception every elected official whose district included the west Village was a Democrat. (The lone man out was a Republican state assemblyman from a district whose core was the silk-stocking Washington Square North part of the neighborhood.) Moreover, the Irish county societies were flourishing, and old St. Joseph's was in the midst of a highly successful building campaign.

But change was in the air. Anti-Tammany candidates had won two out of the last four mayoral elections. Tammany's leaders needed strong support from working-class voters to prevent future defeats, but most of the immigrants who were arriving in unprecedented numbers at the turn of the century were not Irish, and though non-Irish laborers often backed Tammany candidates, they were not so dependably Democratic as Irishmen. Inside Greenwich Village, the impact of these developments was such that by 1900 Italians outnumbered Irish in the Village as a whole by approximately two to one, and Italian immigrants were rapidly taking over parts of the west Village that had once been mainly Irish. If these demographic trends continued, the west Village Irish would soon find themselves in a social and political landscape very different from the one that the Walkers, Culkins, Roons, and other Irish worthies had known at the end of the nineteenth century.[72]

2

For Their Mutual Benefit

I N   T H E   F I N A L   D E C A D E S of the nineteenth century and early years
of the twentieth, hundreds of young American women and men, nearly all
of them college educated and many from wealthy families, made a seemingly curious decision to take up residence in the slums of the nation's
largest cities, including working-class sections of Greenwich Village. The
pioneering generation of American settlement house activists took inspiration from the example of a group of idealistic young Britons, students at
Oxford and Cambridge, who in the 1880s had gone to live among the London poor in order to observe the conditions of urban slum life firsthand
and, as a historian of the movement put it, to "make their settlement in the
slums an outpost of education and culture." Like their British counterparts,
American settlement house reformers were concerned about the enormous
social problems spawned by the growth of modern industrial cities, by the
increasing gulf between rich and poor, and by the increasing ignorance of
and, worse yet, hostility toward workers on the part of the middle and upper
classes. Moving to a working-class neighborhood was seen as a direct, personal act that privileged Americans could make toward fostering cross-class
communication, bringing (as the authors of a New York settlement's constitution described it) "men and women of education into closer relations with
the laboring classes to their mutual benefit."[1]

Settlements everywhere in the United States adopted much the same program in pursuit of their mission to working-class city dwellers. Settlements typically offered classes in subjects ranging from English, civics, and debate to sewing, carpentry, and basket weaving, and they provided organized social activities for both adults and children through settlement clubs. These forms of neighborly outreach were soon supplemented by civic and political initiatives. Settlement workers lobbied city authorities to improve the quality of schools, sanitation, streets, and parks in the neighborhood, and in a further effort to bring these reforms to fruition, many settlement house residents campaigned to elect sympathetic candidates to office. Finally, most settlements conducted fact-finding surveys of local conditions in the belief that well-researched reports would convince the public and the politicians that slum environments seriously inhibited the tenement dwellers' ability to improve themselves.

By the end of the 1890s social settlements were found in most New York City neighborhoods from midtown Manhattan south to the Battery, but the greatest concentration was in Lower East Side tenement districts, which were populated primarily by recently arrived East European Jews. Of the settlements active among this population, three were particularly significant. College Settlement, established in 1889 by seven graduates of elite New England women's colleges, was located on Rivington Street. Less than three blocks away, at 185 Eldridge Street, was the University Settlement Society, organized under that name in 1891 as the successor to the Neighborhood Guild, the first settlement in the United States. The third major Lower East Side settlement house was Henry Street Settlement, founded as Nurses' Settlement in 1893 by Lillian D. Wald, who was still its guiding spirit in 1900.

As of January 1900 there were still no settlements in Greenwich Village, principally because for most of the nineteenth century the neighborhood had not been considered a tenement house district. However, this perception had begun to change in the 1890s as more and more tenements were built south and west of Washington Square. At the turn of the new century, settlement house activists with prior experience among East Side slum dwellers became convinced that the new tenement sections of the Village were promising locales for settlement work. In rapid succession two settlement houses opened their doors for business, one in the south Village in 1900, another in the west Village in 1902.

WEST SIDE BRANCH

In March 1900 James B. Reynolds, the headworker of University Settlement on the Lower East Side, urged his organization's governing council to establish a branch in the southern part of Greenwich Village, just west of University Settlement's traditional area of operation. Reynolds argued that the rapid growth of the West Side Italian immigrant enclave and the economic achievements of its residents—many of whom were moving out of unskilled jobs such as "railroad digger or street shoveler" into trades like barbering—required a supportive response from University Settlement activists. The council agreed, and in June it appropriated $2,500 to organize West Side Branch, a name chosen over the main alternative, Italian Branch, because council members wanted to make it clear that the new branch was open to everyone in the neighborhood.[2]

Reynolds went right to work. Within a short time he recruited Edith Thomas to be the new branch's head resident. The daughter of a New Hampshire judge, she was married to Bond Thomas, a businessman, and had recently been doing volunteer work for University Settlement's legal aid division. To assist her at West Side Branch, Reynolds hired Dorothy Drake, a graduate of Smith College. He leased a house at 38 King Street, which Edith Thomas later described as "a quiet side street" that was "only a stone's throw away from the crowded tenement-house districts" of Bleecker, Thompson, and Sullivan, a south Village neighborhood in which fully 60 percent of the school-age children were Italian.[3]

Although Reynolds had made his case for opening West Side Branch by stressing the growing importance of Italians to Lower Manhattan's economy, political considerations also figured significantly in his thinking. Reynolds had been very active in anti-Tammany politics. In 1894 he served on the Committee of Seventy that successfully backed William Strong's mayoral campaign, and in 1896, excited by the benefits of a reform administration for tenement dwellers (cleaner streets, stronger housing regulations, and less police corruption), he urged settlement activists to follow his example and go into politics. "Be earnest, practical, and be active," he urged. "Political reform is the great moral opportunity of our day." The following year Reynolds helped convince his friend Seth Low to run as the Citizens' Union candidate for mayor, and he served as Low's informal campaign manager during the 1897 election. Although the Croker-led Tammany Democrats won in 1897, Reynolds immediately began to look ahead to the next mayoral campaign. Tammany, he believed, had gained an advantage with downtown Italian voters by backing a prominent Italian businessman, Antonio Zucca, for Coroner of the Borough of Manhattan. Eager to have south Village Italians associate reformers with their best interests, Reynolds wanted to have the West Side Branch up and running before the 1901 municipal elections.[4]

West Side Branch got off to a fast start. An opening reception in December 1900 featured speeches in English by Reynolds and others and in Italian

9. A kindergarten class at a Village settlement house. From Greenwich House, *Annual Report,* 1910.

by prominent representatives of the Italian community. These included Luigi Fugazy, described by Edith Thomas as "one of the best-known Italian bankers in this city" and equally admired in the south Village as the indefatigable patron of New York's Italian mutual aid societies. By March 1901 Thomas and three other women residents had launched a program that was attracting many participants, about a third of them Italians from the tenement district east of the house and the others from the various ethnic groups that lived to the west. Thirty children were enrolled in the West Side Branch kindergarten, and nearly five hundred youngsters had joined the settlement's several dozen clubs and classes, with sewing, debating, singing, drawing, dancing, and gymnastics among the available activities (fig. 9). A brick stable behind the settlement house had been converted into a gym that was used for "dancing-classes, entertainments, musical afternoons and large mothers' meetings," and the settlement's main building housed a circulating library and a penny savings bank. Thomas took it upon herself to plant a large flower garden intended especially for the enjoyment of the local children. Writing in March, she said she was looking forward to spring, when tulips and daffodils could "be picked freely by the chubby little hands which never have been able before to gather growing flowers."[5]

Despite West Side Branch's impressive start, all was not well. Although

Thomas was the branch's chief administrator, she was still an employee of its parent organization, the University Settlement Society, and a subordinate of James B. Reynolds, an ambitious man who showed little patience for anyone who did not come up to his expectations. Unfortunately for Edith Thomas, Reynolds soon became dissatisfied with her performance. The precise cause of his disenchantment was never explicit, but some possible causes can be surmised. Thomas had no previous experience in managing an organization the size of West Side Branch and she sometimes dithered over details, turning to Reynolds for advice on small matters that he may have felt she should have handled on her own. He also may have viewed some of her activities, the flower garden in particular, as frivolous, a poor use of her time. In any event, by early March, less than five months into Thomas's term as headworker, Reynolds had begun to search for a replacement.

Reynolds described the type of upper-middle or upper-class woman he hoped to recruit for the post in a letter he sent to Mary Simkhovitch, the headworker of Friendly Aid House settlement on East Thirty-fourth Street. Although Reynolds may have intended to be ironic or witty, a disdainful tone underlies his words. The new head resident at West Side Branch, he wrote, should be "neither too young, too handsome, nor too stylish, but a fair amount of all these qualities will not be an objection." She should, moreover, "be someone who has for some time been devoted to good works but would like to continue that devotion at sweat shop wages." Given what he called Simkhovitch's "extended acquaintance with the decayed aristocracy," Reynolds wondered if she could suggest a suitable candidate.[6]

When she was informed of Reynolds's decision to replace her, Edith Thomas was devastated. Under great strain owing to obligations that included teaching classes nearly every morning, afternoon, and evening, and despondent over her failure to win Reynolds's approval, she collapsed from "nervous prostration" on three different occasions in March, April, and May. The consulting physician's only suggestion was that she reduce her workload, something she was unwilling to do. Her husband, Bond Thomas, seems to have been of little help during this crisis, in part because he was regularly away on business, returning to the city only every other week.[7]

Around six in the evening of Tuesday, May 14, 1901, Reynolds was talking with Bond Thomas in a first-floor room at the settlement house when they heard a shot, followed by a scream and a heavy thump. The two men rushed upstairs to find Edith, a revolver in her hand, lying on the floor of her bedroom, bleeding profusely from a self-inflicted chest wound. Reynolds phoned a doctor, but she died before he arrived.

The following day the major New York dailies carried stories about Edith

Thomas's life and death. The *New York World*'s headline read: "Lived to Aid Others, Dies by Her Own Hand" (fig. 10). "Childless herself," the *World* article said, Thomas "sought for years to advance the children of the poor." Reynolds, who was doubtless appalled at the bad publicity and fearful that he would be blamed for Thomas's suicide, refused to respond to press inquiries. His coworkers followed suit, leading one paper to comment that "the utmost reticence was observed as to the cause of the suicide" by "everyone connected with the settlement." Lack of information, however, did not hinder speculation, and Democratic papers leaped at the chance to connect leading anti-Tammany reformers with a scandal. The *New York Sun* hinted most directly at Reynolds's role in the affair. "A rumor was afloat," the *Sun* reported, "that Mrs. Thomas took her life because the management expressed dissatisfaction with her work, but this was hotly denied by Mr. Reynolds through a messenger."[8]

Reynolds moved quickly to stabilize the situation at West Side Branch by recruiting a new headworker to take over in the fall of 1901. In Susan W. FitzGerald he found an able individual who during the previous year had held a position at Barnard College that later carried the title Dean of Students.[9]

Approximately six months later FitzGerald reported that West Side Branch's staff and programs were prospering. Where, under Edith Thomas, there had been only four residents, the residential staff now consisted of ten full-time and four part-time workers. The kindergarten's enrollment had grown to fifty, requiring division into two classes. The monthly circulation of library books was nearly one thousand, four times the previous level, and the penny savings bank was attracting depositors in unprecedented numbers. A vacant lot on Houston had been converted to a playground with facilities for basketball and baseball, games that were popular with the local boys. Classes and clubs were packed. The place was humming with activity.[10]

It was, however, disappointing to the staff that many more American-born and Irish immigrant residents of the area were participating in the settlement's programs than were the recent immigrants from Italy. Part of the explanation may simply have been that the earlier immigrant groups, especially English speakers like the Irish, had become sufficiently acculturated after many years in the United States to feel unthreatened by Americanizing aspects of the settlement's programs. Some Italian newcomers may have stayed away initially because they sensed and were offended by a cultural chauvinism in the settlement's staff that was reflected in FitzGerald's description of south Village Italians as "strangely isolated on account of their foreign tongue and equally foreign ideas and way of living." Whatever the case, as late as 1902, the settlement's programs were still attracting

WRITER WHO SHOT HERSELF IS MOURNED BY THE POOR.

Mrs. Bond Thomas, Who Committed Suicide, Was Called "Black Angel" by the Lowly.

The crowd of little Italian boys and girls that gathered in the kindergarten at the University Settlement Branch, No. 38 King street, this morning, missed the cheerful face of Edith Carpenter Thomas, "The Black Angel of the West Side," so-called because of her jet-black hair and eyes.

The fact that the zealous young woman, who had been working six months for the betterment of the tenement children of the lower West Side, lay dead in an upper room of the building, was kept from the swarthy-faced little ones.

Many young men and women interested in Settlement work called at the unpretentious building to offer condolence to the bereaved husband and to the dead woman's co-workers.

They all expressed surprise that Mrs. Thomas, gifted as an authoress, successful in her philanthropic work, should have ended her life by sending a bullet through her heart.

Suffered from Grip.

The responsibility of her work and an attack of grip, it was said to-day by her friends, caused Mrs. Thomas to kill herself.

Mr. Stewart, one of the head workers at the University Settlement Building, No. 184 Eldridge street, to-day said:

"Mrs. Thomas's work was entirely satisfactory. There was absolutely nothing wrong with her accounts. She had been in charge of the King street work since the branch opened last November. Her death is a shock to us.

Husband a Travelling Man.

"Mr. Thomas, her husband, is a travelling man. He is an old friend of Mr. Reynolds, of the University Settlement."

"In a report of her work in King street just published, Mrs. Thomas in reference to the Italian quarter in which she was interested, wrote:

"If the chief object in our national character is a disproportionate commercialism, which measures art and literature, like dry-goods, by what they cost, and gauges all human success in terms of dollars and cents, is it not conceivable that the disinterested love of beauty born in the Italian nature may in a hundred years or so of gradual admixture prevail somewhat against this apotheosis of money? And if our peasant has it in him to do this for us, is it not prudent to cherish him, and do all possible to educate and develop him as quickly as we can?

In her writings Mrs. Thomas preserved her maiden name, Edith Carpenter. Some other published works were "A Modern Rosalind," "Lorenzo de Medici" and "Cross Keys," a play which was produced at a dramatic reading at the Waldorf-Astoria.

WOMAN WRITER WHO KILLED HERSELF.

10. Edith Thomas, the West Side Branch headworker who committed suicide. From *New York Evening Journal*, May 15, 1901.

nearly twice as many non-Italian as Italian participants. This situation, however, like the neighborhood itself, soon changed. By 1907, the continued influx of Italian immigrants had made the surrounding neighborhood "entirely Italian," and most of the settlement's clients were by then also Italian.[11]

But how well fulfilled was the cherished hope of settlement activists that their working-class neighbors would view them less as representatives of an impersonal social service agency than as well-educated friends who happened to live at West Side Branch? Reading between the lines of FitzGerald's 1902 account, it is clear that the services relationship was stronger than the informal neighborly ties, though the latter were not absent. The settlement's clubs and classes were often oversubscribed, and other services were eagerly sought even though they duplicated similar ones available through older institutions within the immigrant community: for example, the settlement's savings bank, which competed with the Italian padrone's traditional role as banker to the poor, and the legal aid society, which competed with the Tammany district leaders' practice of offering legal assistance to constituents. Still, FitzGerald and her coworkers longed for informal friendly exchanges with their neighbors and were delighted when a few began to drop by simply to chat. Every such informal visit, FitzGerald wrote, "makes us feel that we have been accepted frankly as belonging to the neighborhood."[12]

By the time FitzGerald submitted her report in early 1902, major changes were underway at the main University Settlement house on Eldridge Street. The previous fall James B. Reynolds had again campaigned for Seth Low, and following Low's victory, Reynolds had been rewarded with an appointment as the mayor's personal secretary. To fill the now-vacant position of headworker, the University Settlement hired Robert Hunter, a wealthy young Indiana University graduate who had six years' experience in administrative work for the Chicago Board of Charities and who had for the past three years lived at Hull House, the highly regarded Chicago settlement led by Jane Addams. Hunter subsequently recruited a group of talented young men to be his coworkers on New York's Lower East Side. Prominent among these were Ernest Poole, a Princeton graduate and aspiring writer, and two socially progressive individuals with Hull House experience, William English Walling, a University of Chicago graduate, and Leroy Scott, who, like Hunter, had attended Indiana University. These new staff members soon formed lasting friendships with several University Settlement colleagues who were holdovers from the Reynolds period: J. G. Phelps Stokes, a Yale graduate and scion of one of the wealthiest and most socially prestigious New York families, and Miriam Finn, a nonresident staff member in charge of programs for Lower East Side girls.[13]

The young idealists in Hunter's circle came from backgrounds that closely mirrored those of most turn-of-the-century settlement activists, as sketched in a composite portrait by Allen Davis, a modern scholar of the movement. Except for Miriam Finn, a Russian-born Jew, all the rest, like the vast majority of Davis's sample, were college-educated, old stock Protestants born in the Northeast or Midwest. The men, like most settlement workers, came from upper-middle- or upper-class backgrounds, with Stokes, Walling, and Hunter being from exceptionally wealthy families. Also like most contemporary social settlement workers, the University Settlement group was young. Stokes turned thirty in 1902, and the others were still in their twenties. All were unmarried, and most made only a short-term commitment to settlement house life, joining the movement for two or three years and then going on to other pursuits.[14]

Hunter and his coworkers were also typical of the movement in that they became leading advocates of progressive social reform legislation. Shortly after he arrived at University Settlement in 1902, Hunter tapped the city's network of social settlement folk to organize a New York Child Labor Committee that included himself and Stokes from University Settlement, Mary Simkhovitch from Friendly Aid House, and Lillian Wald from Henry Street Settlement. Many social progressives who were not residents of settlement houses endorsed the committee's call for stronger state child labor laws, but the campaign's core group was composed of headworkers and other settlement folk. Leroy Scott and Ernest Poole of University Settlement contributed newspaper and magazine articles in support of the cause. From her outpost in the Village Susan FitzGerald of West Side Branch took responsibility for tracking the progress of the committee's bills in the state legislature. The reformers' concerted efforts were rewarded in the spring of 1903 when the legislature passed four regulatory measures that, though less stringent than the reformers wanted, were among the most rigorous in the nation at the time.[15]

In an unrelated decision taken shortly after the child labor laws passed, University Settlement's council voted to discontinue its West Side branch. The official announcement cited budgetary concerns and the council's belief that money spent on West Side Branch could be put to better use on projects at the settlement's Lower East Side center. To soften the blow, the council agreed to continue paying rent on the branch's buildings into 1904, a gesture intended to give West Side Branch supporters some breathing room while they tried to reorganize on an independent basis. In September 1903, the successor organization opened its doors as Richmond Hill House, a name derived from the historic mansion that had once occupied a site nearby in the Village. Susan FitzGerald stayed on as headworker, and J. G. Phelps Stokes joined the newly formed board of directors. The main settlement house remained at the same location it had occupied for the past year, a building at 28 MacDougal that was slightly closer to the heart of the south Village Italian tenement district than the West Side Branch's previous address had been. The old location on King Street continued to be used by Richmond Hill House as a residence for its staff.[16]

Although West Side Branch was on the southernmost edge of the Village and had a very short existence, the impact of University Settlement and its Italian branch on Greenwich Village history was not insignificant. Part of that legacy was bequeathed through the careers of individuals who came to University Settlement in the Reynolds-Hunter era and subsequently became residents of the Village. By early 1905 most of the members of Hunter's circle were ready to move on, either to marry or to launch their postsettlement work careers. Moreover, by that point in time all of them were becoming increasingly involved in socialist causes, either as members of the Socialist Party or as intellectuals who promoted socialist ideas. Moving to the Village, as nearly every member of the Hunter circle did within a year or two of leaving the settlement, proved an amiable way of maintaining friendships and of facilitating mutual political and intellectual projects. Though few in number, this group of settlement house veterans brought to the Village an invigorating mix of talent, energy, ambition, and political passion that had a substantial influence on Village life between 1906 and the mid-1910s.

West Side Branch's institutional legacy in the Village was also substantial. Richmond Hill House pursued the Italian branch idea with considerable success, and in the early 1910s, when the Russell Sage Foundation sponsored a major study of Italian women in industry, Richmond Hill House not only supplied a majority of the survey's informants but served as home base for several of the principal investigators. Institutionally, West Side Branch had blazed a trail by being the first settlement opened in Greenwich Village. The collegial spirit in the movement was such that University Settlement folk never claimed that their pioneering effort gave them anything like exclusive rights over any or all settlement work on the lower West Side. When Mary Simkhovitch of Friendly Aid House made inquiries in 1902 about the possibility of establishing a second Greenwich Village settlement, she received nothing but encouragement from her colleagues at University Settlement. Robert Hunter, having consulted with Susan FitzGerald of West Side Branch, observed that there was "much work to be done in this neighborhood," and concluded that "if affected at all, we should be benefited by their coming into this district." Having received the blessing of University Settlement's leadership, Greenwich House, which was to have a long and illustrious history, opened for business on Jones Street in the west Village in November 1902.[17]

GREENWICH HOUSE

Residents of West Side Branch and Greenwich House were, like their settlement colleagues throughout the United States, optimists. Far from being disheartened by the social problems associated with conditions in America's industrial cities—sprawling slums, huge numbers of non-English-speaking immigrants, corrupt municipal governments, crime, and working-class unrest—settlement workers preferred to see the opportunities inherent in the urban scene. From this perspective no city offered greater challenges or more promise than New York, a metropolis that was rapidly becoming not just the nation's largest urban center but its financial and cultural capital as well. Mary Simkhovitch spoke for many of her contemporaries when she observed that upon arriving on the Lower East Side in the late 1890s, she had experienced a "vivid sense of a new and overpowering vitality" that exceeded anything she had encountered in Boston and London slums. Life in New York's tenement districts was heady stuff, and certain that she wanted more than just a taste, Simkhovitch in 1898 launched her career as a New York City social worker.[18]

She was well prepared for what was ahead. Born Mary Kingsbury in Chestnut Hill outside of Boston, she was the daughter of a politically active Civil War veteran and a mother she described as more intellectual than domestic. While an undergraduate at Boston University, she was influenced by social gospel Protestants who were committed to Christian-inspired social reform. She also met individuals who were active in the settlement house movement, one of whom, Wellesley College economics professor Emily Balch, became a mentor and friend. After graduation Kingsbury taught high school Latin for two years, did a year of graduate work in sociology and economics at Radcliffe College, and received a fellowship to continue her studies in Berlin. Although her mother insisted on accompanying her, Kingsbury nevertheless found her year abroad an eye-opener in ways both small (seeing a woman smoking a cigarette) and large (attending, with Emily Balch as her guide, the London International Socialist Trade Union Congress of 1896). Upon her return to the United States, Kingsbury enrolled in graduate courses in sociology and political economy at Columbia University, sharing an East Side apartment on Irving Place with another Boston University alumna, Anne O'Hagan, a reporter for the *New York World*.[19]

In September 1897 Kingsbury became a resident at College Settlement on the Lower East Side and soon thereafter assumed the post of headworker. With characteristic thoroughness, she had prepared for living in a predominantly Jewish neighborhood by studying Yiddish. She quickly established friendly relations with the residents of nearby University Settlement. James B. Reynolds, the headworker there, became a trusted colleague, although she never completely shared his hostility toward Tammany Hall's influence in the neighborhood. Kingsbury felt that Tammany politicos such as the local ward boss, Big Tim Sullivan, provided their constituents with many services for which anti-Tammany crusaders, bent simply on throwing the rascals out, offered few substantial substitutes.

In December 1898 Kingsbury left College Settlement to become head-worker at Friendly Aid House, a settlement located in the East Thirties; a month later, on January 7, 1899, she married Vladimir G. Simkhovitch, a Russian-born political economist she had met while both were students in Berlin. She stayed at Friendly Aid House for three and a half years, but her experience there was not entirely satisfactory. The settlement was funded by rich Unitarian philanthropists and viewed by them as a charitable activity in which they gave and others received, quite different from the credo of reciprocity between the classes to which Simkhovitch subscribed. Moreover, the most influential contributor was a staunch Republican, whose refusal to allow the premises to be used for any program critical of his party provoked an unpleasant confrontation with Simkhovitch, who had arranged for and then had to cancel a speech at the house by an opponent of McKinley's foreign policy. These philosophical spats, however, helped Simkhovitch sharpen her thinking about what a settlement should or should not be. It should not, she concluded, simply be an avenue for the wealthy few to demonstrate their altruism. Rather it ought to be an enterprise in which settlement residents and working-class neighbors joined forces in "a cooperative effort for social betterment."[20]

By early 1902 Simkhovitch was ready to test her ideas at a settlement that she would found and lead, and she asked Paul Kennaday, a coworker at Friendly Aid House, to scout Greenwich Village for a site for her new enterprise. Kennaday was typical of the well-educated young men who set aside promising professional careers to devote themselves for a time to the settlement house movement. Born in Brooklyn, New York, in 1873, Kennaday grew up in a family that was deeply committed to academic pursuits, public life, and the urban scene. His father was a lawyer who served in both the New York State Assembly and Senate. His mother had taken some college courses without completing a degree. The younger Kennaday graduated from Yale in 1895 and completed a Bachelor of Law degree at New York Law School in 1897. For the next six years he practiced law in the city; however, his first love was social work, and in pursuit of that interest he had joined the staff at Friendly Aid House.[21]

From May to early July 1902 Kennaday, often accompanied by another settlement worker, Mary Sherman, canvassed the Greenwich Village area to find a suitable location for Simkhovitch's settlement house. He finally heard about a building at 26 Jones Street that seemed perfect. Anything farther south in the Village would have been too close to West Side Branch and its Italian enclave. East of Sixth Avenue was too middle-class, north of

11. Greenwich House on Jones Street. The settlement was in one of the three-story buildings on the near side of the paper box factory. Greenwich House Collection, Tamiment Institute Library, New York University.

Washington Square too upper-class; and the Village west of Hudson Street too cluttered with the many factories and warehouses near the Hudson River docks. Jones Street, however, was in a working-class neighborhood, and the three-story house at number 26, though run-down and filthy, was not only just the right size but available to lease in the fall. Mary Simkhovitch, vacationing in Maine with her husband and their first child, made a quick trip to the city and put her stamp of approval on Kennaday's find (fig. 11).

Bounded on the south by Bleecker and the north by West Fourth, Jones Street was only one block long. This meant that the street had the kind of manageable proportions that might help settlement residents develop friendly relations with their neighbors. The nightly visits of the man who lit the gas lamps that were still in use and the regular passage of horse-drawn streetcars on the Bleecker and West Fourth lines at either end of Jones gave the street a pleasant old-fashioned ambience, but the buildings that lined both sides of the block were a mix of old and new, a hodgepodge of architectural styles and residential and commercial uses. About half of the buildings were older three-story structures like number 26, but the rest were five- or six-story tenements, several with walls flush to those of the adjacent building, a form of construction that left interior rooms without direct access to light or fresh air. Although most were apartment houses or boardinghouses, there were five saloons on the block. Another building just two doors down from number 26 was in active use as a box factory.[22]

Nowhere were the features of a modern industrial city more apparent than in the mixed ethnic composition of the street's population. At the beginning of the century the largest ethnic group on Jones Street was made up of Irish Americans, who comprised about 40 percent of the whole. Another 25 percent of the block's residents came from other western European countries, mainly Germany, France, and England. African Americans and Italians, the latter an advance guard of the most rapidly expanding nationality in the neighborhood, were found in almost equal numbers, about 12 percent each. The remaining 10 percent or so of Jones Streeters were either third-generation Americans or immigrants from scattered locations around the globe: Liberia, Algeria, Hungary, Turkey, Russia, China, and the West Indies. That there was little neighborly communication across ethnic lines was one of the urban social problems that Simkhovitch and her coworkers intended to address.[23]

Naming her settlement Greenwich House, Simkhovitch guided every step of its organizational phase with great care. To fill the largely honorific role of signing the settlement's incorporation papers, she chose distinguished individuals from varied ethnic and religious backgrounds—Felix Adler, a German-born Jew who founded the Society for Ethical Culture, Bishop Henry C. Potter of the Episcopal church, Judge Eugene Philbin, a prominent Roman Catholic, and Jacob Riis, the newspaper man and housing reformer—to indicate that Greenwich House was a nonsectarian organization open to all its neighbors regardless of race, religion, or ethnicity.

Although one in eight of Jones Street's residents were blacks, and many more lived on nearby streets, no African American was included among the incorporators or, for that matter, on any other board of the fledgling settlement. Nevertheless, the omission of blacks did not reflect any antipathy on Simkhovitch's part toward the settlement's black neighbors. With blacks, as with Villagers of every ethnic background, she drew a distinction between good neighbors and bad neighbors. She expressed admiration for the "dignified manners" of the African American "ministers from the South" who lodged at a boardinghouse across the street from Greenwich House, and she described the black residents of Jones, Cornelia, Gay, and West Third streets as "for the most part highly respected and law-abiding citizens." But almost from the first she waged a campaign to "wipe out the

Minettas Street, Lane, and Court" by razing run-down buildings that housed "lawless and shiftless" blacks and building a park on the site. In 1904, she encouraged the settlement's Committee on Social Investigations to provide Mary White Ovington, a young social worker friend who was eager to launch what became a lifelong career working for racial justice, with seed money to start researching her book, *Half a Man*, on New York City's blacks. Moreover, in the second year of its existence, Greenwich House rented a room on Cornelia Street for local blacks to use as a social center and library. No rationale was given for not using a room at the main settlement, but it seems likely that Simkhovitch, though wishing to establish friendly relations with black neighbors, was not willing to challenge directly the conviction strongly held by Americans of all classes, including most of the settlement's working-class clientele, that racial segregation should prevail in the social sphere.[24]

In choosing Greenwich House's governing board, Simkhovitch rejected the practice followed by most contemporary settlements of having boards and councils that were composed almost exclusively of wealthy individuals who had little if any direct contact with the day-to-day work of the settlement. Remembering her unhappy experience with just such a governing system at Friendly Aid House, Simkhovitch insisted that Greenwich House must be a "Cooperative Social Settlement Society" that included resident workers on its policymaking council. Consistent with this principle, the members of Greenwich House's first Board of Managers were a representative mix of young residents—Paul Kennaday, Louise Egvert, and Annie Noyes—and wealthy contributors, two of whom, Gertrude Vanderbilt Whitney and Frieda S. Warburg, remained loyal supporters of the settlement for many years to come.[25]

The house at 26 Jones Street needed a thorough cleaning, interior painting, repairs, and the services of a pest exterminator before it was ready for occupancy in November 1902. Simkhovitch had recruited a staff of fifteen residents, eight women and seven men. Since the main building could not house everyone, she made a virtue of necessity by distributing the overflow to three nearby addresses, describing them as "little colonies" of college graduates in a working-class neighborhood. She, her family, and five women residents moved into 26 Jones, with the young women assigned small bedrooms on the building's third floor. A visitor during the first year reported that each woman was provided with the bare necessities (a chair, a table, a chiffonier, a bed, and bedding) and encouraged to supplement these items with "pictures, rugs, hangings, desks, etc." acquired on her own. The visitor added that none of the idealistic young residents complained about these conditions.[26]

Five of the seven male residents rented rooms in a house about a block and a half away at 88 Grove Street. This handsome Greek Revival home, like its twin next door at 90 Grove, dated from the 1820s and had had distinguished owners. In 1902, number 88 belonged to Ferruccio Vitale, a well-known landscape architect and friend of Greenwich House. Number 90 was the property of Robert Blum, an artist whose studio occupied the back of the lot. Vitale's five Greenwich House tenants—two lawyers, a banker, a stockbroker, and a jeweler—were only the first among many well-to-do social progressives to occupy either 88 or 90 Grove Street over the next decade.[27]

During the first year of the settlement's history, the five Greenwich House men used their rented rooms at 88 Grove mainly as places to sleep. Much of their workday was spent at 26 Jones, including their morning and evening meals. Thinking back to the first of these communal meals, which was on Thanksgiving Day, 1902, Simkhovitch remembered the mood of excitement that prevailed. "We felt," she recalled, "somehow born again. We were all young together. Everything was ahead of us. Full of enthusiasm and zest, we plunged into the life of Jones Street."[28]

Settlement work on Jones Street had a threefold focus: sociability, services, and surveys. Informal socializing began within the community of Greenwich House and played a crucial role in building a strong esprit de corps in its ranks. The daily ritual of taking meals together, especially the less hurried evening meal at 6:30 every night, provided an opportunity to exchange ideas with coworkers and guests, to share stories from the day's activities, and to plan what needed to be done next. Lasting friendships and even marriages were byproducts of these collegial exchanges, but the broadest impact was educational. A veteran settlement activist spoke for herself and many colleagues when she wrote that these contacts with like-minded women and men opened to her "new worlds of thought and understanding."[29]

Greenwich House residents gradually established trusting relationships with their neighbors, even though success on that score was not universal. Things got off to a positive start the day the settlement opened when Mary Simkhovitch arrived, pushing the carriage with her firstborn in it and six months pregnant with her second child. Wary Jones Streeters, who had been wondering why these upper-middle-class people wanted to live on a working-class street, dropped their guard a bit at the unthreatening sight of a mother and her baby. Several neighbors soon became friendly: Mrs. King, an Irish woman with a large brood of her own, Mr. Zimmerman, the owner of a Bleecker Street delicatessen, and Mr. Kelley, who ran a respectable saloon (no drinking to excess and no unaccompanied women allowed) at the West Fourth Street end of the block.[30]

Even so, conflicting cultural assumptions occasionally led to misunderstandings between the settlement folk and their neighbors. When Simkhovitch, acting on the best contemporary public health advice about the benefits of fresh air, put her baby, warmly wrapped and in a bassinet, out on the fire escape at 26 Jones, the young women box makers in the factory next door were appalled, convinced that Simkhovitch was a neglectful mother. Similarly, on hearing the screams of a woman being beaten by her husband, a young female resident called the police to have him arrested. The wife was indignant and refused to press charges. In a jibe aimed at the settlement worker, the woman declared, "Sure I'm going back to my husband. She ain't got any, and don't know."[31]

The services Greenwich House offered its neighbors were similar to those found at most contemporary settlements. Within the first two weeks of operation, Greenwich House residents organized a wide array of clubs and classes, the clubs mostly social in character and the classes ranging from practical (cooking) to recreational (dancing) to academic (New York City history) (fig. 12). A kindergarten was opened for preschoolers, and school-age youngsters were invited to borrow books from a children's reading room. A Penny Provident Bank was established to take deposits of sums too small to be accepted by regular savings banks, and twice-weekly hot lunches were served to women workers from the box factory next door. Simkhovitch firmly believed that in an ideal world Jones Streeters would have either organized such programs themselves or taken the initiative in asking public or private agencies to help them do so; but the reality, she wrote, was that "there are so many neighborhood needs which no one else can or will undertake except neighborhood houses such as Settlements" (fig. 13).[32]

By the end of Greenwich House's first year Simkhovitch was confident that the services then in place were meeting many of the neighborhood's immediate needs, and she was ready to move forward toward her long-range objective, which, in her words, was nothing less than "to make Jones Street one of the most desirable streets to live on in New York." To find out what it would take to reach this ambitious goal, she needed precise information about the neighborhood, and this was where the third leg of the settlement triad of sociability, services, and surveys came into play. Systematic investigations of carefully targeted subjects could, Simkhovitch felt, document local conditions and stimulate discussion of what, if any, ameliorative action needed to be taken. The surveys had another largely unanticipated result, which was to give later generations of readers some insight into the lives of otherwise anonymous working-class Villagers. However, since settlement workers generally judged their neighbors' behavior as good or bad based on middle-class standards that working-class Villagers did not always share, these surveys need to be read for what they reveal about the survey takers,

12. A Greenwich House cooking class taught by Louise Bolard, 1902. Greenwich House Collection, Tamiment Institute Library, New York University.

as well as for what they reveal about the lives and values of the workers being surveyed.[33]

Two such surveys were conducted by Greenwich House researchers during the settlement's second and third years (1903–1905). The first was *Wage-Earners' Budgets*, a detailed report on the incomes and expenditures of two hundred working-class families in the Village. This survey was conducted between November 1903 and September 1905, with Louise Bolard as principal investigator. Bolard had come to New York City after graduating from Allegheny College in Meadville, Pennsylvania, and had worked with Simkhovitch at Friendly Aid House before becoming a member of Greenwich House's first group of residents. Shortly before her monograph came into print, she married Charles H. More and chose to use her married name, Louise Bolard More, on the title page.

More's study contains a wealth of information about ordinary Villagers. After describing her methodology, More echoed an observation that Simkhovitch had made in her first annual report, namely that the occupational profile of Greenwich Village workers was significantly more diverse than that found among Lower East Side residents. "There is [in the Village]," More wrote, "no one highly concentrated industry as that of the garment-makers of the East Side, but a great diversity of trades and occupations." Virtually every type of unskilled and skilled labor was represented, including jobs in "candy, paper-box, and artificial-flower factories" and many occupations related to the Hudson River docks: longshoremen, warehouse workers, and truck drivers. The heads of More's two hundred families divided almost equally between American-born and foreign-born individuals. Income depended on many factors, but larger families tended to have higher annual incomes, mainly because of the contributions made by older children who had part- or full-time jobs.[34]

More limited her survey to working families, leaving the study of entirely destitute Villagers for other researchers. She found that the incomes of her two hundred working households, and consequently the quality of their lives, varied greatly. A small number, only 5.5 percent of the whole, earned what she called "a pitifully small amount" ($400 or less annually) and en-

13. Kindergarteners in Greenwich House's backyard playground. Greenwich House Collection, Tamiment Institute Library, New York University.

dured great hardships. Those with relatively high incomes (14.5 percent earned $1,200 or more per year) generally lived very well. The large middle group, which was very diverse, included a significant number (ca. 25 percent of the total sample) whose annual incomes were within one hundred dollars of the average figure for all families, $851.38. On this sum, More reported, "some families live comfortably, other suffer privations," and since the wife was responsible for most of the family's ordinary expenditures, the difference between comfort and privation, according to More, "depends upon whether the mother is a good manager or not." She added, however, that husbands could also affect the family's standard of living for good or ill. Those who drank heavily often spent so much at local saloons that, in More's opinion, they significantly injured their family's quality of life.[35]

More's findings clearly delineated what workers spent on basic items. The most basic, and most expensive, were housing and food. On average, More's families paid about twenty percent of their income for housing. Rents ranged from $7 to $32 a month ($84–$384 annually), with the average family paying about $13.50 a month for a three- or four-room unfurnished apartment. Food costs were the biggest budget item, comprising 42.3 percent of an average family's expenses. Family size, of course, was a major variable, and many of More's respondents explained that, as a general rule, they needed $1 per week for each family member's food (i.e., $5 to $6 a week for an average sized family). After spending close to two-thirds of their income for food and shelter, families used a large part of what was left for three other relatively big budget items: clothing (10.6 percent), fuel and light (5.1 percent), and life insurance (3.9 percent). Only tiny sums, if anything, went for church contributions, a fact that seems to bear out More's contention that most families in her sample displayed massive indifference toward organized religion, except, perhaps, for the religious education of their children. A few high-income families spent freely for recreation, especially theater, but most working-class budgets showed almost no expenditures for commercial entertainments. The main locales for the leisure time activities of the workers with low and middling incomes were places that did not charge admission, and within that general category the available choices were further restricted along age and gender lines. "Men," More reported, "have saloons, political clubs, trade-unions, or lodges for their recreation." Children played street games (fig. 14). But, More added, "mothers have almost no recreation, only a dreary round of work, day after day, with occasionally a door-step gossip to vary the monotony of their lives."[36]

In the second half of her book, More included a chapter on twelve typical

14. Boys from a neighborhood gang on Minetta Street, with Our Lady of Pompei church visible at the end of the block. From Greenwich House, *Annual Report*, 1910.

families to illustrate how representative households from different income groups lived. Although More scrupulously tried to protect the anonymity of her informants by referring to them by the initials of their surnames only (e.g., "Mr. and Mrs. B."), her account includes so many details that a modern researcher can readily identify some of her families in the 1900 census and add full names to her stories about these working-class Villagers.[37]

Frank and Katherine Brodrick of 25 Jones Street were members of More's high-income group, workers who made $1,200 or more annually. In 1905 Frank was fifty years old and Katherine thirty-eight. Katherine described herself to Greenwich House investigators as a second wife who was much younger than her husband. Frank was a native New Yorker, the son of Irish immigrants. Katherine had been born in Ireland and had been brought to the United States when she was eleven. She married Frank four years later and bore him their first child at the age of sixteen. The Brodricks had seven children, ranging in age from three to twenty.[38]

The Brodricks' annual income in the survey year was $1,500. The eldest children, Mary (20) and Frank Jr. (15), contributed $9 a week as factory workers. (In 1900 Mary, then sixteen, is listed in the census as a box maker, her age, gender, and marital status typical of the nine box makers who lived on Jones Street that year, eight of them teenagers, and all of them unmarried women living with their parents.) Frank Sr. was an oysterman whose job was to sort and select oysters for market, seasonal labor that brought in as much as $75 a week from September to February but required him to work as a watchman and at other odd jobs during slack times. The family's expenditures rose and fell with the seasons as well, and More noted disapprovingly that Katherine Brodrick was willing to go into debt each summer, counting on paying off the loans when her husband was making "big money" again in the fall and early winter.[39]

The nine Brodricks occupied a four-room apartment on the top floor of an old tenement, the two interior rooms of which were windowless bedrooms. This was low-quality housing for a family with such a high income, and, in fact, the Brodricks moved to a larger place in 1906. During the survey period, however, they lived under very cramped conditions. Meals were taken in the kitchen at an oilcloth-covered table that could not seat all nine family members at once. Although Katherine Brodrick was described as "a good manager," Greenwich House investigators expressed surprise at some of her budgetary choices. The family obviously skimped on rent, and Mrs. Brodrick also cut corners on food, serving mainly bread, butter, potatoes, milk, coffee, tea, and little meat, a diet that More described as "wholesome and sufficient, but monotonous." Although she pinched pennies elsewhere, Katherine Brodrick did not stint on clothes for herself, explaining that she was determined to "look well and dress well even [though she had] seven children." Since she did not sew, her outfits were bought ready-made or from a dressmaker, an "extravagant" expense, in More's opinion. However, Katherine Brodrick doubtless would have been pleased by More's observation that when the oysterman's wife went out for a walk, "no one would imagine that her home was on [Jones] Street." Modest expenses for fuel, light, insurance, furnishings, and recreation filled out the Brodricks' budget.[40]

Joseph and Annie Bailey, a young couple who lived downstairs from the Brodricks at 25 Jones Street, had an annual income of $850, almost exactly the average for families in More's sample. Joseph, a native New Yorker, was thirty-one, and his Irish-born wife was twenty-five. They had two children, ages four and one. For the past seven years Joseph had worked as a draftsman for the same company, earning a salary of $15 a week that he supplemented by doing odd jobs for his firm and other customers. The Baileys' apartment consisted of three dark, cramped rooms. Their bedroom had just one window, which looked out into an interior hallway. The small kitchen's only window opened into an air shaft, and their two parlor windows faced a Barrow Street factory at the rear of the building. The Baileys' monthly rent of $13 was just below the average for More's families.[41]

Joseph and Annie Bailey spent nothing for union dues, church donations, or furniture during the reporting year, but their outlays for food and entertainment were considerably higher than the norm for working-class families with middling incomes. By the rule of thumb that decreed food should cost $1 a week per family member, Annie's expenditures should have been only $4 a week, but hers ran closer to $7, a sum that More said let the Baileys eat "extremely well for a family of four" and to have "more fruit and pastry than most families of their class." For entertainment Joseph liked to read penny dailies and to take Annie to the theater once a week in wintertime. Annie liked to dance, so she and Joseph went to six or seven balls that year at a cost of fifty cents each. The Baileys also took their children for trolley rides twice a week, occasionally visited Coney Island, and splurged on a two-week summer vacation at Far Rockaway Beach, where they rented rooms for $9. Although the Baileys were disappointed to have saved only $7 by the end of the year, they had done better in this respect than nearly 80 percent of the families in More's sample.[42]

In 1900, another of More's families, John and Annie Harron, had lived at 15 Jones, just five doors down from the Brodricks and Baileys; however, the very next year they found a nicer place in the neighborhood, a four-room apartment on the third floor of a well-maintained rear house. Although the Harrons' annual income of $870 was nearly the same as the Baileys' $850, John and Annie Harron had to struggle to make ends meet because by 1905 they had eight children, ages six months to thirteen years. They paid the same rent, $13, for their four rooms that the Baileys paid for their three, but the Harrons were definitely more crowded in their apartment than the Baileys were in theirs. Like the Brodrick family, the Harrons could not sit down to a meal together in the space available. The family's income came mainly from John's work as a harness cleaner at a local stable. He made $14 a week, and his oldest son, Charles, added $2 a week to the family's income from his earnings delivering laundry. In a short time, of course, Charles, then thirteen, and his brother Robert, age twelve, would have full-time jobs, and the Harrons' income would predictably increase.[43]

John and Annie Harron were natives of Ireland who had immigrated to the United States in the 1880s. Greenwich House investigators were favorably impressed with both, particularly Annie, whom they described as "a most attractive Irishwoman, bright, capable, neat, and a splendid manager with so large a family." Her food budget was kept under tight control, averaging only $8.50 a week for a ten-person household. She also made all the childrens' clothes, as definite a plus mark for her as Katherine Brodrick's and Annie Bailey's failure to sew had been, in the settlement workers' view, marks against them. This thrifty family stretched its limited resources in many ways. John abstained from alcohol; Annie saved on food and clothing; and the family spent almost nothing on recreation, budgeting about $5 annually for carfare to send the older boys to a park where they played baseball on Sundays in summertime. The only unusual expense was $8 given annually to the local Catholic church, St. Joseph's. This relatively large amount, and the fact that the Harrons tried to be "good Catholics," distinguished them from many neighbors who maintained, at best, a lukewarm attitude toward religious practice. The Harrons were doing all right and would continue to do so as long as John Harron kept his steady job; however, More observed of the Harrons that "if the man should be taken ill or lose his employment, they would be forced to become dependent upon charity."[44]

If workers with middling incomes were economically vulnerable, those who made below $400 a year were even more so. "They are," More wrote, "under-fed, poorly clothed, wretchedly housed, and have the barest necessities of life." To illustrate these generalizations, More chose several examples, one of which was the Schumacher family. The head of this family, Anna Schumacher, was a German-born widow whose husband had died at the beginning of the survey period, leaving her with four young children to support: daughters age twelve and eight, sons age eleven and four. The family's annual income in the period after Mr. Schumacher's death was barely $300; of this Anna contributed about $5 a week as a washerwoman and her older children perhaps $1 a week doing odd jobs. Rent for two rooms in a shabby house was a rock-bottom $7.50 a month, yet this took nearly one-third of the family's income. With little left for everything else, Anna tried to feed herself and four youngsters on $2.25 a week, less than half the normal expenditure for a family of five. Greenwich House investigators described the Schumachers' diet—mainly bread, milk, and vegetables, and nothing in large amounts—as "wholesome, but not adequate in quantity."[45]

Faced with formidable challenges owing to their inadequate income and the squalor of their immediate surroundings, Anna Schumacher's family coped better than most did under similar circumstances. Much of the credit belonged, More believed, to the mother's indomitable spirit. Anna Schumacher set high standards for herself and insisted on the same from her children. "Mrs. S.," More wrote, "is a very neat, quiet, nice-appearing woman, and the children are pretty and well-behaved." The children were also a resourceful lot. To keep the family's fuel bills down, the boys scavenged the neighborhood for discarded wood, and the older children earned petty cash by doing errands. Anna Schumacher refused most charity, even from the church the family attended, but she accepted used clothing and skillfully altered these items for her children's use. As a consequence, More and her coworkers described the children as "well dressed."[46]

The Schumachers were positive thinkers. Their apartment's rear window overlooked a garden behind 88 Grove Street, the Greenwich House men's annex in 1902–1903. Even though they had no access to this yard except visually, the Schumacher children referred to it as "their park" and took delight in watching the flowers bloom each spring, and each summer, when the garden's well-to-do owners left for the country to escape the city's heat, the youngsters entertained themselves with fantasies about how their mother could become the garden's "caretaker." Thus, in spite of the family's marginal present circumstances, More was optimistic about the Schumachers' future, especially since, as she observed, "the two older children, who are both industrious and ambitious," would soon get jobs that would raise the family's income to a more satisfactory level.[47]

More's positive prognosis, accurate though it apparently was (five years later the family had a new address and three children were working), seems even more remarkable after reading the second Greenwich House survey, *A West Side Rookery*, an investigation conducted by Elsa Herzfeld in 1904–1905. Herzfeld, a resident of Hartley House, another West Side settlement, had just completed *Family Monographs* (1905), a study of twenty-four working-class families who lived near Hartley House in the West Forties, when Mary Simkhovitch invited her to do research on substandard housing in Greenwich Village. As it happened, the place Herzfeld singled out for

15. A rear house "rookery" on a back lot on Bleecker Street between Mercer and Greene streets. This three-story wooden building was similar to the one in which the Schumachers lived in 1905. Museum of the City of New York, Jacob A. Riis Collection #75.

study was a cluster of run-down houses in an alley off Washington Place, about a block from Greenwich House. One building in "The Alley," as Herzfeld called it, was 133R Washington Place, the rear tenement in which the Schumachers' apartment was located (fig. 15).[48]

To reach 133R Washington Place, visitors had to squeeze through a narrow passageway between two buildings that faced the street. The first glimpse of number 133R, the dilapidated three-story wooden house in which the Schumachers lived, came as one emerged into the narrowest part of The Alley, a courtyard that measured about twelve by thirty feet at ground level but gave the impression of being smaller because the second stories of several neighboring buildings overhung the open space. Number 133R itself was divided into five apartments, each with two rooms. There were no bathing facilities on the premises, and the only access four apartments had to running water was at two leaky sinks in a narrow hallway. "Eight broken and unsanitary water-closets" that were used by the residents of all five buildings around the Alley's courtyard were located outdoors. For these filthy, drafty, foul-smelling accommodations, the Schumachers and other tenants were paying $8 a month in 1905, the rent having gone up fifty cents a month since More's earlier survey.[49]

The seaminess of life on The Alley rivaled that of the notorious Minettas. Obscene shouts and the sounds of drunken quarrels were frequently heard at night coming from the courtyard, and on the occasions when Anna Schumacher had to go out, her frightened children locked the door and barricaded it with pieces of furniture. The occupants of the other four apartments were something less than model citizens. "Nellie" (her real first name) claimed to be a waitress and lived with a man who said he was her husband, although Nellie told investigators that she was married to "Dub," another man who showed up from time to time. Nellie's sister Mary lived with a fellow who listed his occupation as "bartender"; however, neighbors believed that Mary, Nellie, and a third woman who lived on the first floor were prostitutes whose male companions "lived by the women."[50]

Yet a third Canswell sister (Herzfeld used fictitious surnames, but the sisters' mother was listed as Annie A. Canswell, an Irish American widow, in the 1900 census) occupied an apartment on the top floor with a man named "Flaherty" (Herzfeld's invention), who had recently been arrested for stealing a diamond ring. Flaherty abused their six-month-old baby boy, beating him until he went into convulsions. Greenwich House residents, responding to the mother's pleas, arranged for the boy to be examined by doctors at Bellevue Hospital, where he was found to have "thirty-seven bruises, a broken collar-bone, two blackened eyes and blackened cheeks." In March 1905 Greenwich House asked the Society for the Prevention of Cruelty to Children to intervene, but by the time officers arrived to arrest Flaherty, he had fled to New Jersey. Two months later, without ever having been released from the hospital, the boy died. When Flaherty returned to his wife in December, Greenwich House notified the S.P.C.C., which had him arrested, but his wife refused to testify against him, and a judge ruled that the evidence against Flaherty was therefore insufficient to warrant pursuing the case.[51]

Herzfeld closed *A West Side Rookery* with a brief section titled "What Can Be Done?" Her answer, one doubtless endorsed by her coworkers at Greenwich House, was that the city's government had to do more for the neighborhood, providing better schools and expanding local services: public libraries, public baths, and recreational piers. Mary Simkhovitch, Herzfeld's mentor during the survey period, certainly agreed, but had she written the conclusion, she would have strengthened it by spelling out how the neighborhood's needs could best be presented to municipal officials. The settlement's surveys were only the first step in that direction. The next step required an organization that envisioned a more inclusive neighborhood than did the traditional community interest groups, most of which were based on ethnic ties or party affiliations.

To promote a new spirit of inclusive neighborliness, Simkhovitch in 1903 took the lead in organizing the Greenwich Village Improvement Society, the first neighborhood association in New York City. From its formation onward, the society tried to recruit members from all local constituencies: Catholics, Protestants, and Jews, Democrats and Republicans, and every major ethnic group. Although the society's most active and productive years did not come until the early 1910s, the vision of a new neighborhood that it represented had begun to take shape much earlier. The starting point was the thinking of Mary Simkhovitch and other college-educated women and men who, in the process of living and working on Jones Street, themselves became, for a time, Greenwich Villagers.

3

The Patrician Response

O N THE NORTH SIDE of Washington Square, on the square itself
and on streets adjacent to lower Fifth Avenue, were the homes of the upper-
class Villagers. These patricians were Protestants of Dutch, English, and
French stock, some of them heirs to old wealth and to the handsome residences that their parents or grandparents had built before the Civil War.

Culturally, religiously, and politically, the north Village gentry had little
in common with most of their near neighbors, the working-class and immigrant Villagers who lived south and west of the square. Italian immigrants
and Irish Americans worshipped at Catholic churches, while the gentry attended Sunday services at Protestant edifices along lower Fifth Avenue,
elite congregations such as the First Presbyterian Church and the Episcopal
Church of the Ascension. Irish, Italian, and African American Villagers
gathered to drink and socialize in the numerous working-class saloons of
the west and south Village, while the Protestant elite socialized in the elegant drawing rooms of their homes. These cultural and class contrasts were
reflected in political rivalries, especially between the Irish Villagers loyal to
the Democratic machine and the patrician Villagers who deeply distrusted
Tammany rule. Again and again the Village gentry, whether they were Republicans, Independents, or Democrats, organized to challenge Tammany's
control of the city.

By the turn of the twentieth century, the future of this upper-class north

Village enclave seemed increasingly uncertain. Tenement housing and Italian immigrants were invading the Village from the south, and commercial buildings were encroaching on the square from the east. The novelist Henry James, a famous native son who in 1904 and 1905 visited his youthful haunts in the Village after more than twenty years' absence, found to his dismay that his "birth-house" had been, as he put it, "ruthlessly suppressed," torn down to make way for a ten-story loft building, "a high, square, impersonal structure." The sight of a few familiar places north of Washington Square brightened his mood, and upon venturing into the Church of the Ascension on Fifth Avenue, he declared himself "hushed to admiration before a great religious picture," John La Farge's representation of Christ's ascension. Still, his account of his visit repeatedly returned to his sense of disquietude at the relentless way that urban progress "amputated" all signs of the past and replaced them with towering structures dedicated solely to "mere economic convenience."[1]

Well before James's visit changes in the neighborhood and the attraction of newer elite residential districts farther uptown had led many of the old gentry to abandon their north Village homes. Nevertheless, a substantial number of patrician Villagers remained devoted to the neighborhood, and their continuing presence had the practical effect of slowing the expansion of tenements, factories, and commercial buildings north of Washington Square. Moreover, the patrician Villagers' response to the changing times— particularly to the invasion of the Village by immigrant and working-class New Yorkers—was not entirely passive, a matter of simply staying put. On the contrary, in the waning years of the nineteenth century and first years of the twentieth, Village patricians pursued a variety of cultural and political initiatives in an effort to affirm values that the gentry held dear and to preserve, if possible, the north Village as an elegant residential district.

THE NORTH VILLAGERS

A visitor to Washington Square on Saturday, April 28, 1900, could scarcely have failed to be charmed by the scene. A light breeze stirred the leaves of the giant elms in the middle of the square, and bright sunlight filtered through the luminous green canopy of leaves to fall on the pedestrians strolling below. Washington Arch, only five years old, its marble still fresh and white, dominated the north side of the park. Although the era of horse-drawn vehicles was entering its final years, only a few automobiles passed through the square. April 28 was a Saturday, but the city's commerce moved briskly, with trucks, delivery wagons, and small carts everywhere in evidence. Now and then a handsome carriage owned by one of the patrician families made its appearance. Driven by coachmen in formal attire, complete with top hats, these fine turnouts—"the barouches, victorias or coupes, the shining horses, sometimes even a four-in-hand"—emerged from their stables in the alleys behind the mansions facing Washington Square. The high-stepping horses proceeded to the front of their owners' homes, stopped, and stood alertly, waiting for well-dressed patricians to come down the front steps and climb in the carriages.[2]

Of the twenty-five fine homes that remained of the twenty-eight that had once graced Washington Square North, at least four were still occupied in 1900 by the original owner's children or grandchildren. The most venerable resident of these four was Serena Rhinelander, who lived in number 14, the mansion on the west corner of Fifth Avenue that had been built for her father in 1839–40. A descendant of early Dutch settlers, William C. Rhinelander was able, through judicious investments (mainly in real estate), to leave each of his three daughters an inheritance of more than a million dollars. His daughter Serena became a formidable figure in New York society and used her considerable fortune to promote high-minded causes. A member of Reverend Percy Stickney Grant's Church of the Ascension nearby on Fifth Avenue, she contributed substantial sums to a remodeling project that included the commission of John La Farge's mural "The Ascension," a grand and harmonious work that reflected the aesthetic and religious sensibilities of the late-nineteenth-century elite (map 3).

Miss Rhinelander was equally lavish in her support of patriotic events. The old New York elite, she believed, had an obligation to demonstrate its allegiance to old republican virtues—simplicity, honesty, and hard work—of which she feared later immigrants might be ignorant. To encourage participation in the Washington Centennial held in May 1889 to mark the hundredth anniversary of the U.S. Constitution, Miss Rhinelander had a private viewing stand of "terraced seats" erected on the Washington Square and Fifth Avenue sides of her mansion. Eight hundred guests, more than half of them children from poor families and local Sunday schools, viewed the huge parade that passed by on Fifth Avenue.[3]

Serena Rhinelander's nephew, William Rhinelander Stewart, lived a few doors down the block at 17 Washington Square North. With a comfortable income derived from inherited wealth, Stewart was free to devote most of his time to civic causes. In the late 1890s he was president of the New York State Board of Charities and admired for his efforts to improve the quality of the state's institutions for poor women and children and the physically or mentally impaired. A prominent Episcopal layman, he served for many years as a vestryman of Grace Church, an upper-class parish located at Broadway and East 10th Street, the outermost edge of the patrician Village of Stewart's day. A Republican, he generally remained aloof from local party

—Blackmer—

16. Group atop Washington Memorial Arch to lay the last stone of the attic, April 5, 1892. *From right:* the fourth man (wearing a top hat) is Richard Watson Gilder, the sixth (also in a silk hat), William Rhinelander Stewart, and the eighth, Stanford White. Museum of the City of New York, Print Archives.

battles, the chief exception being his membership on the Committee of Seventy, the ad hoc panel of prominent New Yorkers who spearheaded a successful anti-Tammany campaign in 1894. On May 5, 1895, Stewart doubtless felt great personal satisfaction as he handed the keys to one of his pet projects, the Washington Memorial Arch, to the very mayor, William L. Strong, whom his efforts had helped elect to office (fig. 16).

Stewart's involvement in the Washington Arch project dated from the Washington Centennial celebration for which his aunt had built the huge private viewing stand. At that time a temporary wooden arch had been built astride Fifth Avenue directly across from Washington Square for the May 1889 ceremony. Inspired by the success of the centennial celebration, Stewart proposed that a permanent marble arch be constructed with funds from private donors. Stewart's patrician neighbors endorsed the plan, and a site on the northern edge of Washington Square was selected. The architect chosen to design the arch was Stanford White, a native of the Village and a man to whom the New York elite often turned for their public projects. In the Village he was responsible for the Church of the Ascension's redesigned chancel in 1888 and for the Washington Arch and the Judson Memorial Church in the 1890s.

Every step of the Washington Arch's construction was marked by a ceremony: laying the cornerstone (May 1890), placing the capstone (April 1892), and dedicating the completed arch (May 1895). At each ceremony representatives of the elite described the project's rationale, which was rooted in the north Village gentry's conviction that moral virtues could be inculcated through public art. At the cornerstone ceremony in 1890 the principal speaker was George William Curtis, the editor of *Harper's Weekly* and a man whose public addresses epitomized the elite's ideal of oratory. Curtis quoted words attributed to George Washington—"Let us raise a standard to which the wise and honest can repair"—and applied them to the enterprise at hand, suggesting that raising a beautiful piece of public art would also raise the moral and aesthetic standards of the general public that viewed it. Five years later, at the dedication of the completed arch, the featured address was given by a Civil War veteran, General Horace Porter, who, echoing Curtis's sentiments, succinctly summarized the thinking that lay behind patricians' arch project. "There is nothing," he asserted, "which cultivates a more refined taste in a community than the public display of deserving artistic structures. They speak a universal language and impart a lasting pleasure to all. They appeal to our highest senses and awaken our noblest emotions."[4]

But why an appeal to "our noblest emotions" at this particular time and place? Precisely because the elite's ideal of what Porter called "a universal language" was almost daily being called into question in local and national affairs. Conflict, not unity, was everywhere in evidence in the early 1890s: bloody clashes between labor and capital, a depression that left 25 percent of the industrial workforce unemployed and angry, and the swift growth of urban slums whose immigrant inhabitants had only a limited familiarity with the language and culture of their adopted land. In introducing Curtis at the cornerstone ceremony in 1890, Henry Marquand, a wealthy philanthropist and patron of the arts, made a direct connection between the working-class tenements that were gradually closing in on Washington Square and the aesthetic and civic purpose of the Washington Arch:

> The spot has been aptly chosen, and not a valid objection can be urged against it. It is true some one has remarked that 'the neighborhood in a few years will

be all tenement houses.' Even should this prove true, no stronger reason could be given for the arch being placed here. Have the occupants of tenement houses no sense of beauty? Have they no patriotism? Have they no right to good architecture? Happily there is no monopoly of the appreciation of things that are excellent any more than there is of fresh air, and in our minds' eye we can see many a family which cannot afford ten cents to go to . . . [Central P]ark taking great pleasure under the shadow of the arch.

Having praised the monument for its aesthetic virtues, Marquand went on to invoke its potential as a force for unifying the neighborhood socially: "This is," he said, "the arch of peace and good will to men. It will bring the rich and poor together in one common bond of patriotic feeling."[5]

Five years later, at the May 1895 dedication of the completed arch, the invocation, given by Reverend Henry C. Potter, Episcopal bishop of New York and a resident of Washington Square North, alluded to the social turmoil that was daily grabbing headlines: "Save us from violence, discord, and confusion, from pride and arrogance, and from every evil way," Bishop Potter prayed. He then echoed Henry Marquand's earlier sentiments as he prayed that "the multitudes brought hither out of many kindreds and tongues" might be fashioned "into one happy people."[6]

The gentry's goal of reducing social conflict was closely intertwined with their commitment to anti-Tammany politics. In the public rhetoric of the time, when the gentry's representatives spoke of educating the public to patriotic ideals, they were making coded references to virtues felt to be lacking in Tammany-controlled regimes. If, the thinking went, patricians succeeded in educating slum dwellers (especially recent immigrants) to the gentry's version of high-minded civic virtue, then working-class New Yorkers would cease to back the Irish-led Democratic machine.

One individual in whom the social and political strands of patrician civic activism were combined was Edward Cooper. His mansion at 12 Washington Square North stood just across Fifth Avenue from Serena Rhinelander's residence. Cooper was a member of the platform party at the dedication of the arch in 1895, both in recognition of his long-standing support of the project and because he was esteemed as a former mayor of New York City. A Democrat but an opponent of the party's Tammany wing, he ran as the candidate of a coalition of Republicans and Democrats and was swept into office in 1879, benefiting in part from the aftermath of revelations of the notorious Tweed Ring's corruption. However, by the time the next election came around, anti-Tammany fervor had faded, and Cooper did not win a second term.

After his failed reelection campaign, Cooper remained a prominent public figure in New York City, less because of his one term as mayor than because he was a multimillionaire philanthropist. Alone among the Washington Square elite—all the rest of whom had made their fortunes in banking, retailing, real estate, and, in some instances in the younger generation, the professions—Cooper derived his wealth from manufacturing. His father, Peter Cooper, had been an industrialist who amassed a huge fortune making iron and glue.[7]

Once he had earned it, the elder Cooper used his wealth to support worthy civic causes. Chief among these was the construction of Cooper Union, a large meeting hall and classroom building completed in 1859 at Astor Place, a few blocks east of Washington Square. Cooper Union became, in the words of one modern commentator, "the nation's first free nonsectarian coeducational college." Classes and public lectures were offered free of charge to make education accessible to all, particularly to workers who, as Peter Cooper and his son Edward saw it, were being demoralized by the impact of rapid industrialization. Especially at risk, the Coopers believed, were craftsmen whose skills were becoming obsolete as the old manufacturing system based on small shops owned by master craftsmen was being replaced by an industrial economy in which semiskilled laborers tended machines in huge factories. Self-help in the form of educational opportunities, the Coopers hoped, would enable workers to ride out the wave of change. Such was the rapidity of change, however, that by the early 1890s the workers about whom the patrician speakers and their Washington Square audiences worried most were no longer the embattled traditional American craftsmen but the throngs of southern and eastern European immigrants who were swarming into the city. In response to this new challenge, Cooper Union targeted Lower East Side immigrant masses with new programs intended to introduce them to the basics of American political and social thought.[8]

Despite their support for the Washington Arch project and Cooper Union's educational mission, most Village patricians had little direct personal contact with the non-English-speaking newcomers they hoped to reach. The Village elite, however, did have daily and intimate contact with another group of working-class people—the butlers, chefs, grooms, coachmen, lady's maids, chambermaids, and kitchenmaids who lived and worked in their homes. Ex-mayor Cooper's household in 1900 consisted of Cooper, his daughter, her husband, three grandchildren, and sixteen servants. Although this was the largest staff of servants in any Washington Square North household, it was not extraordinary. William Rhinelander Stewart employed twelve servants, and his aunt Serena Rhinelander had eight house servants plus a groom and a coachman who lived in the carriage house in back of the Rhinelander mansion.[9]

At the turn of the century the typical servant in the Village gentry's households was a young, foreign-born woman. Nearly half of the servants employed by Washington Square patricians in 1900 were in their twenties, and barely one in six was more than forty years old. Only one member of the Washington Square North elite, Mrs. Sarah Livingston of number 20, still employed African American servants, although before the Civil War blacks would have been the preferred choice of many patrician employers. By 1900 blacks had been replaced by white servants, all but a handful of them born abroad, half of them in Ireland. Immigrants from other northern European countries (England, Germany, Sweden, France, and Finland) filled most of the remaining positions in the patricians' households. Only one servant in 1900 was Italian, and none were East Europeans, a reflection of the fact that women from these so-called new immigrant groups generally did not seek employment as domestic servants. Still, many of the gentry's servants were quite recent arrivals, approximately 60 percent of them having been in the United States ten years or less. Moreover, with the exception of males employed as butlers, grooms, and coachmen, Washington Square servants were nearly all female, testifying to the fact that household service was by far the largest job category for young foreign-born women at the turn of the century.[10]

Two doors down from Cooper's sixteen-servant household was Reverend Henry C. Potter's residence at 10 Washington Square. Its occupants consisted of Potter, his wife, their six children, and four female servants, two from Sweden and two from Ireland. The family had moved to the Greenwich Village area in 1868, when Potter had become rector of Grace Church. After fifteen years he had been named assistant bishop of New York and soon thereafter bishop. As the leader of an old-line Protestant denomination from 1888 to 1908, Potter faced many challenges. Not the least of these arose from the fact that the Episcopal church had a strong following among the city's upper class but little appeal to a broader public in an era when most working-class New Yorkers were Catholic or Jewish immigrants. Potter's response was to adopt a broad church approach, reaching out to both the upper- and lower-class constituencies in his diocese. He energetically supported the elite's ambitious project of constructing the Cathedral of St. John the Divine. At the same time he insisted that privileged Episcopalians had an obligation to contribute generously to social programs that benefited the working-class poor, a viewpoint that won him a reputation as a friend of New York's workers and led them to accept him as an arbitrator in labor disputes.

An articulate and thoughtful man, Potter was a welcome guest at a Village institution that represented turn-of-the-century elite culture at its best.

This was the literary salon hosted by Richard Watson Gilder and his wife, Helena de Kay Gilder. Both of the Gilders were well known in artistic and literary circles, she as a painter who helped found the Art Student's League of New York, he as a poet who, since 1881, had edited *Century Magazine*, which under his leadership became one of the great American magazines of the day, a bastion from which high moral and literary standards were tenaciously defended.[11]

Every Friday evening the Gilders opened the drawing rooms of their handsome East Eighth Street home to guests who constituted, as a young writer later recalled, "one of the most civilized and cosmopolitan groups in the city." Although the Gilders fostered a relaxed, homey atmosphere by having their daughters distribute modest refreshments (tea, coffee, chocolates, and small cakes) to guests, there was nothing modest about the reputations of many who attended. Among the luminaries were the sculptor August Saint-Gaudens, the naturalist John Burroughs, and the architect Stanford White, who, incidentally, had designed a mantlepiece for the Gilders' drawing room. Moreover, the evenings were not limited to conversation; well-known artists were invited to perform, creating particularly memorable evenings. On one such occasion, Jan Paderewski played a grand piano that the Steinway Company had loaned for the evening. On another Friday, Helena Modjeska, a leading actress, recited parts she had made famous.[12]

Richard Watson Gilder's commitment to setting standards was not limited to trying to influence what the public read. He also attempted to shape public policy. His first venture into politics came in 1884 as a Mugwump, one of the Republicans who voted for the Democratic presidential candidate, Grover Cleveland, on the grounds that his own party's standard-bearer, James G. Blaine, had betrayed the public's trust by using his office for personal financial gain. During Cleveland's two terms as president (1885–1889, 1893–1897) Gilder remained his admirer and became his friend as well. But Gilder did not entirely share Cleveland's unwavering laissez-faire conservatism and in the 1890s came to believe that city and state governments needed to pass regulatory laws to protect citizens against some of the worst effects of industrialization.[13]

The most dramatic example of Gilder's support for regulatory laws came in 1894 after his appointment as chair of a New York State Tenement House Commission charged with investigating housing conditions in New York City. Determined to observe for himself the conditions faced by the slum dwellers, he asked the city's fire department to notify him whenever they answered an alarm from a tenement district so that he could follow fire trucks to the blaze. He also showed a flare for publicizing the commission's findings when he singled out tenements owned by Trinity Church, one of the city's wealthiest and most prestigious Episcopal parishes, as examples of poorly ventilated, unsanitary, and unsafe housing. Several of the most noxious rookeries owned by Trinity were located on Hudson and Charlton streets in the southernmost part of Greenwich Village. Convinced by personal observation that urban poverty was not, as laissez-faire theorists maintained, simply the result of individual laziness or immorality, Gilder came to believe that poor people were often victimized by slum conditions that could be ameliorated through legislation. With this in mind he helped to draft and press through the state legislature a new housing law that corrected some glaring deficiencies in the previous building code and set the stage for passage of much tougher and more comprehensive regulations that were part of the Tenement House Act of 1901.[14]

Much of the credit for the latter law must go to another Village patrician, Robert W. de Forest. De Forest and his wife, Emily Johnston de Forest, lived at 7 Washington Square North. Like many north Village patricians, the de Forests and Johnstons associated themselves with "Old New York," a term that referred to life in the city before the Civil War and to the families, many of them with colonial era roots, who set the tone of prewar society. Robert de Forest's ancestors were French Huguenot exiles who emigrated to New Amsterdam in 1636. A native of Greenwich Village, Robert had fond memories of his childhood years in the 1850s on Charles Street in the west Village. His father was a successful lawyer, and Robert entered the same profession, doing his undergraduate work at Yale and graduating from Columbia Law School in 1872. Later that year he married Emily Johnston, forming a connection with a family that may have lacked the de Forests' colonial roots but was, on the whole, much wealthier.[15]

Emily's grandfather, John Johnston, had been born in Scotland and had come to the United States in 1804. He made a fortune as an importer and had the house at 7 Washington Square built for himself and his family in the early 1830s (fig. 17). His son, John Taylor Johnston, graduated from New York University (which his father had helped found in 1831) and trained in the law; he chose not to practice, devoting himself instead to investing in railroads. A lover of fine art, he amassed a collection that was regarded as one of the best in the city and put it on display one day a week in a refurbished stable behind his house at 8 Fifth Avenue. Subsequently he became a founder and the first president (1870–1889) of the Metropolitan Museum of Art. A firm believer that works of art could have a civilizing influence on those who viewed them, he donated most of his personal holdings to the new museum.[16]

The de Forests and the Johnstons subscribed to an Old New York ethic

17. Washington Square North, the row of houses to the east of Fifth Avenue. From Emily Johnston de Forest, *John Johnston of New York*. General Research Division, The New York Public Library, Astor, Lenox and Tilden Foundations.

that held public service, discreet behavior, and family ties in high regard. Robert and Emily de Forest were well known for their ongoing and generous contributions to charitable and cultural institutions. They scrupulously guarded their privacy, conducting themselves so that personal and family matters would not become subjects for gossip or, worse yet, newspaper stories. Emily, the family historian and genealogist, only occasionally revealed a glimpse of what life was like inside 7 Washington Square North, and when she did, she said nothing about her own generation but spoke of her grandmother, Mrs. John Johnston, describing her elaborate dinner parties, her exchange of social visits with women friends, and her house's several parlors, each of which had "stiff rows of damask-covered chairs and sofas around the walls, and marble-topped tables in the middle."[17]

Many of the social rituals of Mrs. Johnston's mid–nineteenth century world were still in force among the Old New York patricians who lived on Washington Square North in Emily de Forest's day. The practice of gentlemen exchanging New Year's Day calls was gradually dying out, but the genteel women of the neighborhood still faithfully devoted large parts of one day each week (in the Village that day was Friday) to making formal calls on one another. Hamilton Fish Armstrong, a boy of seven in 1900 and the youngest child of a well-connected Old New York family that lived on West Tenth Street, fondly remembered learning "the geography of polite neighborhoods" while accompanying his mother on such calls. Although food and drink were offered at each stop—"tea and hot chocolate in the dining room, as well as bouillon in a silver urn, also glazed importés and other little cakes from Dean's and such very small, very thin watercress sandwiches that they hardly seemed worth the trouble of eating"—the point of such visits was not to linger over the refreshments but to call at as many homes as possible on the alloted day.[18]

Family was the foundation of Old New York society, and loyalty to family ties often included loyalty to an ancestral home. Such was the case with the de Forest clan. Although Emily and Robert owned a spacious estate at Cold Spring Harbor, Long Island, they spent most of the year at the Washington Square mansion Emily's father had given them as a wedding gift. Emily's siblings also continued to live in the Greenwich Village district to which their grandfather had moved his family seventy years earlier. In 1900, Emily's sister Frances (Mrs. Pierre Mali) still occupied their father's white marble house at 8 Fifth Avenue, and her sister Eva (Mrs. Henry E. Coe) lived two blocks north at 5 East Tenth Street. Before the end of the decade their brother, John J. H. Johnston, moved into 18 Washington Square North (once the residence of Henry James's grandmother) and Emily's daughter Frances (Mrs. William Stewart) set up housekeeping at 1 Washington Square North, remaining at that address from 1906 to 1935.[19]

By 1900, Emily's father, John Taylor Johnston, had been dead seven years, and Robert de Forest had long been the principal manager of the Johnston–de Forest clan's investments and the most conspicuous public spokesman for the family's philanthropic interests. The process by which the mantle of family leadership shifted to Robert's shoulders dated back to at least 1889, when poor health forced Johnston to resign as trustee and president of the Metropolitan Museum of Art, and de Forest took his father-in-law's place on the museum's board. (Later, in 1913, de Forest would be elected the fifth president of the museum, his immediate predecessor being J. P. Morgan.) An able corporate lawyer and shrewd investor, de Forest also succeeded his father-in-law as president of the Central Railroad of New Jersey, which Johnston had founded before the Civil War. Quite separate from such inherited roles, de Forest helped organize the Charity Organization Society of the City of New York, and in 1888 he became its president, holding that post until his death in 1931. By that time the major civic organizations he had served as an officer or board member numbered in the dozens. On two occasions he accepted political appointments. One was the chair of the New York State Tenement House Commission that produced the Tenement House Act of 1901, and the other was the post of New York City Tenement House Commissioner charged with administering the new law. Before de Forest could be offered (and accept) these posts, however, three broad developments had to take place: the emergence of the so-called scientific charity movement, an upsurge in support for urban housing reform, and a renewed assault on Tammany Hall's control of New York City politics.[20]

De Forest's involvement with the scientific charity movement dated from 1882, when he helped a wealthy young widow, Josephine Shaw Lowell, establish the Charity Organization Society of the City of New York. The organization's goal was to replace "unscientific" charity (that is, impulse giving) with a system of assistance that coordinated the efforts of the city's public and private relief agencies. Based on interviews with prospective aid recipients and a centralized list of all names currently on the rolls of local charitable agencies, the C.O.S. made recommendations regarding who should receive aid and which agencies could best assist them. In its early years the society took the traditional stance of trying to differentiate between the morally "deserving" and "undeserving" poor, but in 1896 its leaders voted to abandon this old-fashioned vocabulary. After de Forest became president in 1888, the C.O.S. modernized its programs in other ways as well, making a major contribution to the emergence of social work as a profession through its sponsorship of the Columbia School of Social Work and through the society's journal, *Charities Review* (which after several name changes became *The Survey*).[21]

For a time in the 1890s, the Charity Organization Society's supporters and partisans of the settlement house movement tended to regard each other as rivals and to be critical of each other's methods. Settlement house residents tended to dismiss alms-giving as patronizing and elitist: patronizing because it implied that the benefactor was superior to the beneficiary, and elitist because it required no direct contact with the impoverished recipient. Charity workers, for their part, initially derided the settlement house residents' belief that college-educated individuals could help the poor by living in slum districts. A pat on the back and a sympathetic word from a well-off neighbor, the charity workers charged, was of little practical use to a jobless tenement dweller. In time, the less doctrinaire adherents of each movement began to see that they could function as allies who pursued somewhat distinct, though by no means mutually exclusive, strategies for dealing with urban social problems.

By the late 1890s, the end of de Forest's first decade as its president, the

C.O.S., which earlier had depended almost exclusively on volunteer labor, had professionalized its ranks. The organization had a rapidly expanding central office staff and more than a dozen district offices, each employing a head agent, an assistant agent, and a stenographer. The Greenwich district, whose borders varied over the years but generally included the West Side south of Fourteenth Street to at least Canal, was a major operation, dealing in any given year with hundreds of active cases. Each of these required an initial interview, follow-up visits to the applicant's home address, and correspondence with relevant agencies. People who knew de Forest only in his later years sometimes formed the false impression that he had no personal dealings with poor people. For instance, an interviewer reported that a former administrative assistant of de Forest's who had worked for him in the 1920s, when he was a very reserved man in his seventies, said that "she never knew him to come into direct contact with the poor." During the 1880s, however, de Forest served on several district committees, members of which were responsible for doing follow-up interviews with recent applicants. In the course of such interviews, de Forest certainly gained firsthand knowledge of how working-class Villagers lived.[22]

De Forest did not have to go many blocks from his Washington Square mansion to find the homes of the poor. At the turn of the century the sections of the Village under the C.O.S. Greenwich district office's jurisdiction had more than 3,600 tenement buildings occupied by nearly 95,000 Villagers. Even the blocks just south and west of de Forest's home, an area still not considered a dense tenement district, had more than 500 buildings and a population of almost 16,000.[23]

Despite the publicity that Jacob Riis's *How the Other Half Lives* and Richard Watson Gilder's tenement house investigation had brought to dangerous and degrading housing conditions in the city, the movement for housing reform stalled in the late 1890s. The Greater New York charter, which consolidated Manhattan, Brooklyn, Queens, the Bronx, and Richmond into a single metropolis, required the new city government to draw up a unified building code for all five boroughs. However, in the 1897 municipal elections—the first under the new charter—the Tammany Democratic ticket headed by Robert Van Wyck won. With the new mayor's backing, the Tammany-dominated Board of Aldermen first proposed and then in the fall of 1899 passed a weak building code that, according to housing reformers, offered little protection for tenement dwellers.

De Forest used his position as president of the Charity Organization Society to promote a reform alternative. When he was approached by Lawrence Veiller, a twenty-six-year-old housing activist who was regarded as a radical innovator, de Forest did not hesitate to place resources at the young man's disposal. In December 1898 a special C.O.S. Tenement House Committee was established with Veiller as its chairman. Less than a year later Veiller's committee was ready with recommendations for a comprehensive reform of the city's housing laws.

Since the city government was controlled by a Tammany regime committed to its own housing code, de Forest and Veiller appealed to Governor Theodore Roosevelt, a Republican, for help. Roosevelt appointed a New York State Tenement House Commission to investigate housing conditions in New York City and to propose remedial state legislation. With de Forest as its chair and Veiller as his assistant in charge of most details, the commission soon produced a draft of a new state housing code that the legislature used as the basis for the Tenement House Act of 1901.

As for the results of the new law, no simple generalization can accurately sum up its impact on literally millions of New York City tenement residents. Critics note that the law's higher standards raised construction costs, leading some builders to drop out of the low-end market and exacerbating a shortage in low-cost housing that drove rents up prior to World War I. Consequently, the poorest of the poor continued to be housed in tenements built before the new law. Nevertheless, the New York Tenement House Act of 1901 was landmark legislation, widely copied by other states as representing the best thinking on housing reform at the time. It led to some upgrades in older tenements and required major improvements in the physical features—light, air, sanitation, and fireproofing—of tenements built after its passage. A recent history of New York City housing concluded that "for the general public, [the new law] radically improved the quality of tenement housing."[24]

Despite Robert de Forest's role in securing the new law's passage, his name would never have received serious consideration for the post of Tenement House Commissioner established under the law had not its passage coincided with the election of Seth Low, the Citizens' Union candidate, in the 1901 mayoral election. One month after his victory at the polls, the mayor-elect announced de Forest's appointment as his administration's Tenement House Commissioner. Initially very reluctant to accept the post, de Forest was eventually persuaded to take it by his fellow patrician, Josephine Shaw Lowell, who in a manner worthy of a character in a Henry James novel said little but conveyed much when she met de Forest at a gathering and spoke four words only: "Mr. de Forest, please do." Lawrence Veiller, who had wanted the post and thought it should have been his, was angry, but he accepted de Forest's invitation to be his deputy.[25]

Reporters who sought the new commissioner out at his Washington Square residence on the day of the announcement were treated to a typical de Forest performance. He had been hesitant to accept, he said, but had decided that it was, as he put it, his "duty to do so," even though "acceptance involved some sacrifice" of time from other commitments, including his work as C.O.S. president. When asked how he would administer the new law, de Forest displayed the moderation that Low so valued in him. He promised to meet with opponents of the law to see whether their complaints could be met without undermining its overall intent. And what was that? According to the new commissioner, simply to "secure to the tenement dwellers, who number more than one-half of the population of Greater New York, more light, better ventilation, and better sanitation."[26]

De Forest's reference to one-half of the city's population quite rightly placed his duties in a citywide frame of reference, but housing reform also had ramifications for his own neighborhood. De Forest and Veiller had written in 1900 that "in former years" the area near Washington Square "was not distinctively a tenement house district (fig. 18). It has, however, recently become so, and this tendency is fast increasing." This statement about the number of tenements in one part of the neighborhood also reflected trends in the Village as a whole. In the first decade of the twentieth century, however, the pace of new construction varied greatly from year to year. A building boom in 1903 and 1904 added nearly 1,200 apartments to the neighborhood's housing stock, but from 1905 to 1910 only about 200 apartments were built annually, a slow pace that reflected the citywide drop-off in tenement construction.[27]

The north Village elite's response to the changing demography of the neighborhood had begun well before de Forest and Veiller wrote their appraisal in 1900. Throughout the late nineteenth century, members of the north Village gentry, believing that their privileged status obligated them to assist their less fortunate neighbors, had involved themselves in many philanthropic and civic activities. Although their civic activism had conservative origins in that it sought to blunt social unrest, reform-minded patrician Villagers were not reactionaries who lacked sympathy for their working-class neighbors. De Forest's efforts to help the poor through the Charity Organization Society programs, the gentry's campaigns to improve housing conditions for tenement dwellers, Bishop Potter's work as a labor arbitrator, and ex-mayor Cooper's commitment to providing Lower East Side immigrants with free access to educational opportunities: these late nineteenth-century actions produced very real benefits for lower-class Villagers.

As the neighborhood continued to change in the first decade of the twentieth century, the north Village patricians' response to the neighborhood's transformation also evolved. Two innovative responses received significant

18. Washington Square Arch, looking south, with the tower of the Judson Memorial Church to the right of the arch. Photograph by Arthur Chapman, 1915. Museum of the City of New York.

backing from Village gentry between 1907 and 1910—Ascension Forum, sponsored by an elite Protestant church, and the Washington Square Association, a group organized by north Village taxpayers. Neither initiative had entirely satisfactory results for either the north Village elite or working-class Villagers, but the very fact that patrician Villagers sought new ways of responding indicates that they realized that in a time of change the goal of preserving a bit of Old New York required that they, the Village gentry, change too.

Ascension Forum

During its heyday, October 1907 to June 1910, Ascension Forum caused quite a stir. Contemporary observers were astonished when the Church of the Ascension, a fashionable Fifth Avenue Episcopal church whose leading parishioners included some of the wealthiest Villagers, proposed to open its doors every Sunday night to a motley crowd of street people, socialists, cranks, and laborers, many of whom were Jewish or Catholic immigrants. Given the social and economic gulf that existed between the city's Protestant elite and the working class, it was perhaps even more remarkable that the Ascension Forum actually got off the ground. (That it eventually foundered surprised people less.) Nevertheless, during its three-year existence Ascension Forum provided a practical test of how patrician Villagers would respond to several pressing issues: the yawning social gap between upper- and working-class Villagers, the growth of socialist sentiment among workers, and the future of old-line Protestant denominations in neighborhoods like the Village where the proportion of working-class residents was rising.

The question of how a Protestant religious institution whose members were drawn from the upper-middle and upper classes could survive in the Village was a subject of great concern to the Church of the Ascension's leaders. When the parish had dedicated its church at Fifth Avenue and Tenth Street in 1841, the surrounding Washington Square and lower Fifth Avenue district had been well on the way to becoming the exclusive residential neighborhood it would remain for many decades. By the end of the century, however, many of the area's patrician families were departing for newer elite districts above Fourteenth Street, and this fact, coupled with the encroachment of industrial buildings and working-class tenements east and south of Washington Square, forced several north Village Episcopal and Dutch Reformed churches to close their doors between 1890 and 1910. Although the Church of the Ascension also felt the impact of these changes, at the turn of the century it remained, in the words of its principal historian, "a rich, fashionable parish." As late as 1916, the year the church celebrated the seventy-fifth anniversary of the completion of its Fifth Avenue building, nearly 20 percent of the 1,064 individuals on the parish rolls were named in the *Social Register* for New York City.[28]

Ascension met the challenge of the times through a process of internal reform that was led by its rector, the Reverend Percy Stickney Grant. A graduate of Harvard College (1883) and the Episcopal Theological School in Cambridge, Massachusetts (1886), Grant came to Ascension in 1893 with strong opinions about what the parish needed to do. As a condition of his acceptance of the rectorship, he insisted that Ascension abandon its policy of having pews owned as the private property of individuals and families. Though this practice was still the norm in New York's elite parishes, Grant argued that it was an anachronism that made Ascension seem unwelcoming to newcomers and guests alike. Critics responded by warning that Grant's goals of openness and democratization might bankrupt the church, already in trouble financially as a result of the depression of the 1890s. Grant plunged ahead anyway, and for years thereafter his annual reports usually included at least a brief comment on the growth of contributions that had come with the introduction of the free pew system.[29]

At Grant's urging, Ascension also expanded its charitable activities among the Village's poor. Practically speaking, the growth of the neighborhood's immigrant and working-class population was sufficient to justify devoting more resources to local philanthropic causes, but for Grant the religious rationale for doing so was even stronger. Charitable enterprises, he argued, were the deeds by which Christians worked to make God's kingdom of love and justice into an earthly reality. This interpretation of Christian responsibility, widely known at the time as the social gospel, had emerged in American churches in response to the injustices and inequities brought about by rapid industrialization. At Ascension, putting the social gospel into practice meant launching or enhancing a wide variety of parish social services: material assistance (cash, clothing, coal purchases, food, and rent), support for institutions for the poor (hospitals and nursery schools), education (especially vocational training for children), holiday gifts (particularly Thanksgiving and Christmas dinners), and even pensions for aged or infirm individuals.

Grant's views on some aspects of Christian charity evolved dramatically between 1905 and 1907. During that period he began to urge the parish to follow the lead of the Charity Organization Society and other major New York social agencies by adopting a more professionalized approach to philanthropy. Simple "kindheartedness," he suggested, needed to be supplemented by techniques—community surveys and careful record keeping—

drawn from the emerging field of "trained philanthropy." To help educate the church's charity agents in these methods, Grant invited leaders from local social agencies (e.g., Greenwich House and the C.O.S.) to Ascension for annual conferences on emerging trends in social work.[30]

An even more radical shift in Grant's thinking was evident in 1906–1907 when he announced that Ascension's response to urban poverty should no longer be limited to philanthropy. The problem with charity, he argued, was that it kept the poor at arm's length rather than inviting them to become participants in parish life. The Chapel of the Comforter, Ascension's mission for workers, was located on Horatio Street in the west Village. Although this building was only eight blocks from Ascension's main church on Fifth Avenue, the social distance between the Chapel's working-class clientele and Ascension's elite parishioners was much greater. The appropriate response to the gulf between the classes, Grant argued, was for Ascension to pursue a bold policy of "inclusion." What he proposed was that Ascension's regular Sunday evening service be redesigned specifically to attract working-class New Yorkers to the church's Fifth Avenue location. The format for these gatherings, to be known as Ascension Forum, would be a brief prayer service and homily in the main chapel followed immediately by a lecture and discussion meeting in the parish hall.[31]

Grant's plan was not without precedent. The most notable example of a similar program was People's Institute, the brainchild of a public-spirited retired Columbia University professor, Charles Sprague Smith. People's Institute had been in operation since the late 1890s at Cooper Union. From a relatively modest beginning of twice-weekly lectures on Fridays and Sundays, it gradually expanded its offerings until classes and lectures were scheduled nearly every day of the week all year. Variously labeled by contemporaries as "A Practical School of Democracy" and "An East Side 'College,' " People's Institute aimed to attract the largest possible audience of Lower East Side residents and then, as one newspaper put it, "teach the masses correct social and economic views." "Correct" in this context meant the anti-Tammany political perspective favored by Smith and the north Village patricians.[32]

Although People's Institute was very popular, attracting more than 100,000 participants annually, it was a secular organization with a mainly political focus. Grant and other religious leaders might speak to People's Institute audiences, but there was a major difference between occasional addresses given at People's Institute and an effort to draw workers into parish life at Ascension on a regular basis. Moreover, the chief focus of Ascension's program would not be on weaning workers from Tammany but putting into practice the church's teachings about brotherly love.[33]

Grant's pursuit of his plan to transform Ascension's evening service into a working-people's forum enabled him to play one of his favorite roles, that of the liberal gadfly whose proposals were meant to prod parish traditionalists into rethinking their conservative views. In the context of 1907, a depression year during which many working-class Villagers were unemployed, Grant urged his parishioners to see that their church had a unique opportunity to dispel laborers' distrust of Christianity in general and Ascension in particular. The simple act of opening Ascension's doors invitingly to the poor, he insisted, would convey in no uncertain terms the message, as Grant put it, "that the Church is not a rich man's club" that sought to exclude workers. Moreover, he hoped that candid dialogues at Ascension would show that cross-class fellowship and understanding was possible, proving "that some of the most serious present-day problems which seem to involve class bitterness and conflict can be solved by bringing together men who differ, and letting them discover the sincerity and good will of their supposed antagonists."[34]

No matter how good Grant's rationale for starting a people's forum might be, his plan would not succeed if laborers refused to participate. As a first step toward winning laborers' confidence, Grant sought to recruit an assistant minister who was well regarded by working-class people. He found his man in the person of a street evangelist and Socialist named Alexander Irvine. During the spring of 1907 Irvine had conducted several services at Ascension's West Side mission, the Chapel of the Comforter, and his particular approach, preaching first and then soliciting comments from his audience ("an incipient People's Forum," Grant later called it), had been very well received.[35]

One source of Irvine's common touch was his ability to speak eloquently from personal experience. Born in Northern Ireland, the son of impoverished parents, Irvine told heartrending stories of a childhood spent "shoeless, hatless, and in rags." At the age of nineteen, after working at a variety of low-paying jobs, he joined the British navy, fought in several campaigns in the eastern Mediterranean, and returned on furlough to England, where he attended classes for a brief time at Oxford and, once his furlough ended, continued his studies at various military schools. He emigrated to the United States in 1888. For a couple of years he flitted from job to job—elevator operator, milk-wagon driver, warehouse worker, and editorial assistant at a publishing company—all the while pursuing his primary interest: honing his skills as an evangelist by preaching from streetcorners to down-and-outers in the Bowery slums. His success as an urban missionary launched him on a career in religion that led in fairly rapid succession to ordination as a Congregational minister, brief stints as a pastor in Iowa and

19. A standing-room-only crowd at an Ascension Forum meeting in the church's parish hall. Church of the Ascension.

Ohio, several years of study at Yale, and finally his return to New York City, where he resumed his activities as an evangelist preaching from streetcorners and at homeless shelters.[36]

Grant and Irvine conducted Ascension Forum as a team. Grant took responsibility for readings from the prayerbook and the benediction, Irvine for the sermon. After the chapel service ended, attendees adjourned to the parish hall where, after brief remarks from Irvine, the session was thrown open to comments from the floor. At the early meetings in October 1907 the audience numbered only thirty or so, but it soon grew to the hundreds, crowding the parish hall to capacity (fig. 19). Workers came in large numbers, but the audience also included some of Irvine's Bowery followers, a sprinkling of middle-class social workers, writers, and artists, and even a few well-to-do Wall Street businessmen. The vast majority of the participants were men, although according to Grant, who couldn't resist a chance to take a swipe at traditional prohibitions against letting women speak in church, "Women are heard in and after the meetings, St. Paul to the contrary."[37]

The "after meetings," as Grant called the parish hall sessions, were as volatile as they were popular. Grant tried to impose a rule that everyone who wished to speak would get a chance to and would be listened to respectfully, and for the most part the rule was observed, despite the eagerness of many to take the floor. However, a few participants were, in Grant's words, "rampant individualists, not so eager to learn as to teach, hot headed, fiery tongued and impatient of control, no matter how tactfully exerted." Irvine's skills in dealing with crowds, developed through years of experience with the rough-and-tumble of street meetings, enabled him to squelch most speakers who did not want to yield to others. At least twice during the forum's first year, though, meetings ended in disarray because of disruptions caused by a few "fanatics and egotists," as Grant called them. These were probably the same sessions to which the local precinct station had to send a small squad to remove particularly obdurate members of the audience.[38]

The year's best documented meeting took place on March 29, 1908. It was orderly, even though it was held immediately after a nasty incident involving police brutality toward working-class New Yorkers. The previous day a large crowd of unemployed workers and their sympathizers had assembled at Union Square (five blocks north of Ascension) to protest the authorities' failure to alleviate working-class misery during the depression of 1907–1908. But as Irvine and others who had been at Union Square reported to Ascension Forum the next evening, the rally had scarcely begun when police moved in to break it up, swinging clubs and knocking onlookers to the ground. When the March 29 forum assembled, working-class participants were still seething about the incident, and a sometimes heated debate continued for more than an hour and a half. Nevertheless, according to a middle-class observer, Madge Jenison, the "meeting was the most effective one of the winter" because a consensus was reached between wealthy and working-class members on the point that "free institutions can be preserved only by free speech."[39]

Toward the end of Ascension Forum's first year, Grant reviewed his project's progress. Except for the few occasions when chaos had reigned, he felt that everything had gone to his satisfaction. Having earlier identified American laborers' alienation from Christianity as one of the most serious problems faced by mainstream denominations, he was especially pleased to report that many workers who "had not been inside the portals of a church for many years" had come to Ascension Forum. He was also glad to note that regular members of the parish showed up too. The large crowds at forum meetings, the "catholicity" of the audience's composition, and the fact that popular demand often kept the sessions going long past the appointed ten o'clock closing hour—all of these, he felt, testified to the success of the Sunday evening service's new format.[40]

Not all of Grant's parishioners shared his enthusiasm. Neither the negative attention caused by the disorderly meetings nor the reports that Irvine and his radical followers espoused socialist ideas sat well with a conservative core group in the parish. In a bold attempt to reply both to newspaper criticism and his grumbling parishioners, Grant allowed himself to be interviewed by the *New York Sun* and then reprinted the article in the parish *Year Book* for 1908.

Early in the interview Grant went to the heart of the matter, stating unequivocally: "I am not a Socialist [and] the Sunday night meetings at the Church of the Ascension on Fifth Avenue are not Socialist meetings, nor is any attempt made at Socialistic propaganda." Grant conceded that socialist views were often expressed during forum meetings, but this, he contended, was simply a natural consequence of the presence of many workers who, like workers in every American industrial city, had in recent years shown an increasing interest in socialism. Moreover, he insisted that openness to everyone's opinions was crucial if members from different classes were to learn from one another. Pressing this point further, he used himself as an example. Before participating in Ascension Forum, he said, he had been as ignorant about socialism as most of his critics apparently were, having thought of it as "a dangerous, doctrinaire and revolutionary propaganda." However, in the course of forum sessions he had learned that quite the opposite was true, that American socialism was, as he put it, "a peaceful and evolutionary program . . . [founded on a] social ideal which is one of cooperation rather than conflict."[41]

Notwithstanding his stout defense of Ascension Forum, the good reverend was in fact a bit chastened by the attacks on his project. In an effort to blunt further criticism, Grant modified the format of the forum's sessions during their second year. Greater reliance was placed on invited speakers, who were described as "distinguished specialists in sociological matters." Most of the forum's "after meetings" now opened with a formal address by one of the guest experts, a structured approach calculated to prevent the sessions from moving immediately into the free-for-all debates that had sometimes caused trouble in 1907–1908. Without exception the speakers were middle- or upper-class men and women rather than workers. Politically, all the guests represented some variety of reformist or progressive thought, mostly well to the left of center. Two reform-minded speakers, Arthur Bullard and Rheta Childe Dorr (one a Socialist and the other soon to be) spoke on Russia and on child labor. Charlotte Perkins Gilman, a radical feminist and social critic, gave an address titled "The Social Conscience." E. R. L. Gould, an economist, devoted his talk on model tenements to the proposition that socially conscientious individuals could both make a profit and improve workers' lives by investing in tenements built to high standards.[42]

Ascension Forum's second and third years passed without the turmoil of the first, but conservative parishioners who found any connection with socialism an embarrassment remained restive. Their discontent finally coalesced in the form of an attack on Irvine by Ascension's vestrymen, members of a twenty-four-man body that included many of the church's wealthiest individuals, among them August Belmont, the banker-financier, John Claflin and Edwin N. Tailer, dry-goods merchants who lived on Washington Square North, and John H. Flagler, an industrialist, all of them millionaires. Precisely which vestrymen spearheaded the attack is unknown, but in the spring of 1910 the parish's disgruntled lay leaders made their move and demanded Irvine's resignation. Stung by the implicit rebuke to his leadership of the parish, Grant made a fervent appeal to the vestrymen to reconsider; however, having started on a course of action they knew their minister would oppose, the vestrymen did not back down. Irvine, who was convinced that his job couldn't be saved and that continuing the controversy would only hurt Grant's standing with Ascension parishioners, resigned at the end of June 1910.[43]

Irvine's admirers responded by denouncing Ascension's vestrymen. On June 24, the Friday night before his last scheduled pulpit appearance at Ascension, Irvine was the guest of honor at a dinner attended by 250 of his supporters. The after-dinner speakers expressed anger and disappointment at the conservative political thinking that had led to Irvine's dismissal. Master of ceremonies Robert Bruère, a Socialist and social worker, lamented the decision: "It is a terrible pity that the first church to open its door to the broader Democracy . . . should now be the first church to close that door." Sol Fieldman, described in *New York Times* reports as a "Socialist agitator" and "the son of a Jewish rabbi," asserted that no one should have been surprised by the vestrymen's power play given the fact that "the [Episcopal] Church is owned by the ruling classes, and . . . a church in Fifth Avenue cannot be an exception to the rule."[44]

The evening's main speaker was Lincoln Steffens, best known as a muckraking journalist but introduced on this occasion as the president of the Liberal Club, a debating society he and Grant had organized for left-of-center intellectuals and opinion leaders. Steffens was no less caustic in his remarks about organized Christianity. Of "the Church" (a generic term he used for all major denominations), he said, "It has been corrupt. It has voiced the desires of a part of the people only. It belongs to the same people who control our Government and our politics. . . . We know there is a social crisis approaching, but the Church does not. It sees the viewpoint of only part of the people."[45]

Irvine got off a few parting shots of his own. On Sunday evening, June 26, 1910, Ascension's chapel was jammed to near overflowing with his friends. During the hymns and prayers that preceded Irvine's sermon, the radicals in attendance, unfamiliar with the order of service, struggled gamely but awkwardly to follow along. Then Irvine rose to speak. Taking as his text the biblical injunction that "ye cannot serve God and Mammon," he assailed his critics, answering their charge that his work had been "too sociological and not spiritual enough" by reminding his listeners that "Jesus himself was sociological, and his greatest sermons teemed with economic truth." In America, he thundered, Mammon was "a slimy beast called Money, that ruled the land" from the White House and the New York legislature's chambers right down to the pulpit at Ascension. Those who had voted to remove him from that pulpit because of his Socialist views, Irvine charged, failed to acknowledge that money, not socialism, was "the force that is driving us into warring factions and splitting the country into rival camps." After expressing his appreciation of Grant for having invited him to serve at Ascension, Irvine, the happy warrior for socialism, closed with a promise to continue to fight the good fight for his cause.[46]

Caught in a no man's land between the vestrymen and Socialists, Grant scrambled to minimize the damage done to his relationships with the rival camps. Initially he worried most about losing credibility with laborers, and in addresses made to working-class audiences he described himself as sorely disappointed by the vestry's actions. However, he soon tried to smooth things over with his conservative parishioners. "I must also make public record," he wrote in his parish report for 1910, "of my happiness in my personal relations with the vestrymen of the Church of the Ascension," who, he added, had for many years raised fifty to sixty thousand dollars a year for church projects. He also expressed gratitude to the vestry for having always allowed him "untrammeled freedom of expression," and if the phrasing rang a bit hollow in the aftermath of Irvine's forced resignation, Grant was determined to show that his freedom was real. Specifically, he followed through on a pledge made to Irvine's Socialist friends in 1910 by continuing to sponsor a weekly Sunday night "People's Forum" at Ascension through the early 1910s.[47]

Ascension Forum's history in the Irvine era was just one small episode in a larger drama being played out in the United States during the early 1900s. Massive immigration from southern and eastern Europe and the harsh working conditions these new immigrants encountered in the nation's industrial cities exposed inequities in American capitalist society that greatly heightened class tensions. An increasingly visible Socialist Party voiced the workers' discontents and, aided and abetted by caustic attacks on the status quo by middle- and upper-class intellectuals, the party grew by leaps and bounds. Nationally, the Socialist presidential vote rose nearly fourfold from 1900 to 1908. Over the next two years the growth of electoral support for Socialists was even more impressive locally in New York City, where the vote cast for the party's gubernatorial candidates nearly doubled from 1908 to 1910. It was perfectly obvious to the Village patricians who comprised the core of Ascension parish's membership that the old American elite's standing in society was being challenged by working-class radicals, some of whom were Ascension's near neighbors from the south Village and the Lower East Side.[48]

Given this background of class tension, Grant was being exceedingly optimistic in hoping that his experiment in cross-class communication could succeed and that he could make both the "conservative classes" and the "radicals" (as he called the two groups) feel welcome at Ascension. With Irvine at his side, Grant had a reasonable chance of attracting working-class participants to Ascension Forum, but even with Irvine's help he had no assurance that he could keep them coming to a north Village church they distrusted on both religious and class grounds. Meanwhile, his regular parishioners, the middle- and upper-class worshipers who filled the pews at Ascension on Sunday mornings, were also a problem. Ascension's wealthy vestrymen did not like anticapitalist sentiments when spoken at street-corner rallies or printed in Socialist papers such as the *New York Call*, but they found it even harder to bear when their own church's sanctuary was the site of such pronouncements. The strain of playing host to Irvine and his radical friends was severe from the very first.[49]

Eventually the strain became too great. For three years Ascension's lay leaders and ordinary parishioners had hosted a people's forum and even participated in its meetings—behavior at odds with any glib characterization of them as uniformly hostile to their less privileged neighbors' views. Working-class men and women had come to Ascension Forum and kept coming in large numbers to the very end. They not only showed up; they enjoyed themselves, some because the forums offered an opportunity to bait the wealthy face to face, and others because they were eager to learn what they could from the meetings. Regardless of whether they came to denounce or to learn, these participants were products of a working-class culture in which ideas were taken very seriously, and even though many radicals were skeptical about the sincerity of Grant's invitation, they treated it as worthy of being put to the test. In the end Ascension Forum's wealthy hosts ceased to welcome their radical guests, and these guests were naturally displeased. Grant was at least half right, however, when on the Sunday of Irvine's last pulpit appearance he declared, "I cannot think of this termination of our experiment here as a failure."[50]

THE WASHINGTON SQUARE ASSOCIATION

The Washington Square Association, a neighborhood taxpayers' organization sponsored by and for north Village patricians, was established in 1907. It differed in many respects from its older counterpart, the Greenwich Village Improvement Society, which had been the first neighborhood association in the city. Generally, the society's geographical focus was on the middle- and working-class areas south and west of Washington Square, while the newer association concentrated its attention on the north Village district in which its members lived. Of even greater significance in distinguishing between the two groups was the difference in their philosophies with regard to which neighborhood interests they should represent. The society's founders, led by Mary Simkhovitch of Greenwich House, embraced their neighborhood's diversity and attempted to reflect it by recruiting representatives from every major local ethnic group (except African Americans) for its governing board. By contrast, the Washington Square Association's membership was composed exclusively of north Village patricians who made no effort to admit non-elite neighbors to their ranks. As a result, though both the Greenwich Village Improvement Society and the Washington Square Association acted as neighborhood advocacy groups seeking to improve the quality of streets, lighting, public services, and the like, the Washington Square Association's projects placed primary emphasis on the Village gentry's interests, which frequently clashed with the interests of working-class Villagers.

The Washington Square Association's membership list reads like a roll call of the north Village's most prominent citizens. Among those who lived on Washington Square North were a millionaire drygoods merchant, John Claflin; a banker, Eugene Delano; and Robert W. de Forest, the president of the Charity Organization Society. The members who lived on Fifth Avenue included one of de Forest's brothers-in-law, Pierre Mali; a wealthy investor, Amos F. Eno; and the nationally known financier and Democratic Party power broker Thomas Fortune Ryan. Nearly every side street off Fifth Avenue north to Twelfth Street had at least one representative in the organization. East Tenth was home to several lawyers, among them Joseph Auerbach and Henry E. Coe (another de Forest brother-in-law). Another lawyer, Joseph L. Delafield, who served for many years as the group's corresponding secretary, lived on West Twelfth. All these men were well-to-do and several (Claflin, de Forest, Eno, and Ryan) were millionaires. Politically, the association's members were fairly evenly divided between those like de Forest, Ryan, and Auerbach who were anti-Tammany Democrats and those like John Claflin and Henry E. Coe who were Independent Republicans.

Moving in the same upper-class circles, these north Villagers belonged to such elite social clubs as the Union League, Union Club, and University Club and supported such major civic institutions as the Metropolitan Museum of Art.[51]

The Washington Square Association's first bulletin, issued in February 1907, announced that the organization's goal was to "maintain and improve the character of the neighborhood." The association's main modus operandi was to send letters to city officials: the Manhattan Borough President, the commissioners who headed the Department of Health and the Department of Street Cleaning, and the police captain in charge of the Sixteenth Precinct, which was located at 253 Mercer Street, a block southeast of Washington Square. During the association's first year most letters addressed matters of safety or the neighborhood's physical appearance. Officials were urged to fill potholes, restore sidewalks promptly after construction projects were completed, remove loiterers from the area, enforce laws against spitting in public places, and require manufacturers and merchants to keep sidewalks clear of commercial debris. Apparently some progress was made. The association's final bulletin for 1907 included a self-congratulatory note claiming that "the great and visible improvement in the conditions of the streets" was traceable to the association's efforts.[52]

These physical improvements in the neighborhood's streets presumably benefited all local residents, poor and wealthy alike. So, too, did the association's demand for better traffic movement, to which the police responded by adding patrolmen at congested intersections. The association's secretary applauded such action as proof that police could be "alert, intelligent and efficient" when properly motivated. But he went on to complain that the police did not act energetically on other matters of concern to the Village gentry. Police, he wrote, "behave as if they were half-witted and half-blind" when they encountered cases of littering or of children breaking the city ordinance against using streets as playgrounds.[53]

Competing values came into high relief in June 1908, when the association launched an initiative against street vendors and pushcart merchants of every type: bootblacks and newspaper vendors whose semipermanent stands had established locations, pushcart operators who moved into place daily, and the even more temporary and more mobile holiday peddlers who were allowed to set up booths or tables during the Easter and Christmas seasons. According to the association's spokesmen, street merchants took business away from the more established local stores. Sidewalk booths inhibited easy access to shops along major thoroughfares, and the booths' shabby appearance discouraged wealthier patrons from shopping in the neighborhood. The street vendors also enjoyed an unfair competitive advantage over store owners, who had to charge higher prices to cover the cost of property taxes that street merchants did not have to pay. On top of everything else, many sidewalk stands were operating illegally, taking up space in excess of that allowed under their permits.

The first targets of the clear-the-sidewalks campaign were two concession stands operating at the exits to the Sixth Avenue Elevated line's Eighth Street station. On the northeast corner of the intersection stood a newsstand owned by Charles Gordon and a three-chair bootblack stand run by Antonio Mastrino. According to the Washington Square Association, both booths were positioned in such a way as to nearly block the sidewalks at the base of the station's stairways. Initially, the association's letters to the Manhattan Borough President and the Commissioner of Public Works did not ask that Gordon and Mastrino be deprived of their licenses to do business, only that they be required to modify the dimensions of their stands or move them to new locations so as to cause less inconvenience to pedestrian traffic and to shoppers who wanted access to nearby stores.[54]

It might seem that the balance of power in the battle between the Village gentry and the street vendors greatly favored the Washington Square Association. Not only were its ranks filled with wealthy members of the city's social elite, but they had some support from storefront merchants who believed they were losing business. In addition, when the association began its campaign in mid-1908, the mayor of the city, George B. McClellan Jr., was a neighborhood resident, living at 8 Washington Square North (next door to the de Forests).[55]

The vendors, on the other hand, were mainly lower-middle-class immigrants. Antonio Mastrino, known to his friends and customers as "Tony," was thirty-one years old, an Italian immigrant brought by his parents to the United States in 1888. Before entering the shoeshine business, he had worked as a hotel bellhop. He and his wife of four years lived in a small flat on West Eighth Street between MacDougal and Sixth Avenue, where north Village residents of modest means clustered. Charles Gordon, the newsstand owner, was a thirty-year-old Russian Jew who had come to New York City in 1899. In 1908 he and his wife, Minnie, and three young children lived on West Eighth, a few doors down from the Mastrinos; income from his stand soon enabled him to move his family to a large West Fourth Street apartment house whose occupants were a mix of small entrepreneurs and lower-class wage earners.[56]

In June 1908, Joseph L. Delafield, the lawyer who served as the Washington Square Association's corresponding secretary, launched the organization's campaign against street concessionaires by writing Manhattan Borough President John F. Ahern to ask that something be done about the

Gordon and Mastrino stands at the Sixth Avenue elevated line's Eighth Street station. Over the next year he pursued the matter through correspondence with the Commissioner of Public Works, the New York City Police Commissioner, the local police precinct's captain, the Bureau of Licenses, and the city's Assistant Corporation Counsel. Despite this barrage of complaints, at the end of 1910, a year and a half into the campaign, Mastrino and Gordon were still doing business as usual at their old locations.[57]

Three sources of resistance frustrated the village gentry's efforts to tidy up the neighborhood by controlling the activities of street merchants. Bureaucratic inertia and red tape constantly delayed decisive action. Many city officials simply did not regard placing restrictions on street vendors as a high priority; others, though apparently sympathetic with the association's overall goals, stressed the fact that nothing could be done at the double-quick pace the association expected. For example, an administrative assistant in the borough president's office wrote Delafield to say that even if some street stands were in violation of regulations prohibiting "obstructions outside stoop lines," these transgressions could not be corrected except through a fairly elaborate procedure. Stands said to be in violation of their licenses had to be visited by a city inspector, issued a citation if something was amiss, given a reasonable period to correct violations, and then inspected a second time—all this before legal proceedings could begin. Many street vendors simply moved to different locations, or made slight changes to existing stands that, even if they were not judged satisfactory, nevertheless required a whole new round of citations, waiting periods, and reinspections. Perhaps, one official suggested, a more direct route to cracking down on street vendor violations would be to ask the police to intervene.[58]

Police action struck the Washington Square Association's members as a viable alternative to the License Bureau's cumbersome procedures, and Delafield's initial correspondence with high-ranking Police Department officials produced seemingly helpful offers to have cops on the beat serve notices to stands that were in violation of municipal regulations. In April 1909, Police Commissioner Thomas Bingham wrote Delafield that patrolmen in the Sixteenth Precinct had begun to issue citations, and in June a group of approximately sixty vendors were summoned to hearings in municipal court.[59]

The trouble was that ordinary patrolmen and municipal court judges— both groups more beholden to the Democratic machine than to reform-minded Village gentry—showed considerable sympathy to the beleaguered vendors. When the first sixty cases were reviewed, one judge immediately ruled that no vendors' licenses could be revoked nor their holders fined without giving the defendants ample time to correct deficiencies. As for those caught operating without a license, they were simply instructed to apply for one. And when hearings were held on citations given for stands that exceeded legal size limits, police proved to be totally unhelpful as witnesses. In several instances the judge dismissed cases after patrolmen said they could not properly identify the defendant as the licensee, and others were dismissed because the officer who served the notice admitted that although the stand had appeared too large, he had not actually measured it. By way of explanation one such policeman told the court that he had had "no yard stick with which to measure" the booth. Reading between the lines, it appears that police went through the motions of carrying out their superiors' orders to enforce regulations, but did so in such a way that they knew the vendors would not lose their licenses.[60]

Even as they moved ahead with the process of taking vendors to court, patrician Villagers pursued another method of curbing the presence of street merchants in the neighborhood. By long-standing practice, permits for activities or structures that might encumber sidewalks—shoeshine booths and newsstands, peddler's carts and tables, barbershop poles, cigar store Indians, and sandwich board advertisements—were subject to a two-stage approval process. Applicants first got a permit from the city licensing bureau, and then took it to the alderman of the district in which the activity or structure would be located for his endorsement. Though cumbersome, the system embodied an old-fashioned form of direct democracy in which aldermen identified themselves with their constituents by providing them with valuable personal services. Under this system, however, aldermen could be caught in double binds. Applicants whose requests were approved went away inclined to repay the favor by voting for the man who had helped them, but it wasn't possible to please all the people all the time. Many applications were rejected because objections were raised in a convincing fashion by other valued constituents—existing license holders opposed to additional competition, or property owners objecting to a potential eyesore near their homes or stores. As one alderman who served the Washington Square district recalled, "Sometimes the pressure from the two forces [the applicants and the property owners] felt like a giant pair of scissors closing about my neck."[61]

Starting in March 1909, the Village gentry applied increased pressure with the blade of the scissors that they controlled. They began to make a particular issue of their alderman's biannual approval of thirty-day licenses for vendors who hawked flowers, chestnuts, candied apples, trinkets, and the like from pushcarts and tables on the neighborhood's busiest commercial streets—Sixth Avenue, Fourteenth Street, and Broadway—during the

Easter and Christmas seasons (fig. 20). In general, these holiday street vendors were economically much more marginal than businessmen like Antonio Mastrino and Charles Gordon who operated year-round from fixed locations; however, as remembered by one north Villager, the small-time street merchants contributed local color to the neighborhood scene at holiday time:

> In Christmas week, all Sixth Avenue from Macy's at Fourteenth Street to Siegel-Cooper's at Eighteenth was lined solidly with little stalls lit by kerosene lamps. Most were trimmed with greens and all were piled with useless gifts like brass paperweights, miniature Statues of Liberty or huge glittering gems pinned to cards, while the wires above were hung with necklaces and handkerchiefs and rows of striped peppermint canes. The hawkers called out their last-minute bargains, the smell of scorched holly and roasting chestnuts hung deliciously on the frosty air, and even the most garish objects seemed desirable in the flickering light.[62]

Although the street vendors were a well-established feature of the holiday season, two circumstances gave the Washington Square Association's members reason to think that the vendors could be removed. Holiday peddlers had to reapply each Easter and Christmas, which enabled the Washington Square Association to renew its appeals to the alderman twice a year. The Twenty-fifth aldermanic district, in which the north Village gentry resided, was also an unusual Lower Manhattan ward in that it generally voted Republican, and in 1909 it was represented by a Republican, Tristam Johnson. Tammany's police department and municipal courts might be slow to defend the Village gentry's interests, but surely, the association believed, Johnson would respond sympathetically to its pleas.

Any hopes that Johnson would simply do the gentry's bidding were doomed to disappointment, however. In an exchange that became a bi-annual ritual, Delafield sent Johnson the association's request that he cease to approve licenses for holiday peddlers, and Johnson answered with a carefully worded reply. He understood the concerns expressed by the association's members, he said, and he wanted them to know that he kept the number of approvals down in a variety of ways. He refused to approve license applications from individuals who lived outside the district, and, as they were welcome to observe if they would visit him at his district Republican club office, he turned down many requests from new applicants. However, he was not about to abandon altogether the long-standing custom of granting licenses to holiday street vendors, especially those who had held the licenses in previous years.[63]

Johnson's successor as the district's alderman was Henry H. Curran, the same Curran who had made his debut as a public speaker campaigning for

20. Everett Shinn's *Sixth Avenue Shoppers* shows the crowds that jammed north Village sidewalks during the Christmas and Easter seasons. Santa Barbara Museum of Art, Gift of Mrs. Sterling Morton to the Preston Morton Collection.

Seth Low during the 1903 mayoral election. A critic of Tammany rule, a Yale graduate, and a prosperous lawyer, Curran might also have been expected to side with the Washington Square gentry and against the immigrant vendors who did business from shabby sidewalk stands, pushcarts, and folding tables. But Curran proved no more willing than Johnson to drive the small vendors from the neighborhood's streets. He had populistic inclinations, derived from political activities that had made him aware of and sympathetic to the needs of his grass-roots constituents: several years spent as a district Republican organizer for Johnson, a vigorous but futile campaign for Congress in 1910, the beginning of his alderman career when he was appointed in March 1911 to fill the vacancy created by Johnson's resignation, and his successful campaign for reelection as alderman in fall 1911.[64]

Curran's memoirs contain a section on what he called the "trouble" associated with the alderman's duty to endorse licenses for the approximately three hundred fruit, soda water, shoeshine, and newspaper stands in his district. He was well aware that store owners resented the competition and home owners disliked having the street vendors' "dirty little shanties" near their property, and he knew that the arrival of even more peddlers each Easter and Christmas season only exacerbated the property owners' bad feelings. However, he was unwilling, as he wrote Delafield, to "put out of business the immigrant family that could not yet do anything in this strange new world but run a little sidewalk stand," since to do so would condemn them to "starvation."[65]

Curran used several individuals to exemplify all the immigrant entrepreneurs who sought and received his endorsement on their vendor's licenses. One was an old Italian whom Curran nicknamed Garibaldi. The old man ran what Curran described as "the most gypsylike looking stand of them all," and had but a few words of English to communicate with patrons at his umbrella repair booth. However, Garibaldi had eight children (and an uncountable number of relatives and friends in the district), and Curran knew that an alderman who turned down such license-seekers would be perceived as an enemy of the common folk. Curran surely had constituents like Garibaldi in mind when he replied to one of Delafield's appeals. "I have your annual letter about Christmas booths," Curran wrote. "As you know, I consider myself subject in this matter to the will of the people in the neighborhood"—by which Curran obviously meant the ordinary folk, not the Village gentry. Aware that its anti-vendor campaign had not succeeded in driving the unsightly stands and pushcarts from the streets, the association had to be content with claiming that at least it had prevented them from proliferating.[66]

A parallel effort by the association to control the use of Greenwich Village's largest open public space, Washington Square, also produced inconclusive results. As in the street vendor controversy, the debate over the square's present and future use was shaped by the unusual circumstance that, as one contemporary put it, "the Washington Square neighborhood contains . . . a small first-class residential district contiguous to a large proletariat neighborhood." Lying as it did between the upper- and working-class parts of the Village, the square itself could legitimately be claimed by both patrician and proletarian Villagers as their turf—and both did claim it, for largely incompatible purposes. Occupants of the fine homes north of Washington Square wanted it to be a tranquil haven from the bustling commerce of the city, a park where visitors sat on benches or strolled quietly along well-marked paths, finding respite amid attractive lawns, tidy flower beds, and well-cared-for greenery. Working-class Villagers, many of whom lived in tenements south of the square, saw it as a scarce commodity: the largest of the few open public spaces in the neighborhood, a patch of green amidst the concrete, a place where their children could play and where they might picnic, nap, and even, on hot summer nights, sleep outdoors on a lawn.[67]

Park or playground? On behalf of the Washington Square Association, Joseph Delafield expressed dismay at behavior in Washington Square that violated the gentry's notion of what was proper in a well-ordered park. Some of his complaints were directed at adult users—the drunks, both men and women, who slept on park benches, and the working-class Villagers who lunched or picnicked on the lawns and left unsightly litter behind: discarded newspapers, fruit peels, glass shards, pieces of cardboard. However, the majority of his grievances concerned "tough horse-play and rowdyism" by children, especially boys. As he put it to Park Commissioner Charles B. Stover in March 1911: "[with spring's arrival] the boys take advantage of the lawn, especially on the south side of the Park, for the purpose of playing ball and other games." Two months later his pleasant stroll through the park with his wife and their child was disturbed by an annoying sight: "Boys and girls romped over the lawns, digging here and there." In July 1911 he wrote Mayor Gaynor to complain that the practice of allowing tenement dwellers open access to the park's grassy areas on hot nights had the effect of giving "free reign to the rowdy element to play ball and rough it on the lawns." More letters in the same vein, requesting that city officials crack down on the "crowd of rough boys" who roller-skated on the square's walkways and played baseball on its lawns, followed in 1912.[68]

Several factors explain why the Washington Square Association's protect-the-park campaign gathered momentum in 1910. By that summer the war on street vendors was making little headway, and Delafield apparently felt that a new focus was needed to reenergize the association's effort to impose genteel standards of public decorum. Summer was also the season during which the park was most likely to be used (or abused, depending on one's viewpoint) as a playground. In addition, the new city administration was led by Mayor William Gaynor, a Democrat elected with Tammany backing but somewhat independent of Tammany control, and a number of newly elected officials—Manhattan Borough President George McAneny and John Purroy Mitchel, the president of the Board of Aldermen—were so-called Fusionists, reform Democrats who had Republican backing in running against Tammany's regular slate in 1909. The anti-Tammany politics of these leaders may have encouraged the Village gentry to believe that their views would now be more favorably received.[69]

The association's hopes were only partly realized. It seemed that every time a city official responded positively to the association's program, a related action was taken or opinion expressed that alarmed the Village gentry. On the positive side, Park Commissioner Charles B. Stover ordered a variety of renovations at Washington Square: reseeded lawns, extensive landscaping, and the installation of a new drinking fountain, all of which North Village patricians applauded. But even as he secured these improvements, Stover, a former resident of University Settlement, revealed a soft spot for working-class children by suggesting that specified sections of municipal parks should be set aside for baseball games and organized play (fig. 21). Similarly, although Lieutenant John Shay, commander of the Sixteenth Precinct, seemed eager to assure Delafield that his officers did and would vigilantly patrol Washington Square, he added that as far as he knew there was "no evidence of torn sod or misuse" resulting from the practice of opening the park's lawns to tenement dwellers on hot nights. In March 1911, Delafield and his patrician neighbors were encouraged by reports that a sympathetic mayor and his police commissioner were going to crack down on baseball games, but it soon became obvious that cops on the beat were doing little to prevent ball playing in Washington Square.[70]

During 1911–1912, the peak years of the Washington Square Association's preserve-the-park campaign, it became clear that the association's members faced both practical and ideological obstacles to achieving their goals. Given the park's location near rapidly expanding tenement districts, Washington Square was inevitably going to be used by the neighborhood's working-class residents for relaxation and recreation. This was a fact of life recognized by Alexander H. Spencer of the City Club, a civic watchdog group whose members boasted impeccable upper-class credentials, when he urged the Washington Square Association to take what he called "a charitable approach" to the needs of Village tenement dwellers. Acknowledging that the gentry's desire to keep "a handsome park well preserved" was completely understandable, he asked them to give serious consideration to the question of what was to be done for "the hoi polloi and their children who must overflow somewhere."[71]

As Spencer's remarks suggest, the Washington Square controversy was not simply a confrontation between patrician and proletarian Villagers and their political allies. An ideological divide also existed among middle- and upper-class New Yorkers over whether the city's open spaces, especially those in or near slum neighborhoods, should be used primarily as parks or as playgrounds. By advocating a pristine park, the Washington Square Association identified itself with an ideal articulated by the renowned nineteenth-century landscape architect Frederick Law Olmsted, the designer of

21. William J. Glackens's *For the Championship of the Back-Lot League* depicts tenement district children at play. From *Collier's*, November 11, 1911.

New York City's Central Park. Olmsted and his allies held to a romantic view of nature, one in which the beauty and serenity of natural landscapes, set aside as parks in cities, would provide, as the historian Paul Boyer has termed it, "a 'natural' counterweight to the morally destructive pressures of urban life." Progressive Era urban designers updated Olmsted's approach by insisting that truly modern parks needed aggressive management through the provision of highly structured experiences (plays, concerts, and talks by naturalists) to interpret and reinforce nature's uplifting qualities.[72]

In the early 1900s, both of these versions of the park ideal were challenged by a second group of progressives, supporters of the playground movement. Their alternative program for using open spaces in industrial cities as children's play areas had the backing of most leading members of the social settlement house community, including Mary Simkhovitch of Greenwich House. A member of the Parks and Playgrounds Association of New York City's board of directors, Simkhovitch argued that directed play activities would not only enhance the physical health of slum children but also inculcate in them moral values essential to a democratic society: team play, respect for others, and self-control.

A March 1912 incident in Washington Square brought these competing ideas into sharp focus. A woman social worker employed by the Parks and Playgrounds Association had gathered a small group of working-class children in the park and was leading them in organized games. A prosperous-looking man approached, reproved her, and then enlisted the aid of a passing policeman to prevent the games from continuing. According to Eugene A. Philbin, the Parks and Playgrounds Association's president, the gentleman also told the play leader that "children of the Sullivan Street district should not be encouraged to come to Washington Square Park," and suggested that "she confine her work to the children accompanied by nurses."[73]

A prickly exchange followed between Philbin and Delafield. Delafield denied that the man who had objected to the games was a member of the Washington Square Association, but he acknowledged that the association's members shared some of the man's views. Although they did not dispute the need for a playground for working-class children from the south Village, they strenuously objected to designating Washington Square as that space. To do so, he insisted, would "needlessly destroy the traditional character" of Washington Square and would lead to a "general removal" of the better class of people from the neighborhood. Philbin responded that the area had already changed radically and that some concessions regarding the use of the park needed to be made "by both the old residents and the new."[74]

In the end, the only common ground the two sides found was agreement that more playground space was needed in the Village for working-class youngsters. Unable to achieve its original goal of a total prohibition on games in Washington Square, the association gradually adopted the view that the best way to preserve the square as a park would be to help find alternative locations for a playground. This newfound pragmatism became most apparent in 1913–1914, when the association backed a proposal from Mary Simkhovitch and the Greenwich Village Improvement Society that city authorities raze several tenement blocks in the Minettas to provide play space for south Village children.[75]

In the same years that the Washington Square Association pursued its largely inconclusive campaigns to rid the north Village of street vendors and Washington Square of unruly youngsters, the organization enjoyed considerable success in its ongoing effort to bring improved public services to the neighborhood. Local streets were upgraded in response to persistent demands that potholes be filled, broken sidewalks repaired, abandoned horsecar tracks removed, stone block pavement replaced by asphalt, missing street signs restored, and new trees planted on residential streets. Police took positive action on requests for better traffic management and for suppression of late-night noise. Ambulance and fire truck traffic was, when possible, redirected away from residential side streets; the clock in the Jefferson Market Courthouse tower was repaired; companies engaged in construction projects or industrial activities were forced to move quickly to eliminate unsightly rubbish piles or sources of noxious odors; and, in general, the collection of ashes, garbage, and dead animal carcasses was dealt with more efficiently by the responsible city departments. After five years of existence, the association had good reason to express satisfaction regarding its achievements. "We feel justified," the March 1912 *Bulletin* declared, "in assuming that the general conditions [in the neighborhood] have never been better."[76]

The features that distinguished the association's successful projects from its failures provide clues into the way political and group relations operated inside Greenwich Village in the early years of the century. When the Washington Square Association campaigned for such goals as cleaner, safer, and more attractive streets that served the interests of a majority of the area's residents, city officials usually acted quickly to secure the requested improvements. By contrast, when the interests of working-class Villagers were threatened by the association's campaigns to impose controls on street vendors and park-goers, those initiatives achieved minimal results. The relationship between the Village gentry and their working-class neighbors remained basically adversarial. Nevertheless, the association's campaigns, by preserving and even enhancing the quality of the neighborhood's physical environment, produced substantial benefits for both groups.

4

Allies

A CARTOGRAPHER marking a Greenwich Village map to show where the neighborhood's largest ethnic groups lived in 1900 would have begun by shading in four large areas: an Italian section in the south Village, an African American enclave south and west of Washington Square, a west Village Irish district, and the blocks on Washington Square North and lower Fifth Avenue where the Protestant gentry lived. This exercise would have left one section in the center of the Village largely untouched: the east, south, and west sides of Washington Square and the streets between it and Sheridan Square, and the blocks north of Sheridan Square between Waverly Place and Sixth Avenue. This L-shaped borderland between the Village's most readily identified ethnic enclaves was mainly a middle-class residential district whose inhabitants included many of the reformers, social activists, and writers who are the focus of this chapter.

Although they came to their adopted causes by a variety of paths, these reform-minded Villagers shared certain traits and beliefs. They were cosmopolitans, well above average in their educational attainments, and intensely interested in national and international affairs. Their conviction that an old world was passing and a new one emerging was inspired by events that are largely forgotten today: the growth of Socialist Party strength in the United States, the Russian Revolution of 1905, and the panic and depression of 1907.

Few of the reform-minded Villagers stayed permanently in the neighborhood. Unlike Robert de Forest, Serena Rhinelander, Father Demo, Billy
Walker, and Charles Culkin, all of whom lived in the Village for decades,
many of the middle-class reformers came and went. They might rent rooms
in the Village through the winter, summer elsewhere, and then, perhaps
after a period spent somewhere else, return to the Village for a time.

An extreme example of such transitory Villagers would be Neith Boyce
and Hutchins Hapgood, the young journalists mentioned in chapter 1.
Both rented rooms on Washington Square in 1898, Boyce spending the
better part of the year at the Judson Hotel and Hapgood living at the
Benedick (a bachelor hotel at 80 Washington Square East) for a few months
in the fall. After they married, Hapgood and Boyce (she retained her
maiden name) moved to an apartment in Chelsea, the neighborhood just
north of the Village. They never again lived in the Village, although their
ongoing connections with the neighborhood—their summers at Provincetown with Village friends and their frequent visits to the Village in connection with literary and political activities—were so numerous that they
were treated by their contemporaries as honorary Villagers long after they
had ceased to live there.[1]

Practical considerations such as easy access to good transportation, relatively low rents, and pleasant surroundings drew many middle-class individuals to the Village's Washington Square–Sheridan Square district; ties
with friends and local institutions kept them coming back. Madeleine Doty
and Ida Rauh met and became involved in Village life when they enrolled
as students in New York University's law school. There they met another
classmate, Jessie Ashley, forming bonds of friendship based in large part on
a shared ambition to break into the legal profession at a time when it was
exceedingly unwelcoming to women. Even at N.Y.U., which in the early
1900s had one of the few law schools in the country that accepted women
students, men still outnumbered women by a ratio of more than thirteen to
one in Doty, Rauh, and Ashley's class of 1902.[2]

At the time they graduated Doty and Rauh were in most respects still
very conventional personally and politically. Rauh was the daughter of protective Jewish parents, and Doty adhered to the Victorian behavioral
code—women should not smoke, drink alcoholic beverages in public, or
engage in sex outside of marriage—with which she had been inculcated by
her Presbyterian upbringing and Smith College education. Both women
were smart and ambitious, but in 1902 neither had any expectation that
before the end of the decade they would become activists on behalf of the
city's poor.[3]

An evolution from an apolitical outlook to progressive activism was not unusual among the Washington Square–Sheridan Square middle-class Villagers, as the case of Mary Heaton also illustrates. When she married Albert White Vorse in October 1898, she felt that she had failed in her efforts to become an artist but that she had made a highly desirable marriage. Bert seemed perfect: a Harvard graduate (friends with Hutch Hapgood, who was also a Harvard man), an aspiring author, and an editor with connections that gave the two of them entrée to the best of traditional literary culture (the Richard Watson Gilders' north Village salon) and to the circle of bohemians led by James Gibbons Huneker, a well-known literary critic. When she and Bert moved to their first home, a five-room apartment at 210 West Fourth Street (across from Sheridan Square), Mary had no inkling that her writing career would soon be much more successful than her husband's or that she would be actively supporting radical working-class protests.[4]

In all their undertakings, whether local, national or international, the reform-minded Villagers sought to build networks among allies of two types: friends from their own class of educated social critics, and comrades from working-class backgrounds. Few were more important than those they found inside Greenwich Village.

THE A CLUBBERS

In February 1906, a group of eighteen or twenty young writers and social workers bought a mansion at 3 Fifth Avenue, just north of Washington Square, with the intention of entering into a cooperative housing arrangement. The news caused a small stir in the newspapers. The proposed housing collective was so at odds with the individual or familial ways that New Yorkers usually lived that reporters were dispatched to investigate this novel group. When a reporter asked its president, Howard Brubaker, what the collective's name was, Brubaker casually replied, "Oh, just call it a club." Thereafter it became known as "A Club" both in the newspaper accounts and in the popular lore of the group itself. Although the A Club cooperative housing experiment lasted only a few years, it nevertheless brought together and helped solidify a network of individuals whose contribution to Village history far outweighed their relatively small numbers.[5]

Newspaper reporters who interviewed A Club's founders received somewhat contradictory descriptions of the group's purpose and membership. The earliest version came from Helen Todd, a wealthy Chicago settlement worker who had bankrolled the purchase of the mansion. She described A Clubbers as "people who like the bohemian life and are interested in the East Side of New York," and who took the Fifth Avenue house "because it is only a short distance from the 'ghetto.' " The part about wanting to be close to East Side slums was true enough, but the New Yorkers in the group objected to Todd's use of the word "bohemian" in connection with themselves. Charlotte Teller, an editorial assistant at *Everybody's* magazine and a writer of both fiction and nonfiction, emphasized that "Life [at A Club] will not be bohemian, as has been stated, for most of us are old enough not to be childish in that way. . . . We shall lead a perfectly conventional, normal family life." Another woman member also disagreed with newspaper stories that had implied "that we are organized for dilettante, artistic, easy living, which is entirely false." She, for one, hoped to organize women who were employed in the factories of the Washington Square district. "We are here for work," she stated emphatically.[6]

Charlotte Teller and Howard Brubaker gave interviewers additional reasons behind the founding of A Club. "Driven to desperation by New York hotel, boarding house and apartment life," Teller said, "we think this [cooperative arrangement] will be an improvement and it seems to me a perfectly natural thing to do." Brubaker thought that "getting literary people together" would provide a stimulating intellectual environment for all concerned, but added that the club had been founded without any specific public or political purpose in mind. Teller agreed with the latter point, although she acknowledged that because "all the members hold views more or less radical," A Club might become "a radical centre" and its members might join forces to promote some "political, social or industrial movement." But the club's main purpose, she said, was to provide each member with a convenient place to live and do his or her work.[7]

Residents of A Club came to 3 Fifth Avenue by a variety of routes, the two most common being through contacts made in literary circles (Mary Heaton Vorse heard about the club in that way) and through friendships formed among settlement house workers (which was how Helen Todd of Chicago came to join the group). Veterans of University Settlement on New York's Lower East Side provided most of the early recruits, including Howard Brubaker, Ernest Poole, Leroy Scott and his wife, Miriam Finn, Hamilton Holt, Walter Weyl, and Arthur Bullard. Although most of these individuals had ceased to be active at University Settlement before moving to A Club, many of them had continued to work together in activities related to the 1905 Russian Revolution.

Settlement workers who had lived on the Lower East Side could scarcely have avoided being affected by the intense anti-czarist feeling that prevailed among recent immigrants from Russia and Poland, the latter at that time controlled by Russia. Again and again the college-educated American social workers heard their Jewish East European neighbors decry tyrannical czarist rule and the atrocities committed against Jews. In the same period that immigration from eastern Europe had been swelling the population of New York's East Side slums, Russia had been undergoing an economic crisis, and strikes and food shortages were widespread. When Czar Nicholas II's unpopular expansionist program in the Far East led to disastrous defeats in the Russo-Japanese War in 1904, the disaffection of workers, peasants, and soldiers began to approach revolutionary intensity.

In January 1905, thousands of workers marched on the czar's winter palace in St. Petersburg; troops fired live ammunition into the crowd, thus ending any hopes that the czar would hear the workers' protests. Bloody Sunday, as this incident came to be called, left more than a thousand demonstrators dead and triggered a period of rioting throughout Russia. Czarist control continued to weaken as the year progressed. In November, Vladimir Lenin, the leader of the Social Democrats, a Marxist party, returned to Russia, and in December armed uprisings broke out in Moscow and other major cities.

The future A Clubbers in the University Settlement group did not stand idly by as these events unfolded. Immediately upon receiving news of Bloody Sunday, they went into action. Ernest Poole, already known for his pro-labor articles about working conditions in New York and Chicago, asked *Outlook* magazine to send him to Russia as its correspondent. Three weeks later he arrived in St. Petersburg, posing as a representative of an American shoe company but actually bearing money and letters for Russian revolutionaries. After meeting secretly with anti-czarist informants in St. Petersburg, he traveled to Moscow and to the Caucasus, where he continued to find evidence of czarist repression and revolutionary unrest. When Poole returned to western Europe, he was joined in London by English Walling. They traveled to Paris and then to Geneva, where two more University Settlement veterans, Arthur Bullard and Howard Brubaker, showed up. Walling and Bullard set to work to establish a news bureau that would give anti-czarist writers financial support and help them publish their writings in the West.[8]

The young Americans were intensely excited about their campaign. "In 1905," Brubaker recalled, "we were sure that the revolution was just around the corner." Walling and Bullard soon left for Russia, but before their departure and again after they reached St. Petersburg, Walling cabled Anna Strunsky, a Russian-born Californian who had been romantically involved with the novelist Jack London, and urged her to come to St. Petersburg and "lend a hand" in the work of dealing a "possible *death* blow to the old society." Without telling their parents where they were going, Anna and her sister Rose headed for Russia, joining Walling and Bullard in St. Petersburg. Less than a month later, Anna Strunsky and English Walling had fallen in love and decided to marry. When news of the Walling-Strunsky engagement reached New York, it was greeted with a banner headline on the *New York World*'s front page: "Socialism Finds Bride for a Rich Yankee in Russia." In June they were married in Paris, and that fall the newlyweds returned to the United States and stayed at A Club for about six weeks.[9]

By the time English and Anna reached A Club, the most highly publicized moment in the club's history, Maxim Gorky's visit to the United States, had passed. Gorky, the renowned Russian author, had arrived in New York City to an enthusiastic reception on April 10, 1906. His trip, approved by Lenin to raise money and create goodwill for the revolution, owed much to the efforts of English Walling, Arthur Bullard, and their Friends of Russian Freedom organization. The plan was to have a committee chaired by Mark Twain, who lived from 1904 to 1908 at 21 Fifth Avenue and frequently visited his A Club neighbors, sponsor a welcoming banquet in Gorky's honor. Besides Twain, the committee's members included such leading literary figures as Richard Watson Gilder and William Dean Howells. An informal preliminary reception was held for Gorky at A Club shortly after his arrival. The Russian author's visit was off to a good start (fig. 22).

Then the public mood underwent an abrupt change. On April 14 the *New York World* revealed that Gorky's traveling companion, a well-known actress and Bolshevik named Madame Andreyeva, was not his wife and that Gorky was still married to another woman. The fact that Gorky and Andreyeva had a common-law marriage of long standing did not prevent moralists from raising a great uproar about their relationship. Embarrassed, Twain and most members of the honorary committee resigned, and the welcoming banquet was canceled. In quick succession three hotels evicted the Russian visitors. Late one rainy night, left with nowhere else to go, Gorky and Andreyeva went to A Club and asked to be taken in. Details of this memorable episode vary from account to account, but all agree that the two Russian radicals were welcomed at A Club, sheltered there from press inquiries for several days, and then spirited off to other locations owned by sympathetic hosts. Gorky remained in the United States until October, but as an effort to generate goodwill for the revolution, his visit had been, in the words of one historian, "a complete fiasco."[10]

Support for the 1905 revolution was not the only public cause in which the young progressives who lived at A Club were active. Energized by the feeling that the pace of change was accelerating, they played major roles in founding or sustaining organizations—the Women's Trade Union League of New York (NYWTUL) and the Intercollegiate Socialist Society—

22. Although A Clubbers had to cancel their full-scale banquet for Maxim Gorky, they were able to hold a welcoming dinner for him on April 11, 1906. Gorky is second and Mark Twain third from the left in the front row. Culver Pictures.

whose goals were indicative of the direction in which the A Clubbers' social and political thought was evolving during the period.

The NYWTUL was established in 1904 as one of the first local branches of the National Women's Trade Union League, an organization founded in 1903 as a result of lobbying by English Walling and others at the American Federation of Labor's annual meeting. Walling's idea, borrowed from British precedent, was that women factory workers should be encouraged to form or affiliate with unions. As an elite group, the NYWTUL drew most of its active members from among middle- and upper-class women who used their wealth, professional training, and access to the press to further the league's goals. Walling served briefly as the league's secretary and then withdrew from direct involvement in its affairs. However, most of the women who lived at A Club between 1906 and 1910 participated in at least one NYWTUL project, and A Club became a center of women's pro-labor activism in the Greenwich Village area (fig. 23).[11]

A Clubbers also figured prominently in the early history of the Intercollegiate Socialist Society (ISS). Founded in September 1905 at a meeting in New York City, the ISS made spreading information about socialism among college students its principal goal. Although its leaders insisted that their purpose was to educate rather than convert, they encountered considerable resistance from college administrators, who did not welcome ISS speakers or chapters on their campuses. Initial support, therefore, came mainly from eminent American writers and intellectuals. Upton Sinclair, Clarence Darrow, and Charlotte Perkins Gilman were among the group that signed the call for founding the organization, as was Anna Strunsky Walling's husband English, and her old flame Jack London. London was elected ISS president and was succeeded two years later by Graham Stokes, a Socialist Party member with intimate ties to the A Club circle. Among Greenwich Villagers who served as ISS officers during its first five years were Graham's sister Helen, his brother-in-law Robert Hunter, Paul Kennaday, Ida Rauh, and three A Clubbers: Ernest Poole, Leroy Scott, and Robert W. Bruère.[12]

The A Clubbers' comrade English Walling, an inveterate organizer, also helped found the NAACP. In the aftermath of an August 1908 race riot in Springfield, Illinois, Walling, assisted by Mary White Ovington (who was

23. The headquarters of the Women's Trade Union League of New York in 1909–1910. Museum of the City of New York, The Byron Collection.

doing research on New York City blacks with grant support from Green-wich House), brought together a nucleus of reformers with the goal of es-tablishing a biracial organization to promote black civil rights. Although in no sense a Village enterprise, the NAACP in its early years had some sig-nificant ties with the neighborhood. One of the founders' first meetings (in March 1909) was held at the Liberal Club, a debating society with Village roots: of sixteen attendees, half were from the A Club–ISS orbit. In 1914 the NAACP moved its national offices to 70 Fifth Avenue in the north Village.[13]

In supporting the NAACP, the 1905 revolution, the NYWTUL, and the ISS, the young reformers challenged contemporary orthodoxies. By help-ing to establish the NAACP, they attacked the prevailing racial mores of the time. Similarly, A Clubbers who became members of the NYWTUL repudiated the belief (held by most male unionists and many male Social-ists) that a woman's place was in the home, even though the reality was that by the early 1900s many women were wage earners doing industrial labor. A Clubbers who joined the ISS and the Socialist Party in the first decade of the twentieth century did so out of frustration with what they viewed as the largely do-nothing response of the Democratic and Republican parties to the emergence of modern urban-industrial society. The laissez-faire con-servatism of the two major parties, the young Villagers charged, favored the wealthy few at the expense of the working masses. In the interests of creating a truly democratic society, the Socialists endorsed a platform that, by 1912, included proposals for the "collective ownership and democratic management" of the nation's railroads, grain elevators, and telephone and telegraph industries; federal public works projects to employ the jobless; labor laws to establish shorter work days, a minimum wage, stricter factory safety regulations, and to prohibit child labor; and a variety of other re-forms, including women's suffrage, the direct election of the president, and a graduated income tax.[14]

If asked to describe their social and political viewpoint, many A Club residents would have agreed with Charlotte Teller's statement that they were "more or less radical." Teller was typical of her A Club colleagues in using the word in this vague way. In an age of innocence before the Bolshe-vik Revolution gave the word a more specific meaning, many A Club resi-dents used the terms *radical, liberal,* and *progressive* interchangeably to refer to one or another form of advanced thinking. Given the Socialist leanings of most A Clubbers and their advocacy of programs to the left of main-stream opinion, the term *radical* fits them well enough for the 1904–1907 period. Later, however, in a passage written in the mid-1930s, when finer distinctions had come into use, Mary Heaton Vorse observed: "Some of the

A Club members fondly thought of themselves as revolutionists, but we were liberal reformers . . . natural-born New Dealers." In retrospect, Vorse got it about right. By later standards A Club residents were neither radicals nor revolutionaries. Rather, in most of its elements, their version of socialism anticipated the Progressive Era regulatory laws passed in the 1910s and the welfare capitalism programs instituted during the New Deal years.[15]

The opportunity to make common cause politically with other A Clubbers was only one reason the residents of 3 Fifth Avenue were so enthusiastic about life at A Club. There were also practical benefits of a cooperative housing arrangement and the house's convenient location in the city. Above all else, however, A Clubbers enjoyed being part of a small residential community that contributed in important ways to their personal lives, serving as an informal marriage bureau, a writers' collective, and a mutual support group.

Many A Club members arrived at 3 Fifth Avenue as part of an already established couple. This group included two couples—Bert and Mary Heaton Vorse and Leroy and Miriam Finn Scott—who stayed for long periods, and English and Anna Strunsky Walling, who were briefly in residence there. The Scotts and Wallings struck many outside the A Club circle as unusual couples because they consisted of a wealthy Protestant man married to an East European Jewish woman. The Walling-Strunsky alliance had been a headline grabber; other A Club marriages were not high-profile events, but they came along with impressive regularity. 1907 was a banner year. In quick succession Ernest Poole married his sweetheart, a Chicago heiress named Margaret Winterbotham. Then Poole's sister married Walter Weyl, a University Settlement veteran. Finally, Martha Bensley, one of the club's founders, married Robert Bruère, a Socialist who was working as an agent for the New York Society for Improving the Condition of the Poor.[16]

As a writers' collective, A Club was a place where a lot of work got done. 1907 was a big year for books as well as marriages. Charlotte Teller, Ernest Poole, and Leroy Scott all published novels that year. It seemed as though everyone either had just finished a project or had several works in progress. Mary Heaton Vorse completed her first novel, *The Breaking in of the Yachtman's Wife* (1908), and wrote several dozen short stories during three stays at 3 Fifth Avenue. A veritable flood of articles and stories poured forth from the pens and typewriters of other A Club residents between 1906 and 1910. Martha Bensley Bruère produced articles on modern housekeeping techniques and became a recognized expert in that field; her husband, Robert, wrote about education and industrial democracy; Miriam Finn Scott completed several pieces about contemporary labor conditions. Arthur Bullard and Howard Brubaker were productive too, writing mostly about foreign affairs, and Madeleine Doty did weekly book reviews for the *New York Times*.[17]

In their memoirs, Ernest Poole and Mary Heaton Vorse provided particularly vivid descriptions of life at A Club. Poole emphasized the high level of energy that was generated when friends who shared many professional and political goals also shared one roof. "With most of us writing books, stories, or plays and all of us dreaming of reforms and revolutions of divers kinds," Poole wrote, "life in that house was a quick succession of intensities, large and small." One by-product of living together was that one writer's work sometimes stimulated another's. Mary Heaton Vorse, inspired by Arthur Bullard's success in publishing articles based on his travels in Europe, went to North Africa in 1909 to collect material for a similar series of her own. Like Poole, Vorse remembered A Club as both a political and a social community. She particularly valued the A Clubbers' political iconoclasm. "It was the first time," she wrote, "I had been in a large group of like-minded people who questioned the system under which they lived." She also fondly remembered "the mutual kindness and the gaiety of our household. It was," she felt, "a completely successful and civilized experiment in communal living."[18]

As Vorse's words suggest, she found in A Club a very supportive environment. Here was a place in which everyone, men and women alike, was working. The male residents—particularly Leroy Scott and Ernest Poole—were better known to the general public than most of the women residents. But the women A Clubbers certainly held their own and helped to create a residential community in which gender roles did not divide along the conventional lines of men doing the "real" work and women taking care of the kids, meals, and the laundry. When Mary Heaton Vorse hung out an "I am working! Do not enter!" sign, it carried a message that she knew her housemates would honor. The sign also affirmed the importance of her professional endeavors, testifying to the disappearance of her previous diffidence about her writing achievements as she laid claim to her inner creative power. She was delighted when her newfound confidence led her A Club friends to speak admiringly of her as a "dangerous woman."[19]

Vorse and her fellow A Clubbers were Greenwich Villagers of a particularly peripatetic type. For example, just before beginning his three-year stint at the Church of the Ascension, Alexander Irvine lodged briefly at A Club, moving out as soon as he found a place uptown to which he brought his wife and three children. Other A Club residents also came and went, some spending a month at 3 Fifth Avenue, others a summer, and still others living there a year or more. Upon leaving A Club quite a few former residents remained in the neighborhood. Madeleine Doty summered at A Club in 1906 before moving to an apartment on Charles Street in the west Village. Similarly, after he married and left A Club in early 1907, Ernest Poole rented rooms for himself and his bride at 88 Grove Street, formerly the location of Greenwich House settlement's men's annex. When the Pooles later left their Grove Street place for another Village apartment, Mary Heaton Vorse rented the rooms they had vacated.

These comings and goings were not, in and of themselves, particularly significant, but they represented one way that A Clubbers and their allies spread throughout the Village and continued to build a network of radicals and reformers dedicated to furthering the social changes that had begun to surface so forcefully between 1904 and 1907.

THE GREENWICH HOUSE CIRCLE

The network of reform-minded Villagers had three discernible elements: individuals, institutions, and cross-class relationships. Individuals came to join the network through a variety of personal and professional avenues. Certain institutions functioned as anchors or gathering points for collective action. In the Village these included the two local social settlements, Greenwich House and Richmond Hill House, the district office of the Charity Organization Society (C.O.S.), and, for a while, A Club. These institutions then became the organizational bases from which their founders and members, most of whom were well educated, middle- and upper-class Protestants, were able to develop relationships across ethnic and class lines with the non-elite, non-Protestant residents of the neighborhood. This chain of associations is the subject of the remaining sections of this chapter.

In January 1906 Madeleine Doty was sharing a Lower East Side apartment with Ida Rauh, her friend from law school days. Visits to University Settlement, which was nearby, provided Doty and Rauh with plenty of intellectual stimulation. Through conversations with residents there, Doty "first heard about Karl Marx and socialism." Rauh was an enthusiastic participant in the activities of the Women's Trade Union League of New York until early 1906, when she fell ill. At that point her parents intervened and, according to Doty, took her "much against her will" to Europe for rest and recuperation. Unable to afford the rent on their flat by herself, Doty moved to A Club, where many former University Settlement workers now lived.[20]

Doty arrived at A Club just after the April 1906 uproar over Gorky and Andreyeva. Having shed some of her previous prudishness about manners and morals ("I had long since learned to smoke cigarettes," she wrote, "and looked with amusement at my former attitude"), Doty unhesitatingly joined her A Club friends in defending their famous Russian visitors against the moralistic outcry in the American press. Moreover, through daily contact with young members of what she called a "literary artistic crowd," all of whom advocated revolution in Russia and criticized the American capitalist system, Doty gradually adopted more radical positions on political and economic affairs, placing herself on a trajectory that would eventually lead her to join the Socialist Party.[21]

At A Club it was possible to rent rooms on a monthly basis, but most Greenwich Village leases ran for a year that began in the fall. As a result, every Villager in search of better accommodations—and there were always many of them—was on the move in September or October. Doty joined this annual migration in September 1906, leaving A Club for a west Village apartment. She leased a five-room flat on the third floor at 12 Charles Street, midway between Greenwich Avenue and Waverly Place. Since her earnings from legal work barely covered her share of the expenses for a law partnership she had formed with her N.Y.U. classmate Jessie Ashley, Doty supplemented her income with part-time jobs. Her work as a tutor at her former prep school paid poorly, so she dropped tutoring and found two new jobs: teaching at Greenwich House settlement (which enabled her to take some meals there) and reviewing books for the *New York Times*. Rent on her apartment was substantial, $36 a month, and to help defray that expense she planned to sublet two of the flat's three bedrooms. One she held for her friend Ida Rauh. The other she rented to Crystal Eastman, a young woman she met through the Greenwich House connection.[22]

Eastman was twenty-five at the time she moved in with Doty. The daughter of one of the first women to be ordained as a Congregational minister, Eastman had graduated from Vassar College in 1903 and earned a master's degree in sociology at Columbia University a year later. For the next two years she lived with her parents in Elmira, New York, teaching high school to help pay for her younger brother Max's last year at Williams College and for his subsequent treatments for various ailments. Although she dutifully helped her family, Eastman was eager to get back to New York City. As early as February 1905, she visited Greenwich House with Paul Kellogg, a social worker who was a resident at the time. Eastman intended to pursue a law degree at N.Y.U. while teaching classes and taking her meals at Greenwich House. As she wrote her mother, "I like it [the Greenwich House circle] because they are all cranks and reformers, and sooner or later every really interesting and up and doing radical who comes to this country gets down to Greenwich House for a meal." When Madeleine Doty, a graduate of N.Y.U. Law School and also a part-time worker at Greenwich House, invited her to share an apartment, Eastman agreed at once; the arrangement seemed ideal.[23]

Nearly every aspect of Eastman's new situation went well. She managed to earn satisfactory marks in her law school classes without devoting an inordinate amount of time to them. She enjoyed her work at Greenwich House and was delighted with the attention she received from several male members of the settlement's circle. These included Paul Kellogg and Paul Kennaday, both former Greenwich House residents who often dropped by to see friends there. Mary Simkhovitch's husband, Vladimir, also made it plain that he found Eastman completely enchanting. She liked him and wrote her mother that his friendship was one of "the richest things that I have found in New York so far." However, being the object of Vladimir's overt interest was a bit awkward. Fortunately, a partial solution presented itself around New Year's 1907 when her brother Max arrived in the city. He and Vladimir hit it off, so Crystal felt free to invite Max to accompany her and Vladimir to cultural events, the threesome serving to defuse a potentially troublesome situation. "It solves a good many things to have Max here," she confided to her mother.[24]

On learning that Max had come to the city without any job prospects, Crystal's admirers rallied to help. Kellogg and Kennaday worked for the Charity Organization Society, and they combined forces to get Max hired as a lecturer for the C.O.S. Committee on the Prevention of Tuberculosis. Soon thereafter Vladimir Simkhovitch persuaded the philosopher John Dewey, whom he knew as a colleague at Columbia and who was a frequent visitor to Greenwich House, to recommend Max as a replacement for a Columbia philosophy teacher who had died early in the spring term. Appointment in hand, Max moved uptown to be closer to the Columbia campus.

Max's very brief stay in the Village coincided with a variety of changes—some small, others large—in the lives of the women at 12 Charles Street. Ida Rauh returned from Europe in January and occupied the third bedroom at Doty's apartment. She and Crystal's brother were introduced, but neither was especially impressed with the other on first meeting. Crystal, meanwhile, had decided that she was, as she had written Max, "not very fond of Madeleine Doty." Though the reasons for this feeling went unspecified, they probably arose out of small but crucial temperamental differences: Crystal was an early riser and loved to socialize, while Madeleine slept late and had little time in her daily schedule for leisurely chats. By February 1907 the two women were no longer trying to cooperate on meals and other activities.[25]

At this point Doty had so much on her mind that she scarcely noticed her roommate's withdrawal. Her work schedule was extremely demanding. The previous September she had answered a *New York Times* help-wanted ad for a man to interview authors and review their recent books. Although the editors reluctantly agreed to hire her, they insisted that the column's byline show a male name. Doty chose the nom de plume Otis Notman, which stood for "O 'tis not man." She still devoted most daytime hours during the work week to her legal practice, but she now took brief breaks three or four times a week to interview authors. On Sundays and the nights that she didn't have meetings at Greenwich House, she prepared her two- to three-thousand-word articles for the *New York Times Saturday Review of Books.* Even though her multiple jobs made for what she called "a hectic life," she was thrilled by the opportunity that Otis Notman had to meet well-known authors such as Maxim Gorky, Theodore Dreiser, Charles Edward Russell, and David Graham Phillips.[26]

Doty's interview with Phillips set in motion a chain of events that turned her world upside down. Their first conversation took place in early January at his Gramercy Park apartment. Initially they chatted about his political writings, especially *The Treason of the Senate,* an exposé of the influence of large corporations on U.S. Senators that he had published less than a year earlier. However, Phillips soon steered the interview toward his real interest, which was writing novels, specifically novels about love and about the lives of "people who have not become conscious of themselves." They talked a while longer; then, as Doty rose to leave, he startled her by asking, "Aren't [you] going to invite me to come and see you?" Almost speechless with surprise, Doty nonetheless agreed to go out with him for what proved to be the first of many times.[27]

Doty and Phillips were a study in contrasts. He was a worldly forty-year-old who felt that "love is everything. . . . The most creative and vital thing in the world." She was an emotionally immature twenty-eight-year-old who, though she was beginning to find herself professionally, had never had a serious romantic relationship and who, by her own admission, knew almost nothing about "love and sex."[28]

Despite their intense attraction to each other, what Doty called "a great struggle" arose between them. Phillips wanted a companion and lover but not a wife; Doty was not sure she could live that kind of life. When Phillips invited her to accompany him to Paris in June, she declined, but by the time he left for France her eager response to his passionate embraces made her wonder if she had made the right decision. "He left me," she recalled, "a seething mass of emotion. My reason said, married or unmarried, our love was justified. We were hurting no one!"[29]

Coincidentally, about the time that personal upheavals left Doty with little energy to think about her work at Greenwich House, a promising opportunity for meaningful social service came Crystal Eastman's way. Indirectly, Eastman's good fortune was traceable to advice that Robert de Forest, the president of the Charity Organization Society, had given a private client in 1906. This client, Mrs. Russell Sage, had asked for help in establishing a charitable trust in her deceased husband's name. De Forest urged her to give any such trust a broad mandate so that it could respond flexibly to changing societal conditions. She agreed and had him draw up incorporation papers for the Russell Sage Foundation accordingly. In 1907 the trust made its initial grants, and one of the first went to support a comprehensive investigation of industrial conditions in Pittsburgh, Pennsylvania. To direct the project, C.O.S. administrators asked Crystal Eastman's friend Paul Kellogg, then coeditor of the C.O.S. journal, *Charities and the Commons*, to take a leave of absence and oversee what became known as the Pittsburgh Survey. Kellogg, in turn, recruited Eastman to conduct the part of the investigation that dealt with industrial accidents and employers' liability laws. Her duties were to begin in September.[30]

Toward the end of June, her immediate job future secure, Eastman took the bar examination and prepared to spend the summer with her parents in Elmira. As the time to leave 12 Charles Street drew near, she became aware that although she had been a resident of the Village for less than a year, she had begun to think of the area near Greenwich House as home. At a later date she explained her feelings in some detail to Max. "This neighborhood," she wrote, "is *home* to me—partly from habit, partly because my friends are here; (and it does not matter much whether I see them or not, so long as they are within reach); partly because Greenwich House is a center of life and interest with which I feel myself identified."[31]

Eastman's Greenwich House circle was composed of settlement house residents, social workers, and a few intellectuals and academics. At any given time the current residents of Greenwich House comprised the heart of this community of friends and allies. As they collaborated with Mary Simkhovitch to fulfill her goal of improving the immediate neighborhood, their daily contact with working-class Villagers enabled them to fine-tune their programs to the changing neighborhood scene.

From their vantage point on Jones Street, Greenwich House residents were well aware that the west Village's ethnic makeup was not only changing but changing very swiftly. Blacks were moving out of the Jones Street district, as were many Irish Jones Streeters. The block's new residents were mostly Italians, many of them recent arrivals from their native land.

These shifts in Jones Street's ethnic makeup took less than a decade to unfold. Barely a year after Greenwich House opened its doors in 1902, Mary Simkhovitch had observed that although Jones Street was on the "edge of the incoming Italian colony," few Italians lived on Jones Street itself; census records show that at the beginning of the century, about 11 percent of the street's residents were Italian. (This was roughly the same percentage as that of German and African American Jones Streeters, while Irish Americans comprised more than 40 percent of the street's residents.) By 1906, however, Simkhovitch was reporting that "each month brings an increasing number of Italians" to the area, and in 1910 Italians comprised Jones Street's largest ethnic group, one that had taken over nearly half of the tenements on the block. Committed to working with neighbors of all ethnic backgrounds, Simkhovitch made a point in her 1909 annual report of emphasizing the positive impact the growing Italian community was having on the area. The Italian presence, she asserted, was "revivifying [the Village] with new color and stir. . . . The Marionettes come and go. Dried mushrooms, caccicavalla [sic], tortone, pan forte, fresh artichokes and peppers in the shops and on the pushcarts all proclaim us an Italian neighborhood."[32]

Simkhovitch and her Greenwich House colleagues also noted that even as the arrival of Italians was changing the Village, the newcomers were themselves being changed by their encounter with the host culture's economic realities. Traditionally, Italian women neither worked outside the home nor socialized outside their church and family circles. These conservative mores had considerable staying power among Italian Villagers and significant consequences for Greenwich House programs. In 1909 Simkhovitch observed that it was "extremely difficult to establish social clubs among Italian girls. Many of the parents object most strenuously to dancing." Typically too, unmarried daughters of Italian families were strictly chaperoned. Nevertheless, adherence to old country conservatism was gradually being undermined by economic realities; in order to achieve a decent standard of living in their adopted homeland, many Italian families were forced to abandon the practice of not letting their unmarried daughters work outside the home. The result, Simkhovitch wrote in 1909, was "the dramatic, if silent, *entry into industry of the Italian girl.*"[33]

There were times when such gradual social transformations in the neighbor yielded center stage while Villagers dealt with the sudden onset of a social crisis of massive proportions. The panic and depression of 1907–1908 was one such crisis. Beginning on March 13, 1907, an extended period of panic selling in the stock market exposed the weaknesses underlying the general prosperity of the previous ten years. Business bankruptcies, production cutbacks, and rising unemployment followed. By the fall of 1907, all but the most complacent observers had to admit that the economy was in the worst shape it had been in since the depression of the early 1890s. The bad times continued unabated throughout the winter of 1907–1908.

Greenwich Village social workers grimly compiled statistics on the depression's severe impact. The Charity Organization Society's Greenwich district office reported that requests for economic assistance increased dramatically in 1907–1908, running double the norm from recent years and higher than at any time since 1893–1894. What distressed C.O.S. agents even more than the sheer numbers of needy Villagers was that the new applicants were drawn from an unusual source. The groups that typically dominated C.O.S. relief roles were newly arrived immigrants, widowed women with young children, and families that had lost their main breadwinner to disease, old age, or injury. By contrast, aid applicants in 1907 and 1908 were, according to Sophie P. Foote, the C.O.S. district agent, "families containing able-bodied, fairly capable men and women willing to work," but for whom "[work] can not be found." Mary Simkhovitch agreed that conditions were especially bad. Writing many years later, she recalled: "That was the hardest time our neighborhood saw till the close of 1929. The hope of the neighborhood was stunned by the sudden drop in prosperity."[34]

Social workers had few palliatives they could offer to relieve the distress of jobless Villagers. Greenwich House ran a workroom at the settlement where a few working-class women made craft items and clothing, and the proceeds from products that were sold went to assist the workroom participants. Similarly, the C.O.S. expanded its woodlot, a business that provided the agency's able-bodied clients with small stipends in return for their work chopping firewood. Even though these private philanthropic efforts were pitifully inadequate at a time when the needs of the unemployed and their families were so great, few middle-class reformers were ready to demand that the federal government step in (as it did twenty-five years later during the Great Depression of the 1930s, when it became the employer of last resort for jobless Americans). It took a longer and more severe downturn— one that hit even the middle class—to bring that major shift in reform thought.

Nevertheless, the 1907–1908 depression did have an impact on the thinking of reform-minded Villagers, who, in common with most middle-class progressives of the day, looked first to what could be done through private philanthropy and local or state laws that regulated housing conditions and workplace health and safety. With the depression lending urgency to their concern about their working-class neighbors, members of the Greenwich House circle launched new initiatives to deal with two problems associated with urban-industrial life: urban "congestion" (i.e., overcrowding in tenement districts) as a source of disease, fires, and crime, and the dangerous and unhealthy conditions under which many industrial workers had to labor.

The problems attendant to urban overcrowding were creatively addressed through the work of the so-called Committee of Congestion, which sponsored a two-week-long conference and "Exhibit on Congestion of Population" that was held at the Museum of Natural History in March 1908. Although the Committee on Congestion was a blue-ribbon panel that drew its membership from the wider community of social workers and progressive reformers in the city, members of the Greenwich House circle played key roles in the project. Mary Simkhovitch was the committee's chair and three other Greenwich residents—Benjamin Marsh, George Ford, and Carola Woerishoffer—took primary responsibility for planning and preparing the exhibit's displays. The goal of the conference and exhibit, Simkhovitch explained, was to show the public "that overcrowding was responsible for many of the city's ills," including high infant mortality rates, rising numbers of tuberculosis cases, and, more generally, the appallingly low quality of the physical environment in tenement districts.[35]

Simkhovitch acknowledged that the negative impact of overcrowding was most severe on the Lower East Side, but an awareness of similar conditions in Greenwich Village was never far from her mind. "Jones Street," she noted, "was the most densely populated of the lower West Side streets," consisting as it did of a single block with "fourteen hundred people, 975 to an acre." Moreover, as recently as 1903, both the "infant death rate and tuberculosis death rate [in the Greenwich House neighborhood] were the highest in the city." The appropriate response to these problems, according to Simkhovitch and other speakers at the Committee on Congestion's conference, was to recognize the pernicious effects of urban overcrowding, and to go beyond tenement house laws (which dealt with individual buildings only) and create a city planning process to deal with broader issues of urban development.[36]

Carola Woerishoffer's role in the Committee on Congestion and other Greenwich House activities exemplified the dedication and idealism with which the settlement's residents pursued their work. A Bryn Mawr graduate, class of 1907, Woerishoffer became a Greenwich House resident in 1908 and lived there for the next two years. She was the third in a line of dynamic, wealthy women in her family. Her grandmother, Anna Uhl, lost her first husband in 1852. Finding herself a widow with six children to support, she took control of the family's business, the important German-language daily, *New-Yorker Staats-Zeitung*, and edited the paper on her own until the late 1850s. In 1859 she remarried; her second husband was Oswald

Ottendorfer, a veteran of the German revolution of 1848, whom she had named her coeditor in 1858. Anna Uhl Ottendorfer's daughter (also Anna) married Charles Woerishoffer, a native of Germany who amassed a fortune as a Wall Street investor before his untimely death only a year after Carola was born. Both Carola's grandmother and mother were canny financial managers who subscribed to a social ethic that combined liberal politics (the *New-Yorker Staats-Zeitung* had been pro-Union and pro-emancipation during the Civil War) with generous charitable deeds. One of Anna Woerishoffer's philanthropic endeavors was support for Greenwich House, a cause she adopted several years before her daughter became a resident of the settlement.[37]

At Greenwich House Carola Woerishoffer occupied a small upstairs room, and although she was very wealthy, she voluntarily adopted a life of poverty. It was not that she despised all wealth; she simply did not derive any pleasure from lavish surroundings, rich food, or personal luxuries. She was intelligent, athletic, and in the habit of holding others to the same high standards she demanded of herself, but she strenuously avoided publicity about her accomplishments. In an era when the leading newspapers and magazines avidly pursued stories about the foibles, excesses, and activities of rich and famous Americans, this was no small achievement, particularly since Woerishoffer was a representative of a phenomenon the public found endlessly fascinating, the "Revolt of the Young Rich" who chose social service careers over idle luxury.[38]

Woerishoffer's preference for anonymity and her voluntary poverty served her well during the summer of 1909 when she undertook a study of conditions in the city's commercial steam laundries, a business that, like many other urban industries, relied heavily on the labor of women. For her survey Woerishoffer adopted the undercover investigatory style of the era's muckraking journalists. For four months she answered help-wanted advertisements from laundry companies, regularly changing jobs to be sure that she acquired a broad knowledge of diverse shops. No employer challenged the heiress's application, and only one coworker suspected she was something other than what she claimed to be, and that Woerishoffer did not belong in a steam laundry shop. More often, however, Woerishoffer was accepted as just another worker, and she freely participated in the ordinary chatter that her coworkers exchanged about their jobs and social life. (Conversations on the latter topic often ran along these lines: "Say, you got a feller?" "Sure. Ain't you got one?" "Sure.")[39]

Woerishoffer followed a demanding daily schedule during her career as a laundry worker. She rose at six or earlier to play tennis on a court near Greenwich House, hurriedly ate a spartan breakfast, and rushed off to her job. Her workday began at seven-thirty and continued for twelve to fourteen hours, with quitting time often not arriving until nine or ten o'clock in the evening. For sixty or seventy hours of labor each week laundry workers received as little as $3 or as much as $25, the great majority earning $4.50 to $8 (less than fifteen cents an hour). Standing for ten or twelve hours straight at machinery that had to be operated at a fast pace in order to keep one's job, women suffered from fatigue that greatly increased the danger of injury. Woerishoffer found that not even the most experienced workers escaped burns at the sleeve-ironing machines, and that unguarded or poorly shielded mechanisms of pressing machines took a constant toll of crushed fingers and arms. The better-paid work, such as hand starching, was done in extremely hot, humid rooms. Once after a long stint in a starching room, Woerishoffer stepped outside on a sweltering summer day and remarked how refreshingly cool the 96° outdoor temperature felt by contrast with the room she had just left.

Upon completing her research on New York's laundries, Woerishoffer became a special investigator for the New York Department of Labor. During a trip to inspect an immigrant labor camp in upstate New York in September 1911, she lost control of her car on a wet road; the car turned over, pinning her underneath. She died of her injuries the next day. She was twenty-six.

Woerishoffer's colleagues in reform circles had no doubt that they had lost a talented and resourceful ally. Her Bryn Mawr College classmates published a book-length memoir, *Carola Woerishoffer: Her Life and Work*, in 1912, and her mentor at Greenwich House, Mary Simkhovitch, wrote a stirring eulogy of Woerishoffer in the settlement's *Annual Report* for 1911. The tragedy of her death at such an early age doubtless intensified the feelings of loss expressed in these memorials, but the qualities attributed to Woerishoffer—"generous," "entirely fearless," "oblivious to conventional criticism," "a knight errant of industrial democracy"—had a larger import. For in lauding these qualities in their young friend, members of the Greenwich House circle were also affirming the ideals which they believed should motivate their ongoing work in the west Village.[40]

CROSS-CLASS ALLIANCES, 1907–1911

The women of the Greenwich House–A Club circle had male counterparts in the world of social reform, but the proportionate influence of women activists in Village life was greater in the first decades of the twentieth century than it had been at any previous time. Moreover, their contribution to the Village scene was more than just a matter of numbers, of more women involving themselves in public affairs. Progressive Era women Villagers were both working for social change in the public world and redefining themselves in terms of individual standards of behavior instead of obedience to the socially imposed codes of conduct with which they had been brought up. Indeed, it was their pursuit of one or both of these goals—social or personal transformation—that had brought many of them to the Village in the first place.

For the better part of three years in 1907–1909, Madeleine Doty was engaged in a struggle to clarify what she needed to do in both her personal and professional life. Having graduated from N.Y.U. Law School in 1902 and worked both in a private law practice and as a book reviewer for the *New York Times*, Doty seemed to have achieved much for a young woman. Nevertheless she was, by her own description, immature, and she was caught in the crosscurrents between her desires and her ideals that were generated by her relationship with the writer David Graham Phillips.

Phillips wanted her to agree that "a secret [sexual] relation without marriage was right," but Doty, passionately idealistic, could not bring herself to agree. "My conscience," she wrote, "said that if it was real love our relationship should be open," with "no lies, no sense of shame." Unable to resolve this conflict, she fled to Europe with her friend Ida Rauh, who, it happened, was involved in a similar situation with a man who wanted a lover and not a wife. The two women returned to New York in February 1909, but Doty, now suffering from chronic indigestion brought on by emotional conflict, left the city almost immediately and sought refuge in Northampton, Massachusetts, where she lived in "a little rest house" owned by her alma mater, Smith College.[41]

In Northampton Doty took to her bed and, seeking to understand what was the matter with her, read four volumes of *Studies in the Psychology of Sex* by Havelock Ellis, an English physician-psychologist who was a pioneer in the study of human sexuality, and *The Sexual Question* by Auguste Forel, a now largely forgotten writer who at the turn of the century was widely admired as an authority on relations between the sexes. "All the information I had dodged," Doty wrote, "was there," but "the knowledge gained didn't help." She "might read that colitis came from emotional disturbance, but that did not cure it." The cure came when, on the advice of a friend, she went to see Dr. Richard Cabot, a Boston psychologist. He helped bring an end to the deep conflict between her convictions and her desires by urging her to do volunteer work for a Boston hospital with which he was associated. She soon found that "forgetting [her]self and working for others brought peace."[42]

As her health returned, Doty became convinced that social service rather than the law or marriage was her true vocation. Late in 1909 she went back to New York and began to explore ways of becoming a legal advocate for juvenile delinquents, and plunged into doing pro bono work on behalf of working-class women who needed legal assistance. When she chanced one day to meet Phillips on the street, the encounter was entirely cordial. "He seemed very glad to see me," Doty wrote. "I found I could meet him now on a wholly new basis. I had learned it was possible to live without him. I was free and able to stand on my own feet." Their renewed friendship flourished, albeit without any romantic attachment, in the year and a half before Phillips was murdered by a deranged man in March 1911.[43]

While Doty was in the process of discovering her vocation, Crystal Eastman's career in progressive causes continued to flourish. In the fall of 1908, after a year spent completing her survey of industrial accidents in Pittsburgh, she returned to New York City to prepare a written report on her findings. She rented rooms on West Eleventh Street in the Village, sharing the flat with her brother Max and preparing several essays on employers' liability for publication. In April 1909 she was named a member of the New York State Employers' Liability Commission, the sole woman on the fourteen-member panel. The *New York Herald* featured an article on Eastman titled "Portia Appointed by the Governor" that praised her intelligence and dedication. By the fall of 1910 Eastman was hard at work drafting a state workers' compensation law that, once passed, became a model for similar laws in other states. In the meantime she and Max had moved to another Village apartment, located at 118 Waverly Place. Vivacious and attractive, Eastman never lacked for male suitors, although it was not until late 1910 that she met a man who, in her brother's words, "aroused Crystal for the first time physically." This was Wallace Benedict, a Milwaukee businessman, whom she married in May 1911. They moved to Wisconsin, and Eastman, ever the irrepressible activist, became the leading organizer of a campaign (unsuccessful, as it turned out) for women's suffrage in the state.[44]

College-educated Village women played significant roles in the life of Crystal's brother Max. Late in 1909 he had a brief flirtation with Inez Milholland, a Vassar graduate and soon to be N.Y.U. law student who was living with her wealthy parents at 9 East Ninth Street, in the patrician part of the Village. Despite being viewed by their friends as the perfect twosome—both handsome and well educated, and both interested in important political causes (women's suffrage and working people's rights)—they never quite clicked as a couple. However, less than a year after his failed romance with Milholland, Max was strolling through Washington Square and happened to bump into Ida Rauh, who invited him to tea at her nearby apartment. Ida, once the timid little rich girl, was now a confident young woman who not only knew more about both Marxism and love than Max did, but gladly undertook to tutor him on both subjects. They married in May 1911.[45]

Between 1907 and 1909 the writer Mary Heaton Vorse had little time for reform activities. She was the family's main breadwinner, supporting her husband, Bert, two children, a nursemaid, and a secretary-stenographer. Although she was earning a good income from her articles and stories, keeping the money coming in required entrepreneurship. In 1909 she persuaded *Harper's Monthly* to hire her for a series on Morocco, and toward the end of October she left for North Africa by way of Europe. Late the following spring, in June 1910, she was en route back to New York when she received word that Bert and her mother had died only one day apart. After a summer of grieving at Provincetown, she returned to New York City in the fall, moving herself, her aged father, and her children into the apartment at 88 Grove Street, long a popular rental location among members of the Greenwich House circle. She hired a young woman named Rosina to cook for the household, "the first," as she wrote later, "of a line of those magnificent, efficient, noisy, good-tempered Italian girls who brightened [my] life for the next seven years, sending a cousin or sister to take a place left by marriage."[46]

Even as Vorse devoted herself to personal concerns, like many of her friends in the A Club–Greenwich House circle she became caught up in events related to the shirtwaist strike of 1909–1910, a massive labor conflict that further exposed the underside of urban industrialization. Harsh working conditions—six-day workweeks of up to sixty or seventy hours, low wages, and oppressive rules—deeply angered many garment workers, most of whom were young Jewish and Italian immigrant women (fig. 24). Resentment over these conditions had simmered during the depression of 1907–1908, and when better economic times returned, worker militancy increased. In late 1908 and during the summer of 1909 walkouts occurred at several major firms, among them the Triangle Shirtwaist Company, which occupied the top three floors of the Asch Building, a ten-story structure located on Washington Place one block east of Washington Square. (Completed in January 1901, the Asch building was precisely the type of tall commercial building whose construction close to the square so troubled the north Village patricians.)

The Triangle Shirtwaist Company epitomized many negative features of the urban-industrial world that prompted middle-class sympathizers and striking garment workers to form an alliance in defense of the workers' interests. The company's owners were notorious for their tough labor policies: low wages, long hours, and annoying rules, which included a prohibition on speaking to one's neighbor at the workbench and a penalty of being sent home and losing a half day's pay for taking more time for a toilet break than the floor supervisor felt was necessary.[47]

As the worker demonstrations against the company continued into the

24. A shop floor in a New York garment factory. UNITE Archives, Kheel Center, Cornell University, Ithaca, N.Y.

fall, Triangle's owners struck back aggressively. Pickets were verbally and physically harassed by hired thugs and the police, and dozens of strikers were arrested. To add insult to the injury of incarceration and fines, the arrested women were taken to Jefferson Market Courthouse at Sixth Avenue and West Tenth and tried in Night Court, a tactic meant to intimidate strikers through association with the prostitutes whose cases usually filled that court's dockets. "No nice girls go there," one arrested shirtwaist maker asserted.[48]

The tactic did not succeed. On the contrary: not only were the striking women's spirits not broken, but other shirtwaist makers rallied to the cause. On November 22, 1909, a mass meeting of shirtwaist makers at Cooper Union led to a strike pledge that was accepted by more than twenty thousand workers. Faced with a revolt of this magnitude, many employers quickly accepted their operatives' three general demands: a fifty-two-hour workweek, five paid vacation days annually, and union recognition. (Wage hikes, if any, were to be set on a shop-by-shop basis.) By early December, approximately one-third of the companies had settled with their employees.

The strike action continued into February 1910, although with gradually declining strength as more companies agreed to terms and the strikers who continued to hold out over the union shop issue lost public support. Some employers—notably the owners of the Triangle Shirtwaist Company—refused to make any concessions to the union's demands.[49]

Especially in the early phase of the walkout, shirtwaist makers benefited from having the support of a broad coalition that included settlement folk, social activists, women's suffrage advocates, and a few male unionists. The most sustained backing for the strikers from outside their own ranks came from the Women's Trade Union League of New York (NYWTUL). This cross-class organization, its membership composed of a few working-class women and a much larger number of their college-educated allies, undertook a wide range of activities in support of the strike.[50]

Members of the Greenwich House circle participated in or led many of the NYWTUL's major initiatives. When five to ten thousand strikers marched on City Hall on December 2, 1909, to demand that Mayor George McClellan order police to stop the arrests and mistreatment of picketing operatives, Ida Rauh was one of the NYWTUL leaders selected for a delegation of six women who met with the mayor (fig. 25). Rauh also offered

25. A delegation of three shirtwaist workers and three middle-class allies leading a march on the mayor to demand an end to police brutality against striking garment workers. From *New York World*, December 4, 1909.

GIRL STRIKERS IN PROTEST PARADE;
ARE PROMISED JUSTICE BY MAYOR.

free legal assistance to pickets who were arrested, as did Madeleine Doty and Crystal Eastman. Carola Woerishoffer organized a NYWTUL news bureau that disseminated information about the strikers' grievances and goals.[51]

These activities often had places or events in the Village as their primary context. For example, Crystal Eastman and Inez Milholland attended Night Court sessions at Jefferson Market Courthouse to issue reports on the generally harsh penalties handed down in cases involving strikers. When one judge sought to punish detainees by refusing to release them unless they could provide large amounts of bail secured by real property, Carola Woerishoffer stunned the court by producing a deed to property valued at $75,000, after which the women were freed. Past and present women A Clubbers—including Mary Heaton Vorse, Martha Bruère, Miriam Finn Scott, and Bertha Weyl—joined the strikers' picket lines outside the Triangle Shirtwaist Company's factory. The latter tactic proved highly effective in reducing the number of arrests of picketing Triangle operatives, since incidents involving middle- or upper-class women typically resulted in bad publicity for the police.[52]

By taking their protest into the streets, shirtwaist makers and their college-educated allies opened themselves to hostile interpretations of their conduct. As indicated by the response of many male authority figures (factory owners, policemen, and judges), their defiance of Victorian rules of respectable womanly conduct led to charges that they were behaving indecently. Yet reform-minded women were not deterred. It was a time of growing militancy not only for women garment workers on strike, but also for middle- and upper-class suffrage advocates (a term applicable to all the Greenwich House circle women who were aiding the striking shirtwaist workers). Inspired by the direct-action tactics of their British counterparts, New York suffragists from 1907 onward abandoned their former dependence on such genteel methods as petition-writing and formal addresses given in auditoriums and increasingly took to the streets, giving street-corner speeches and launching pro-suffrage marches on the city's major thoroughfares.[53]

The new style of protest caught on with astonishing swiftness. The city's first suffrage parade in February 1908 drew only a few dozen marchers, but in May 1910 (not long after the shirtwaist strike had been settled), more than a thousand women—many of whom, the *New York Times* reported, "had never taken part in anything of the kind before"—joined that year's parade. Three years later, in May 1913, an estimated ten thousand women's suffrage advocates assembled in Washington Square and then marched eight abreast up Fifth Avenue in support of their cause.[54]

Along with direct-action protests, a distinguishing trait of the shirtwaist strike had been the cross-class alliance forged between Village NYWTUL members and working-class women. That sisterhood across class lines had become the order of the day during the strike was acknowledged even by the none-too-friendly *New York Times*, which observed that "a sort of 'you-a-girl-and-me-a-girl' spirit" prevailed between women on the picket lines. "For once," the *Times* reporter continued, "the factory girl and the college girl are making a fight together." It was a high-water mark of cooperation among women that was rarely matched until what came to be called second-wave feminism emerged in the late 1960s.[55]

Second-wave feminist scholars have made important contributions to the reconstruction of the full picture of the campaigns their early twentieth-century predecessors waged. Close scrutiny revealed that the earlier efforts at cross-class and cross-ethnic cooperation had been beset by significant problems. Middle-class NYWTUL allies sometimes found it difficult to bridge differences in language and culture between themselves and Jewish and Italian immigrant women workers. The political agenda of many middle-class allies led them to give a high priority to the goal of women's suffrage, and this was seen by working-class women as a betrayal of their basic economic concerns. Despite the best intentions of the participants, Progressive Era cross-class coalitions were fragile and temporary, strained by reservations and misunderstandings between the two allied camps.[56]

No description of the accomplishments of the middle-class women progressives who became members of the Women's Trade Union League of New York can be considered complete if it fails to note the class and ethnic tensions that limited the NYWTUL's effectiveness. Nevertheless, it is equally true that the combined efforts of the NYWTUL's leaders and rank and file accomplished something truly remarkable. Coming together under the NYWTUL banner, women from various classes and ethnic backgrounds joined hands, however awkwardly and briefly, to fight effectively for a common cause in the factories, streets, and courtrooms of New York City.

There was a sequel to the great shirtwaist strike of 1909–1910. This was the tragic fire at Triangle Shirtwaist Company in 1911, an event that more than any other during the pre–World War I period produced cooperation among representatives of nearly every major group in Greenwich Village. Just as the World War II generation of Americans never forgot precisely when and how they first learned of the Japanese attack on Pearl Harbor, residents of the Village who were in the neighborhood the afternoon of March 25, 1911, always retained vivid memories of the fire at Triangle Shirtwaist Company. Mary Heaton Vorse got her first inkling that something was amiss while trying to phone an A Club friend, Bertha Carter, whom she expected to find at the apartment of a mutual acquaintance, Frances Perkins. But the telephone connection was haywire. All Vorse could hear was women's voices screaming, "They're burning! They're jumping out of the windows!" Alarmed, Vorse telephoned the local police station and learned that a huge fire was raging at a factory building near Washington Square. Not knowing what to expect but fearing the worst, she left her Grove Street flat and hurried toward the square, three blocks away.[57]

By the time Vorse reached Washington Square, Frances Perkins was already there. Perkins, a former resident of Greenwich House and now secretary of the Consumers' League (which had sponsored Woerishoffer's steam laundry investigation), had been at her Waverly Place apartment when she heard the sound of fire engines passing nearby and went outside to see what was going on. Drawn by crowd noise to Washington Square, she could see that the top three floors (the eighth, ninth, and tenth) of the Asch Building were ablaze. Having arrived just as the first of many workers began leaping from the upper stories, Perkins was stunned. "I shall never forget," she said later, "the frozen horror which came over us as we stood with our hands on our throats watching that horrible sight." The crowd, constantly augmented as workers from neighboring factories reached the square during the usual rush at Saturday afternoon quitting time, now numbered in the thousands.[58]

Another A Clubber, Martha Bruère, was walking down Fifth Avenue toward Washington Square. Ahead she could see what she described as "a great swirling, billowing cloud of smoke that swept like a giant streamer out of Washington Square and down upon the beautiful homes in lower Fifth Avenue." Two young working-class women she knew rushed up to her. "Tears were running from their eyes," Bruère recalled, "and they were white and shaking as they caught me by the arm. 'Oh,' shrieked one of them, 'they are jumping. Jumping from ten stories up! They are going through the air like bundles of clothes and the firemen can't stop them and the policemen can't stop them and nobody can't help them at all.' "[59]

This was the grim truth. Unable to escape the building's upper floors because fire escapes were lacking, elevators stalled, and stairwell exits either locked or jammed, desperate Triangle employees were leaping out of windows. Firemen tried to catch them in nets, but the plummeting bodies broke through the fabric and smashed on the sidewalk (fig. 26). The fire and smoke, the thump of bodies landing, and the screams of the crowd created pandemonium. Even the stolid fire truck horses, accustomed to flames, smoke, and general disorder, became alarmed and, wild-eyed, moved nervously in their harnesses.

Ernest Poole, another A Club veteran, was at work in his apartment on West Eleventh, a quarter of a mile away. He heard a horse ambulance coming at a gallop to the entrance of St. Vincent's Hospital just down the block. Then another ambulance approached, its gong sounding; then another. Finally, all sorts of vehicles, cabs, carriages, and automobiles, converged on the hospital entrance. Puzzled, Poole went outside and found that a crowd of onlookers had gathered. It took a few moments for him to grasp what was happening. He saw a taxi pull up and disgorge a man carrying "a huge bundle." Only when Poole saw "a head and a shock of hair" protruding from the bundle did he realize that it was a person; not until later did he learn that the taxi had been carrying a Triangle fire victim.[60]

The death toll eventually reached 146, most of them young Jewish or Italian women. Grief and anger were expressed in all parts of the city but felt with particular intensity on the Lower East Side and in the Village, the districts from which most of the dead and injured came.

The tragedy prompted an outpouring of sympathy and support from individuals and organizations representing every class and ethnic group. Much of the assistance offered to Triangle victims and their families came from traditional philanthropic sources. In the Village, for instance, Robert de Forest, the president of the Charity Organization Society and head of the New York chapter of the American Red Cross, lived two blocks from the site of the disaster. Immediately after the fire, de Forest called on Mayor William Gaynor and urged him to issue a public appeal for contributions to aid fire victims. Subsequently, de Forest assigned many C.O.S. employees to help with the relief effort. The Red Cross drive, led mainly by wealthy New Yorkers like de Forest, directly aided more than a hundred working-class families.

Members of the Women's Trade Union League of New York also swiftly rallied to the cause. NYWTUL members helped to locate affected families and evaluate their needs. Settlement workers from Greenwich House provided information on Italian families that had lost loved ones. Carola Woerishoffer, though she no longer lived at Greenwich House, had retained close ties with the settlement and the NYWTUL, and she took time from her busy schedule as a factory inspector for the state Department of Labor to visit many of the families of victims who had lived in the Village.

Most of the dead were Jewish women from the Lower East Side, but at least eighteen were Italian Villagers and members of Father Antonio Demo's Our Lady of Pompei Church. The roll call of the deceased was grim testimony to the youth of many fire victims: Rosie Grasso and Gaitana Midolo, both age sixteen: Isabella Tortorella, age seventeen; two sisters, Bettina and Francesca Maiale, aged eighteen and twenty-one; Amelia Prato, age twenty-one; Mrs. May Levintine, age twenty-eight, the sole support of a young daughter; and so the list went on and on.[61]

During the months after the fire, priests at Our Lady of Pompei said masses almost daily for deceased individuals at the request of their families. The major commemorative occasion, however, was a solemn high requiem Mass held at the church on Sunday, April 26, 1911. The *New York Times* reported that the church itself was "completely filled and several hundred persons remained at the doors." The wails of bereaved relatives and friends were frequently audible throughout the service, and at one point during the sermon the sobbing became so loud that the priest had to pause until the noise subsided. In a gesture that acknowledged that the tragedy was not simply a private matter for grieving within the Italian community but an event that touched a wider public, Father Demo agreed to let NYWTUL members distribute leaflets to mourners at the church. According to the *Times*, these fliers, printed in three languages (English, Italian, and Yiddish), urged all present to support "a plan to compel the enforcement of proper protective laws" for workers in the city's factories (fig. 27).[62]

Cooperation among Villagers across class and ethnic lines continued for some time in the wake of the Triangle fire. In June 1911 the state legislature voted to establish a New York Factory Investigating Commission, and

26. Police and the bodies of Triangle workers who died when they tried to escape the fire by jumping from the building's upper floors. Tamiment Institute Library, New York University.

MOURNING THOUSANDS MARCH IN SILENCE THROUGH RAIN-DRENCHED STREETS.
The procession starting up Fifth avenue, both sides of the street crowded with spectators.

WHAT ARE YOU GOING TO DO?

Hundreds of thousands of persons stood in the rain or otherwise saw 40,000 men and women workers march through the main

27. The mass funeral procession for the victims of the Triangle fire passes through Washington Arch. From *New York Tribune*, April 6, 1911.

Frances Perkins, a member of the Greenwich House circle, was named the commission's secretary. Responsible for most of the commission's day-to-day operations, Perkins presented its proposals for reform laws to the legislature.

Perkins's efforts received a big boost from having the backing of key Democratic legislators who represented districts in Lower Manhattan. In the past Tammany had played a clever double game, courting working-class voters with promises of jobs and at the same time seeking support from business interests by pledging to oppose laws that regulated the hours and conditions of industrial work. Now, however, Tammany's leadership, fearful of losing the allegiance of Jewish and Italian workers, advocated regulatory reform. In 1912, the Lower East Side's reigning Democratic boss, state senator Big Tim Sullivan, used his considerable influence to secure passage of a bill to limit the workweek of most New York women factory workers to fifty-four hours. Shortly thereafter Sullivan fell ill, and two younger Democrats from Lower East Side districts, Assemblyman Al Smith and Senator Robert Wagner, both of whom were members of the Factory Investigating Commission, took up the campaign for socially progressive laws where Sullivan had left off. Jimmy Walker, another loyal Democrat who since 1909 had represented the west Village in the state assembly, followed Smith's lead and voted for the pro-labor legislation promoted by Tammany's reform wing.[63]

Backed by a broad coalition of middle-class reformers and Tammany Democrats, more than fifty new regulatory measures passed into law from 1912 to 1915. Like the Tenement House Act of 1901, which had not ended the city's housing woes, the so-called Triangle Fire Laws of 1912–1915 did not eliminate every workplace health and safety problem of the time. But the enactment of the new regulations did reflect an important development in American reform, the increased readiness of New York's social progressives to lobby local and state governments for laws that would aid the city's workers.

Although public outrage over the Triangle fire tragedy provided the immediate impetus for this flurry of legislative activity, the groundwork had been laid earlier by reform-minded Villagers and their working-class allies. The numerous surveys of industrial conditions by members of the Greenwich House circle—Carola Woerishoffer on steam laundries, Crystal Eastman on industrial accidents, and Louise Bolard More on wage-earners' budgets—helped shape the climate of opinion in which the Triangle Fire Laws were passed. By documenting the underside of urban industrial life, these studies revealed to all who were open-minded enough to see it that the ready availability of inexpensive consumer goods, taken by many to be a hallmark of the era's vaunted material progress, had been achieved at great cost to the workers who produced those goods.[64]

5

Value Conflicts

Mary Simkhovitch never tired of pointing out that Greenwich Village had an unusually heterogeneous population. She was aware that in the public mind the Lower East Side was more often thought of as the district with the largest concentration of foreign-born residents, but she liked to observe that compared with the Village, the Lower East Side's immigrant masses were quite homogeneous ethnically and economically, being nearly all working-class East European Jews. By contrast, members of every economic class were found in Greenwich Village, and the neighborhood's working-class districts were ethnically very diverse. In addition to large numbers of Irish, Italians, and blacks, there were Villagers from many other ethnic groups; in an early survey of the neighborhood, social workers from Greenwich House identified representatives of more than two dozen nationalities living on Jones Street.[1]

Just as the Washington Square Association's members and many of their working-class neighbors disagreed over what constituted the proper use of public space, Villagers were sharply divided when issues arose regarding sexual mores, alcohol consumption, leisure time activities, and criminality—all of which were significantly influenced by class and ethnic culture. Mary Simkhovitch was well aware that ethnic diversity made it difficult to build a consensus in the Village about values. "The multiplicity of elements forming such a composite district," she wrote, "hinders the development of a common purpose to effect improvement."[2]

Improvement would be achieved, Simkhovitch and her progressive reform allies believed, through efforts to repress prostitution and criminality and to enforce decorous behavior in the era's new entertainment venues—dance halls, movie theaters, and amusement parks. Moral reform campaigns with objectives of this sort were commonplace in the Progressive Era, and such crusades typically reflected class and cultural conflicts between the native-born white Protestants who generally sponsored the campaigns and the working-class Jews, Catholics, and blacks who were the campaigns' targets. But the Village version of this wider conflict was nevertheless unusual in that the moral reformers and the working-class people whose behavior they wished to reform lived in close proximity to each other.

The first section of this chapter describes the progressive reformers' campaigns to impose their view of moral order. A second section examines why Village artists and writers, most of whom were from the same class as the moral reformers, took a more positive view of the emerging urban culture of their time and a more tolerant stance vis-à-vis the moral behavior of their working-class neighbors.

THE IMPROPER VILLAGERS

In the late nineteenth century, Greenwich Village was not a major locale for the illicit sex business. A large part of the neighborhood was still dominated by middle- and upper-class residences, not the type of housing in which prostitution flourished. Still, the area was not totally free of vice activity, and, in fact, in the early 1890s some of the city's most notorious vice dens were located in or near the Village.

The presence and unsavory character of these Village sites was first brought to light by the Reverend Charles Parkhurst, the most persistent and successful anti-vice investigator of the 1890s. Parkhurst, who was the minister of the Madison Square Presbyterian Church, went in disguise to various places of assignation (brothels and concert halls) throughout the city and then launched, in February 1892, a series of headline-grabbing sermons in which he charged that New York was ridden with moral decay. These exposés contributed to the public outrage that led to the victory of William Strong, the anti-Tammany mayoral candidate, in the 1894 municipal election.

According to Parkhurst's findings and those of subsequent investigations over the next ten years, brothels and concert halls were confined to a relatively small section of the Village. This was the black-and-tan Minetta Lane–Minetta Street area, and nearby parts of Sixth Avenue, West Third Street, and Bleecker Street.

The two south Village establishments that most scandalized anti-prostitution campaigners in the 1890s were the Golden Rule Pleasure Club on West Third and The Slide on Bleecker. What made these places especially offensive to Parkhurst and his allies was that both were patronized by males seeking assignations with other males. (Female prostitutes were also available.) On his visit to the Golden Rule Pleasure Club in 1892, Parkhurst took one look at the scene—male prostitutes who wore heavy makeup, spoke in falsetto voices, and called one another by women's names—and, as his guide recalled, "instantly turned on his heel and fled from the house at top speed." Similarly, also in 1892, a *New York Herald* reporter writing about The Slide referred to it as "that most notorious of dens of iniquity in the city" and described the presence of "fashionably dressed young fellows, whose cheeks were rouged and whose manner suggested the infamy to which they had fallen."[3]

The Slide and the Golden Rule were forced out of business by the Strong administration in the mid-1890s, the same years that a police crackdown brought some measure of peace to the heretofore very violent Minettas. However, following the return of Tammany Democrats to power in 1897, the commercial vice trade boomed again in the Bowery–Broadway red-light districts on the eastern periphery of the Village. The election of Seth Low's anti-Tammany administration in 1901 brought another round of crackdowns, which reached their high point in the Village on February 28, 1903, when police officers raided four south Village disorderly houses and rounded up dozens of prostitutes and their customers.[4]

The vice trade, like a hydra-headed monster, soon arose again in the Village. Moreover it took new forms, as did the strategies and organization of anti-prostitution campaigners. Mary Simkhovitch, soon to be one of the neighborhood's most relentless crusaders against vice, had barely gotten her Greenwich House social settlement organized when the Low administration was voted out of office in 1903. Police statistics on citations of houses of assignation during the first decade of the twentieth century show that the Village had one of the lowest citation rates in the city, but Simkhovitch and her staff could see for themselves that prostitutes and pimps were active on streets close to her Jones Street settlement. In 1905, therefore, she became a founding member of the Committee of Fourteen, a group of social workers, businessmen, and clerics whose goal it was to combat the latest institutional form that prostitution had taken in the city, the so-called Raines Law hotels.[5]

Raines Law hotels had sprung up in the aftermath of the New York state legislature's passage of the Raines Law in 1896. This act had created an exception to the state's unpopular Sunday closing laws by permitting hotels to sell liquor to guests in their rooms or with meals served in dining rooms.

All that an establishment needed to qualify as a hotel was to have ten bed-rooms, a dining room, and a kitchen. New York City saloon owners quickly capitalized on this loosening of the excise laws by adding the requisite num-ber of rooms to qualify as hotels. So attractive was the prospect of lucrative profits from Sunday liquor sales that by 1905 more than a thousand Raines Law hotels were operating in Manhattan and the Bronx alone. Since the added rooms were not needed for legitimate guests, they were rented at low rates to prostitutes, with the result that Raines Law hotels supplanted the old-style brothel as the main site for assignations in the city.[6]

During its first five years of existence, the Committee of Fourteen tried a variety of approaches to eliminate the Raines Law hotels. These included seeking the repeal of the enabling legislation, demanding the enforcement of city ordinances to close saloons and hotels that allowed solicitation on their premises, and pressuring beer manufacturers to refuse to give financial assistance to owners of unsavory establishments who needed aid in paying liquor license fees.

Progress was slow both citywide and in the Village. In 1910, the Com-mittee of Fourteen issued *The Social Evil in New York City*, a book-length evaluation of its anti-vice efforts to date. In one section of the report the committee identified five neighborhoods where the city's vice trade was most densely concentrated, often in close connection with commercial en-tertainment districts. Although two of the five neighborhoods were quite close to the Village—Sixth Avenue between Twenty-third and Thirty-third streets, and East Fourteenth Street between Third and Fourth avenues—no section of Greenwich Village made the list. However, prostitutes contin-ued to ply their trade at dozens of locations—seedy saloons, tenements, hotels (both the standard and the Raines Law variety), and streetcorners—throughout the Village.[7]

In 1910, the part of the Village in which prostitutes were active was, as it had been in Parkhurst's day eighteen years earlier, confined to a fairly narrow zone on lower Sixth Avenue and the blocks in and immediately ad-jacent to the Minettas. It was perfectly possible for Frederick H. Whitin, a stockbroker and the long-time executive secretary of the Committee of Fourteen, who also served the cause by doing undercover investigatory work, to visit nearly every significant site in the Village's vice zone in a single night. The following reconstruction of a hypothetical tour, based on reports he and other investigators made on the Village's trouble spots, serves to illustrate the committee's mode of operation and to provide a glimpse of the transgressive culture that survived despite the committee's efforts to eradicate it (map 4).[8]

Traveling downtown from his home on West 113th Street and suitably dressed for his night's work in garish clothes that were also somewhat worn and dirty, Whitin stepped off the Sixth Avenue Elevated train at the Eighth Street station. Looking north he could see, looming above the platform just to his right, the narrow arched windows and pointed roofs of an imposing Victorian Gothic building, Jefferson Market Courthouse, which housed the Night Court where prostitutes were arraigned and tried (fig. 28). (It was also the site, in 1907 and 1908, of the two trials—the first ended in a hung jury—of Harry K. Thaw for the murder of the architect Stanford White, whom Thaw hated because Thaw's wife, the former Evelyn Nesbit, had been seduced by White before her marriage.)[9]

From the downtown platform of the elevated station Whitin could look up Greenwich Avenue, which ran at an angle to the northwest. Standing on the nearest corner (Christopher Street and Greenwich Avenue) was Luke O'Connor's saloon. Not long after the Raines Law passed, O'Connor had added ten bedrooms to his establishment and opened the Columbus Hotel. The saloon offered food along with liquor as was required by the Raines Law, but none of the patrons took the offer seriously. "At the bar," one customer remembered, "was an everlasting stack of sandwiches. One of these was served with every drink but if one had ever been eaten the waiters would have dropped dead." Surveillence by its investigators led the Committee of Fourteen to conclude that the hotel was being used for illicit purposes. Whitin himself, in 1907, observed "many infractions," noting specifically that the hotel was patronized by "unaccompanied women"—that is, probable prostitutes. In 1909 another investigator reported that the hotel's register listed "too many couples to be all legitimate," a large turnover of guests being typical of use by prostitutes and their clients. Under pressure from the Committee of Fourteen, O'Connor agreed that the hotel would in the future be for men only. However, when a committee investigator returned later in 1909, he again found what he called "suspicious" entries in the hotel's register. Revisiting the place in 1910, the committee's agent concluded that the register now looked satisfactory, but that the "rear room [was] suspicious." O'Connor's, like many saloons of the time, had a front room used mainly or exclusively by men and a back room for women or couples. The word "suspicious" suggests that the investigator observed single men and unaccompanied women socializing in a way that might indicate solicitation.[10]

O'Connor's saloon and hotel were at the northern end of the Village's trouble zone. This was a seven-block-long commercial strip along Sixth Avenue from Eighth Street south to the Minettas. Socially, this part of the Village was a borderland between the mixed ethnic (but mainly Irish and Italian) middle- and working-class west Village and the classier residential

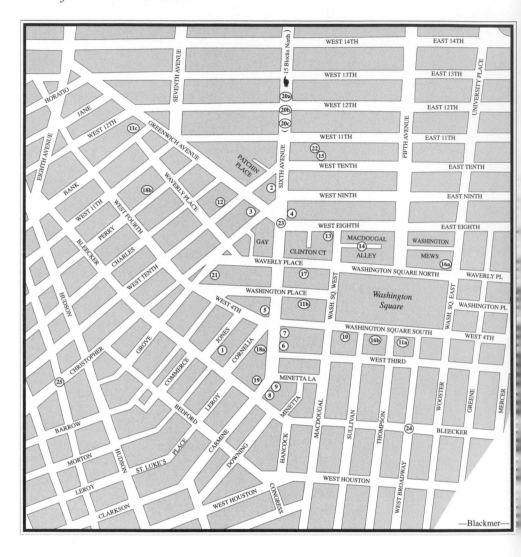

—Blackmer—

area around Washington Square North and lower Fifth Avenue. Since it ran underneath the elevated line's tracks, Sixth Avenue down to West Third, where the elevated turned east, was almost always in partial or complete shade. This, combined with the noise of trains passing overhead every two to six minutes between 5:15 A.M. and midnight, contributed to the avenue's general shabbiness.[11]

At the bottom of the elevated line's stairs, Whitin crossed the street to the east side of Sixth Avenue. On the northeast corner of the intersection were the two small businesses that absorbed so much of the Washington Square Association's attention, Antonio Mastrino's bootblack stand and

Map 4. Important Village Sites, Chapter 5

1. Greenwich House ....26 Jones Street
2. Jefferson Market Courthouse ....Sixth Ave. near West 10th Street
3. Luke O'Connor's ....5 Greenwich Avenue
4. Clinton Place Hotel............................96 Sixth Avenue*
5. Cadigan's...41 Sixth Avenue
6. Curtin's...18 Sixth Avenue
7. Golden Swan, aka Hell Hole...............36 Sixth Avenue
8. Green Cup Cafe....................................6 Carmine Street
9. West Side Cafe.....................................2–4 Carmine Street
10. David G. Phillips's ....Washington Square South
11. Willa Cather's ....a. 60 Washington Square South
                                                                     b. 82 Washington Place
                                                                     c. 5 Bank Street
12. Renganeschi's ....139 West Tenth Street
13. Gonfarone's...MacDougal & West 8th Street
14. MacDougal Alley ....G. V. Whitney at No. 19
15. Tenth Street Studio..............................51 West Tenth Street
16. Glackens's Studios................................a. 3 Washington Square North
                                                                     b. 50 Washington Square South
17. Everett Shinn's......................................112 Waverly Place
18. John Sloan's ....a. Studio: 35 Sixth Avenue
                                                                     b. Home: 61 Perry Street
19. Carmine Theatre
20. Tenderloin Sites ....a. Mouquin's: West 28th Street
                                                                     b. Petitpas': West 29th Street
                                                                     c. Haymarket: 6th Ave. & W. 29th St.
21. Mary Heaton Vorse's ....88 Grove Street
22. Paglieri's ....64 West Eleventh Street
23. Eighth Street Station ....Sixth Avenue Elevated
24. Bleecker Street Station ....Sixth Avenue Elevated
25. Christopher Street Station...................Ninth Avenue Elevated

* All Sixth Avenue addresses are the pre-1920s numbers.

Charles Gordon's newsstand. Immediately behind the stands was the Clinton Place Hotel, one of the Committee of Fourteen's perennial problem cases. In 1909, after receiving repeated reports that the Clinton Place Hotel was the site of suspicious activity, the committee gave it an "AH" designation, an internal rating meaning that they considered it an assignation hotel, one definition of which was a lodging place "whose principal business is furnishing accommodations to men and 'wives' without baggage and staying less than twenty-four hours." Despite pressure from the committee on the police and the surety companies that financed the establishment's liquor license, the hotel stayed in business through the early 1910s.[12]

As he proceeded south on Sixth, Whitin passed two places where the committee's pressure had produced somewhat more satisfactory results.

28. The Sixth Avenue Elevated line at Jefferson Market Courthouse. From *Frank Leslie's Illustrated Newspaper*; courtesy of the Library of Congress.

One block south of St. Joseph's, on the same side of the street as the church, was Cadigan's, a saloon without an attached hotel. Although it was an Irish-owned saloon in an Irish neighborhood, it had a mixed-race clientele and did a booming business. According to the investigator's notes from 1907, the back room was "so full of those of both sexes and races that there was no vacant place." In an example of the uncooperative response the committee initially received from many municipal authorities, Judge Matthew Breen (an honorary member of the County Clare Men's Society) dismissed a police citation against Cadigan. Before much else could be done the owner, Agnes Cadigan, had died, and a new proprietor took control. Two years later conditions had improved somewhat.[13]

One block farther down Sixth, on the other side of the street, was another Irish saloon owned by a woman proprietor, Mamie Curtin. Curtin's was reported as an assignation house in 1905, the first year of the Committee of Fourteen's operation. The committee achieved quick success here because both the brewer and the surety company that had backed the place removed their support and Curtin abandoned the business. By 1907 a new licensee had taken over and the committee's investigator initially reported "all quiet." A subsequent visit turned up evidence of illegal Sunday sales, a less serious infraction than vice activities but still a bad sign from the committee's viewpoint.[14]

Thomas Wallace's Golden Swan, located in the same block as Curtin's, was rarely all quiet. A rowdy Irish pub that also attracted African Americans, Village gangsters, and slumming artists and writers, the Golden Swan came under fire from the committee in 1911–1912. When charged with excise violations, Wallace, an ex-boxer who had owned his Village saloon since the mid-1870s, resolutely defended his interests. He hired Patrick McManus, an Irish American attorney who specialized in cases that arose out of excise violations and had considerable success in winning them. Although the court determined that a violation had taken place, the case was settled out of court and discontinued later in 1912, leaving the "Hell Hole," as it was known to its aficionados, open for business as usual (fig. 29).[15]

As Whitin walked down Sixth Avenue and crossed West Third Street, he reached the Village's most unsavory area. Before the mid-1920s, Sixth Avenue terminated at the corner of Minetta Lane and Carmine Street, the site of two of the worst dives still open in the Village. Both the West Side Cafe at 2–4 Carmine and the Green Cup Cafe next door at 6 Carmine were black-and-tan (i.e., mixed-race) saloons. Committee of Fourteen undercover agents visited both on many occasions and kept more detailed notes on them than on any other sites in the Village.

Investigators usually tried to visit these saloons in the late evening when

29. The interior of the Golden Swan saloon as depicted in John Sloan's *Hell Hole* in 1917. Philadelphia Museum of Art: Purchased: Lessing J. Rosenwald Gift and Farrell Fund Income.

they were likely to be busiest. Of the Green Cup Cafe one undercover agent wrote: "This place is even worse than its twin on the corner [the West Side Cafe]. Coloured prostitutes infest the backroom and bar. It is a most disorderly place and it and No. 2 [the West Side Cafe] should be 'straightened.'" On several occasions when the private detectives visited it the Green Cup's bar room was full of black and white men. Whiskey sold for a nickel a shot and there were many takers. One investigator reported, as evidence of vice transactions in progress, that he saw a black "wench" go out a back door with a white man and that he overheard a black man ask a black woman, "Have you made five yet?" (At fifty cents to one dollar per trick, five dollars would have taken a while to earn.) On another visit, the committee's detective noted the brash insouciance of the black "wenches" who patronized the place. He described one woman as being "seated on top of a table with her clothes halfway up her back" and arguing with another black woman who was standing in the middle of the floor. The detective seemed both awed and appalled by the seated woman's forthright and filthy speech. "Her flow of language," he wrote, "was remarkable, and her use of profanity and obscene expressions baffles description."[16]

The last stop on this hypothetical tour would have been the West Side Cafe on the corner of Carmine and Minetta Lane. "This," one detective wrote, using the slang racial epithets common in the era, "is a bad coloured joint supplied by nigger men and nigger prostitutes from Minetta Lane and its environs," a place "so vicious that a policeman is on the corner for duty." The front room had a piano and a phonograph to provide entertainment for the saloon's patrons. As he entered this room, the committee's agent observed "nigger wenches" drinking at the bar, several "coons" playing dice, and some "white men standing around." The back room he described as "a 'hore house in distress (simply rotten)." An Italian named Nick was hugging Mamie, a black woman. Another black woman came in and said, "Christ, look at Nick loving Mamie." A young white girl, who the investigator estimated to be about twelve years old, came to the back door of the saloon with a pail and some money, and Nick got up to fill her pail with beer or ale.[17]

The detailed notes taken by undercover agents provide rare glimpses of saloon culture, including the language and the social interactions of these lower-class New Yorkers. On one occasion, the committee's agent observed an obviously drunk black woman enter the cafe to buy cigarettes from the black bartender. "Did you hear," she asked the bartender, "that Sadie got 'punched?' " (Sadie had been arrested and taken to night court at Jefferson Market Courthouse to "explain how it happened.") Continuing her monologue, the cigarette buyer added that she herself had just been warned to move on by the policeman on the corner: "About five minutes ago the cop said to me, 'Beat it.' But I said, 'You cocksucker! I can't walk fast; my feet are sore.' He said, 'Don't you see Lennon coming?' I said, 'Fuck Lennon.' "

A short while later the agent overheard another exchange among the bar's patrons. Ida, another black woman, came in to get a half pint of whiskey. Upon her arrival a black man named Jim got up and abruptly left the room. Lottie looked around and asked the crowd, "Did you see Jim blow when Ida came in? Why G[od] D[amn] it, I don't want her Jim." When the detective later got up to leave, Lottie turned to him and addressed him familiarly: "Are you going, Sweety?" He replied, "Sure," and left.

The full identities of most patrons of the Green Cup Cafe and its twin next door are unknown; only Louis Seiderman, the Polish-born Jew who ran the Green Cup from 1905 into the early 1910s, can be identified for certain in the 1910 census. (He lived with his wife and young son upstairs from the saloon.) Whatever else can be said about the individuals who patronized the Carmine Street dives, they showed staying power in the face of repeated assaults on their presence. The reformers expressed disgust with the wide-open practice of prostitution in the Minettas and were repelled by the mixed-race nature of the participants, but even with the law and—as they saw it—morality on their side, the anti-vice campaigners had little immediate success in their efforts to reform the area. Early in their campaign against Seiderman's saloon, the Committee of Fourteen took police evidence to a judge, but he threw the case out on a technicality. By the early 1910s, Seiderman had sold out. Although his successor signed an agreement with the committee in 1915 not to allow solicitation on the premises, the Green Cup Cafe was still on the committee's probation list in 1916 and 1917.[18]

Well before those years, Mary Simkhovitch had concluded that the only way to end debauchery in the Minettas once and for all would be to raze the area and create a playground for Village children. Her idea was finally drawn up as a formal proposal in the early 1910s, at which point it was endorsed by the Washington Square Association and forwarded to the appropriate city officials. In the absence of any immediate action on her playground proposal, Simkhovitch and her allies continued to pursue more piecemeal measures. In 1912, the Committee of Fourteen, the police, and building owners succeeded in closing several brothels and in breaking up a "cadet club" (a gang of pimps) in the Minettas. Prostitutes still frequented "two tough saloons"—the Green Cup and West Side cafes—but, statistically speaking, the number of places where prostitutes were active in the Minettas and the Village as a whole was down by perhaps 40 percent.[19]

In *The Social Evil in New York City*, the 1910 publication of the Committee of Fourteen, the authors reported that although the nature of the vice trade had been changed by twentieth-century urban conditions, the evolving situation was more insidious than before. For most of the nineteenth century, prostitution had been centered mainly in "disorderly houses" and had been tolerated as a necessary outlet for the male sex drive. Now, however, the authors found that prostitution was no longer "the simple process of a man seeking a woman in a place kept for such a purpose," and that it had become "the center of an elaborate system . . . fostered by business interests."[20]

The business interests in question were those associated with the commercial entertainment industry, which expanded at an explosive pace in the first decade of the twentieth century. In that period amusement parks added capacity, hundreds of new dance halls opened, and motion picture theaters spread throughout the city, their numbers growing tenfold (from fifty to five hundred) between 1900 and 1910—all to serve a growing urban audience. But according to the Committee of Fourteen, the expansion of these mass audience commercial entertainments was fostering a culture of freer self-expression and contributing to the emergence of a new morality in which looser sexual behavior was becoming more acceptable among women as well as men. The new culture of pleasure-seeking was, the committee feared, particularly attractive to young people, many of them recent arrivals in the city, whose migration there for work had the effect of "breaking the moorings of the past." In the absence of moral restraints that parents and neighbors once would have enforced, these young people were, in the committee's view, in danger of becoming sexually promiscuous and even of being lured into the vice trade that flourished in the Raines Law hotels found near many dance halls and amusement parks.[21]

Before 1910, Greenwich Village had few such commercial entertainment outlets within its borders. Three movie theaters operated in the Carmine Street–Bleecker Street Italian enclave, and a dance academy that taught the new dance styles did business briefly in the west Village, but the paucity of public entertainments was no obstacle to those drawn to such activities. There were many such establishments within easy walking distance on the Lower East Side, and for a few nickels in carfare one could reach much more distant locales, including Coney Island.

If it was difficult for the Village's moral guardians to clean up their own neighborhood, it was even harder for them to control businesses like the emerging motion picture industry or the burgeoning public dance halls that drew young Villagers to locations outside the neighborhood. The great popularity of these recreational activities is suggested by Louise Bolard More in her 1907 study of Greenwich Village workers' budgets: she noted that as workers' incomes rose above the level required for basic needs, they tended to spend a disproportionate amount of the surplus on recreation.[22]

The Committee of Fourteen's particular concern about public dance halls was that "outwardly they seem fairly respectable to the ordinary stranger." However, appearances were deceiving:

> The greatest danger lies in the fact that hotel accommodations may be easily secured in the same building or nearby, and that women are expected to drink with their partners. Another source of danger to the respectable girl at these dances is the constant companionship night after night with immoral women who predominate in places of this type. They appear in gowns far beyond the reach of the average working girl and she gradually becomes dissatisfied with her own personal appearance, and is soon seeking the acquaintanceship of men who will either give her money or presents.

The committee's concern with the public dance hall environment's impact on young women—rather than its impact on both men and women—is quite revealing. That unmarried men frequented such places was no great change; that respectable young women did so was a disturbing departure from traditional social practice.[23]

Establishing the standards of social conduct and public behavior that would prevail in the new century was not a struggle limited to the public sphere. It was also a matter of discussion between parents and children. Susie Fromella's story is a case in point. In 1910 a Catholic social worker wrote Father Demo of Our Lady of Pompei on behalf of Mrs. Maria Fromella, an Italian-born mother of eight who lived at 19 Jones Street. Mrs. Fromella was having trouble with her daughter Susie, age fifteen. The family was quite poor. Mr. Fromella was a truck driver, and his two oldest daughters, Jennie and Susie, worked in a paper box factory (probably the one that was across the street next to Greenwich House). The trouble, the social worker wrote Demo, was that Susie "wants more liberty than her mother wishes her to have. She works all day in a factory, and like most young people wants some recreation." Traditionally, unmarried Italian girls stayed home and did no socializing outside the family and church. Grace Gazzola, a south Village garment worker who was also the daughter of Italian immigrants, remembered that she had "never [been] allowed to go out. Not even on a Saturday night with her girl friends." But those were the old rules, and Susie Fromella clearly didn't think they applied to a working girl like herself in New York City in 1910.[24]

Freedom to socialize away from the vigilant eye of parents and neighbors was one feature that drew young New Yorkers to public dance halls, but another source of their allure was the new style of dancing. Older dance fashions—the waltz, two-step, Virginia Reel, and barn dance in which partners followed patterned movements—were now replaced by styles that emphasized improvisational movement done to a ragtime beat. The fact that ragtime, a rhythm developed in southern black dives in the 1890s, was gaining such popularity indicated that the new dance styles were percolating up from below. The names of the new dances that surfaced as early as 1910—the Turkey Trot, Bunny Hug, Lame Duck, and Grizzly Bear, a veritable animal kingdom of dances—further reinforced the feeling that old social controls were being cast aside. As one scholar has remarked, "The wonderful nomenclature of the dances, taken from the barnyard, added to the general tone of exuberance, unpretentiousness, and informality between the sexes."[25]

From her vantage point in Greenwich Village, Mary Simkhovitch worried about these trends. She took an active role in repressing what she called the "dubious dancing academy" that set up for business near the settlement. But she found it equally troubling that the Village lacked facilities where young people could gather for wholesome recreation, and in 1907 Greenwich House began to sponsor dances for the youth of the neighborhood. In the next few years, as the number of public dance halls in the nearby Lower East Side and midtown West Side areas grew, Simkhovitch expanded her efforts. In 1911 the settlement rented and refurbished a building at 18 Jones Street. Dances were scheduled for three nights a week, with the settlement organizing the programs and providing chaperones. According to a report written later in 1911, Simkhovitch was not too pleased with the results. "There were," she wrote, "many difficulties in maintaining order and a proper standard of conduct." Perhaps young Villagers accustomed to the freedoms allowed in public dance halls simply were not willing to accept the standards of decorum the settlement folk sought to maintain. But Simkhovitch, ever the pragmatist, went on to say, "It is inevitable that a certain kind of deterioration exist while new standards are struggling to emerge. It is hopeless to maintain the old. The only way is to fight through to the new."[26]

Gangsters, like prostitutes, sex-seeking saloon patrons, and the owners of dubious dance academies, qualified in Simkhovitch's mind as disorderly Villagers. But Simkhovitch recognized that one type of gang, the youth gang, was not in and of itself a disturbing phenomenon. A natural outgrowth of school-age boys playing with neighbors on the same or adjacent blocks, the youth gang was ubiquitous throughout the neighborhood. Hanging out with one's pals often took entirely harmless forms: playing baseball or football in streets or vacant lots, pitching pennies, throwing craps, playing cards, and smoking. (One social worker reported that the typical West Side street urchin "smokes incessantly," starting as early as age six.) Boy gangs also frequently fought rival gangs in turf wars, the usual weapons being fists, "clubs, stones, and beer bottles." More dangerous weapons, knives or revolvers, were not widely used by school-age gang members.[27]

The neighborhood's youth gangs did become troubling to Simkhovitch, however, when their members' activities brought them into conflict with the law. If the lure of the street became stronger than the attraction of staying in school, truancy was the result. Petty theft was widespread, and some forms—stealing lumber from a construction site or coal from an unguarded cellar—had the tacit approval of poor parents who sent their children out to locate fuel and didn't ask questions about where the youngsters found the much-needed combustibles. Pilfering small items from local stores or packages from freight wagons was more likely to produce a police record. These minor crimes did not inevitably lead youths to become criminals as adults, but that choice, if made, generally came quite early in a boy's life— usually around the age of fourteen, when school attendance was no longer compulsory and the boy dropped out of school and either found a legitimate job or joined an adult gang.[28]

Unlike the relatively minor harm that resulted from the unlawful activities of youth gangs, crimes committed by the city's adult gangsters—muggings, major thefts, armed assault, and murder—did serious injury to New Yorkers' property and persons.

As measured by the ratio of police arrests to population, the west Village ranked just below the average level of general criminal activity among city police precincts at the turn of the century. However, the Mercer Street precinct, in which the upscale Washington Square North was located, had a higher crime rate, largely because its boundaries included the south Village slum area around the Minettas and the notoriously crime-ridden Broadway–Bowery district to the east of the Village.[29]

At the turn of the century the principal Greenwich Village adult gang was the Hudson Dusters. The gang's name apparently was derived from its members' home turf, the tough dock area between the river and Hudson Street, and from their liberal use of "dust" (cocaine). A few sources suggest, less persuasively, that the hoodlums were so called because of their practice of using brass knuckles to "dust off" victims. Whatever the case, little is known of the history of this Irish American gang in the years immediately after it coalesced in the late 1890s. Apparently the activities of the original gang went largely unrecorded because the Dusters avoided the spectacular shootouts and murderous feuds that characterized the histories of some of their contemporaries.[30]

Not that the early Hudson Dusters were pacifists. They specialized in violent but low-level crimes such as mugging drunken sailors and other unwary citizens. Although the gang's name did not appear in the newspaper accounts of it, a theft and beating that occurred in 1904 during a band concert in Washington Square had the Dusters' signature written all over it. Joseph Perry, a part-time truck driver and sometime pickpocket, attempted to steal a male concertgoer's gold watch. As Perry lifted the watch from its owner's pocket, the watch's chain broke, alerting the victim to the theft in progress. He shouted an alarm and Perry fled, with a policeman, John P. Shea, in hot pursuit. Shea collared Perry under Washington Arch but was immediately attacked by a dozen or more of the thief's confederates, who stabbed the officer in the forehead and kicked and beat him, breaking three of his ribs. Officer Shea might have suffered even worse injuries, except that other police arrived, routed Perry's pals, and took Perry into custody. Perry gave his age as nineteen and his address as 400 Hudson Street.[31]

In the 1910s the Dusters were still the Village's dominant gang, but such was the violent and often short life of the era's gangsters that although the gang's name and Irish American ethnicity had not changed, its most famous early members (Kid Yorke, Circular Jack, and Goo Goo Knox) had disappeared from the scene. The gang's new leader was Mike Costello, and his chief henchmen were Richard "Red" Farrell, Rickey Harrison, and Robert "Rubber" Shaw.[32]

According to Edward Swann, a municipal judge and a close observer of the city's gangs, the Hudson Dusters were a type of gang he identified as "feudists," which were basically adult versions of schoolboy gangs. The Dusters fought with rival gangs that ventured into the Village, indulged in fairly low-risk criminal activities such as stealing unguarded cargo from the docks, and whiled away their idle hours drinking, dancing, and snorting cocaine at their Hudson Street hangouts. But even as Swann wrote this appraisal, the Dusters were becoming more like a second type of gang composed of "gunmen" who were, as Swann put it, "cold, calculated assassins for hire," specializing in major crimes: murder, armed robbery, and extortion.[33]

The gunman type of gang had recently achieved a new level of organizational development. Shortly after Jack Zelig, the leader of Monk Eastman's old gang of Lower East Side Jewish thugs, was gunned down by rivals in 1912, his successor, Dopey Benny Fein, engineered an intergang agreement that produced a price list for services rendered—murder, extortion, beatings, arson—and tried to establish territorial monopolies within which each gang would operate. Dopey Benny's diplomatic genius was such that he got even the Hudson Dusters to commit themselves to the new scheme of things, and this commitment probably explains why the Dusters suddenly abandoned their tradition of low-profile crime and became a more disruptive force in politics, union-management relations, and public life during the crime wave that hit New York in the mid-1910s.[34]

On primary day, September 17, 1913, carloads of Hudson Dusters and their sometime allies, the Gopher Gang from the West Thirties and Forties, engaged in a shootout from automobiles with members of the Sirocco Gang. Most of the thugs escaped, but the police captured four toughs from the Gopher–Hudson Duster contingent. A search of their pockets produced six bundles of paper slips with the names of registered voters on them. The plan apparently was that the each hoodlum would go to as many as six polling places, claim to be someone named on the slips, and vote for a candidate backed by one of the rival Tammany factions jousting for control of the district. Although the precincts in question were located in the West Sixties, the primary day ruckus there was a ripple effect of a struggle to fill the power vacuum caused by the recent disappearance of the Lower East Side's Democratic boss, Big Tim Sullivan. By venturing so far from their usual turf and engaging in a gun battle, the Hudson Dusters played a small role in the events that, according to the *New York Times*, made the 1913 municipal election "the most violent election in years." Public disgust with well-publicized ties between gangsters and machine Democrats con-

tributed to the election of an anti-Tammany Democrat, John Purroy Mitchel, as mayor in November.[35]

On taking office in January 1914, Mayor Mitchel ordered police to get
tough with gangsters. His words were welcomed by Thomas O'Sullivan, a
patrolman in the west Village's Charles Street precinct. O'Sullivan had already launched a personal campaign against Village gangsters, having arrested "Red" Farrell, a leading Duster, the previous November. O'Sullivan
now set out to bring charges against every Hudson Duster he could, and
over the next eleven months he managed to apprehend nine more members
of the gang. Included in this number was Mike Costello, the gang's leader,
who was picked up and briefly incarcerated at Elmira State Prison for his
part in a violent November 1914 altercation over gambling debts that left
one man dead. Indirect evidence suggests that Costello's right-hand man,
Rickey Harrison, was also arrested during O'Sullivan's anti-Duster crusade.[36]

The Dusters' code required retaliation. Around 2 A.M. on Christmas Day,
1914, two gangsters they had hired for the job (the Dusters couldn't do it
themselves because O'Sullivan would have recognized them and not fallen
into their trap) approached O'Sullivan and claimed to be plainclothes detectives who had a suspect cornered in a nearby building and needed help
in arresting the man. O'Sullivan ran with them to a vacant tenement and
entered it, at which point the two thugs attacked and beat him nearly to
death, breaking his nose, knocking out three teeth, and stabbing him eight
times in the neck and head. The Dusters' Gopher Gang allies were so impressed by this achievement that one thug wrote a poem about it that was
widely distributed; copies were even delivered to the police of the Charles
Street Station where O'Sullivan was posted.[37]

This brazen attack and equally brazen poetic taunt took place as the
Dusters entered the final and most violent phase of their history. In addition
to their participation in political conflicts, they managed to get mixed up in
an often vicious struggle between corrupt labor unions and union-bashing
businesses. Just before the Dusters' attack on O'Sullivan, a wholesale poul-
try merchant named Barney Baff had been murdered at his place of business
in the northwest corner of the Village. Although newspaper reporters and
the police failed to uncover any direct connection between Baff's killers and
the Dusters, the murder had happened on their turf, and for reasons no
one could determine they got caught—quite literally—in the crossfire that
followed soon after the killing. Three months later, in March 1915, Mike
Costello was slightly wounded when he and two other men who had formed
an independent teamsters' union were attacked by representatives of the
national union. One of Costello's companions, Luke Doyle, who also happened to be a material witness in the Baff case, was fatally wounded in the
incident.[38]

The Hudson Dusters' days were numbered. Rickey Harrison, who was listed in the Police Department's Rogues' Gallery as the "Greenwich Village Terror," was arrested in 1918 during an armed robbery; he escaped from jail, only to be immediately recaptured. The following year another leading Duster, "Rubber" Shaw, suspected of having murdered a rival gang leader, was himself gunned down in Hoboken, New Jersey, slain by a barrage of fifteen shots fired from a passing automobile. Mike Costello, thought by the police to have set up his old sidekick, went into hiding. As the decade ended the leading Dusters were either dead, incarcerated, or on the run. New Village gangs arose in the 1920s, but as the neighborhood and the nation had changed, so too did crime and criminals in the Village. The Jazz Age Village gangster, like the Village's overall population, was now more often Italian than Irish, and his crime of choice was frequently bootlegging, a by-product of the era's recently instituted national prohibition law.[39]

Village Artists at Work and Play

Villagers who belonged to one of the neighborhood's artistic or literary communities in the early 1910s generally occupied a middle ground in the controversies that arose regarding personal morality and public entertainments. These artists and writers—a group that included magazine illustrators and journalists as well as novelists, short story writers, painters, and sculptors—were, like the vice reformers, educated, well traveled, and middle class or higher in status. But unlike the vice reformers, the Village artists and writers, especially the younger ones, found themselves more fascinated than repelled by their working-class neighbors' behavior. Where reformers saw debauchery, the artists saw potential for a story or a picture. Where the reformers warned of the dangers of cheap amusements, the artists were more inclined to join in the fun, and when reformers identified behaviors they wanted to regulate or suppress, the artists, as individualists devoted to artistic freedom and self-expression, were more likely to argue for tolerance.

The heart of the matter in each of these differences was that vice reformers sought to establish the boundaries of appropriate behavior, while the artistic and literary Villagers felt that their life's work required the freedom to move back and forth across those boundaries. Hutchins Hapgood, in the introduction to his book *Types from City Streets*, published in 1910, aptly described this boundary-testing spirit when he said of himself, "I have been for several years what I may call an intellectual and esthetic adventurer; and my adventures have led me for the most part among people who are generally regarded as 'low.' "[40]

Of course, living in the Village or using neighborhood scenes in their art did not necessarily lead Hapgood's contemporaries to adopt his unabashed unconventionality. These artists and writers were too numerous and independent-minded to fit any single mold, and for many, particularly the novelists, Greenwich Village served as little more than a picturesque backdrop for stories they wanted to tell. Indeed, the phenomenon of giving novels and stories a Village setting was so common that Arthur B. Maurice, in a series of articles written in 1900 on New York City in literature, declared: "An imaginary circle, with its centre in the white Memorial Arch [in Washington Square] and a radius of five or six hundred yards, would hold fully one-half of what is best in the local colour of New York fiction." Maurice went on to illustrate his point with examples, most of them from books now deservedly forgotten; yet even limiting the evidence to the most important late nineteenth-century writers, his case holds up well. Henry James's classic *Washington Square* (1881) offered readers a masterful description of the patrician Village in the mid-1800s, a world James recalled from his childhood and his visits to his grandmother's mansion on Washington Square North, which he used as the model for Dr. Sloper's house. In *A Hazard of New Fortunes* (1889) William Dean Howells has his expatriate Bostonians, Basil and Isabel March, stay at a hotel near Washington Square while they exhaust themselves searching for a suitable apartment. Among a younger generation of writers, Theodore Dreiser, an occasional Villager himself, used 112 West Thirteenth Street as the place where Carrie Meeber and George Hurstwood lived in *Sister Carrie* (1900).[41]

Many Village authors used scenes from the neighborhood not simply because they were picturesque, but because they lent themselves to the exploration of a liminal cultural landscape. Washington Square South, which Howells had described as composed of "lodging-houses, shops, beer gardens, and studios," is a case in point. Where patrician members of the Washington Square Association saw signs of the neighborhood's decline, the young writer David Graham Phillips, who lived in a Washington Square South rooming house while writing his first novel, *The Great God Success* (1901), viewed the scene from his window in a very different way. Below him, he saw what he called the "panoramma of the human race." Visible on the south side of the square were "actresses, dancers, shop girls, cocottes, touts, thieves, confidence-men; artists and students from the musty University building, tramps and drunkards from the 'barrel-houses' and 'stale-beer shops;' and, across the square to the north, representatives of New York's oldest and most noted families." This juxtaposition of aspiration (and also failure) on one side and established wealth on the other appealed to Phillips and offered dramatic contrasts that he exploited in his fiction.[42]

Besides its dramatic possibilities, the south side of the square attracted young artists and writers like Phillips because rents were relatively low, inexpensive restaurants were near at hand, and a loosely knit artists' colony composed of men and women in their twenties and thirties existed among the residents of Washington Square South's boarding houses. In 1910, for instance, more than 60 percent of the lodgers in the best-known rooming houses (numbers 45, 60, and 61) were artists, illustrators, magazine writers, newspaper reporters, musicians, music teachers, or playwrights. In this setting, fact and fiction mirrored each other. David Graham Phillip's Howard of *The Great God Success*, like Neith Boyce (who had once lived on Washington Square South), was a journalist; Stephen F. Whitman's Felix Piers, the central figure in a melodramatic novel, *Predestined* (1910), was, like Phillips, a newspaper reporter hoping to become a novelist; and Willa Cather's Don Hedger in "Coming, Aphrodite!" (1920) represented another familiar Washington Square South type, the aspiring artist who supported himself as a magazine illustrator while trying to launch his career as a serious artist.[43]

Willa Cather moved into a small rooming house at 60 Washington Square South in 1906. She was nearly thirty-three years old, had published short stories and a book of poetry, and had come to the city to join the staff of a major monthly magazine, *McClure's*. The magazine's dynamic and sometimes irascible owner, S. S. McClure, had recently had a falling out with his senior editors and writers, four of whom, led by Lincoln Steffens, had resigned, leaving McClure in desperate need of new staff. He recruited Cather, whom he knew through her writing, and soon promoted her to the job of managing editor.

In the years that Cather served in that capacity, 1906–1911, the magazine business was undergoing a dramatic transformation. Just as entrepreneurs in nonprint entertainment businesses (theaters, movies, and dance halls) were reaching for a wider audience, so too were the publishers and editors of magazines. By lowering their cover prices to ten cents or even a nickel, capitalizing on advertising revenue available from huge consumer products companies that were seeking to promote their goods to an emerging national market, and using livelier graphics and photographs to attract general readers, magazines tapped what one scholar called "a vast new audience" of subscribers. Part of Cather's task as managing editor was to recruit authors, both established writers and neophytes, whose work would keep *McClure's*, known for its muckraking articles and quality fiction, competitive with folksier and visually more flashy journals such as *Collier's*.[44]

One of the novices Cather encouraged was Elizabeth Shepley Sergeant, a 1903 graduate of Bryn Mawr College who showed up at *McClure's* offices one day in January 1910. Cather—"youngish, buoyant, not tall, rather square"—met Sergeant in an outer office and led her to her private office.

There she began to scan Sergeant's manuscript, a piece of investigatory journalism on sweatshop conditions in New York City tenement districts. Cather soon said she liked the objective tone of the piece, but then demanded to know why Sergeant was drawn to exposé journalism rather than to short story writing. Sergeant protested that the social wrongs she wrote about were too terrible to be ignored.

An example of the type of situation Sergeant had in mind was the story of the Rapallos, an Italian family of nine, who lived in a three-room apartment on Macdougal Street in the south Village. Mr. Rapallo had been out of work for two years, so Mrs. Rapallo and the five oldest children eked out a marginal existence by earning $4.50 a week making artificial flowers for hat decorations and corsages. (73 percent of the work in this large American industry was done in Italian sections of the Village and the Lower East Side.) Sergeant had heard through a mutual acquaintance that Cather, while on a visit to Italy, had admired Italian women "sitting in the sun, by the fountain in Naples, brushing their long black hair," and she reminded Cather of this, pointing out that the same women, once they immigrated to New York, had to work themselves nearly to death in "vile, dark tenements below Washington Square." According to Sergeant, "Miss Cather brooded and rather gruffly replied that she knew the Italian children, because they splashed in the fountain in Washington Square of a summer evening when she often sat on a bench with a book. She lived in Washington Place, right up against the Italian Quarter I was talking about, and she loved the big brown eyes, dark smooth skins and Latin voices of the youngsters." Sergeant's essay became the lead article in *McClure's* July 1910 issue, complete with a photograph of Mrs. Rappolo and three of her children making artificial flowers.[45]

Cather remained a Villager for more than three decades. In September 1908, she and her friend Edith Lewis rented an apartment at 82 Washington Place. While still living at that address, Cather, in 1910–1911, reached a turning point in her career. Growing restive with editorial work that distracted her from her own creative development, she took a leave of absence from the magazine. Remembering the advice "to find your own quiet centre of life, and write from that" given her some two years before by the writer Sarah Orne Jewett, Cather discovered her own original voice and began her brilliant exploration of midwestern themes, the first of which was a long short story called "The Bohemian Girl," published in *McClure's* in 1912. About a year later, she and Lewis moved to yet another Village address, 5 Bank Street, where they remained until 1927. Though all of Cather's greatest books—*O Pioneers!*, *My Ántonia*, *The Professor's House*, and *Death Comes for the Archbishop*—were written during the years that she lived in the Village, their subjects were definitely not of it. Only one short story, "Coming, Aphrodite!," published in 1920 as the lead piece in *Youth and the Bright Medusa*, used a Village setting, the Washington Square South house where she roomed from 1906 to 1908.[46]

This finely wrought story operates on several levels. It is a superb description of the physical setting: the seedy, cramped house whose inhabitants live in an atmosphere of forced intimacy, sharing sounds, smells, and the common bath, for which they must stand in line outside the door in their dressing gowns waiting for their turn to come. Then, in what is surely the most erotic passage in all of Cather's work, there is the scene of the artist-illustrator, Don Hedger, watching through a keyhole as his new neighbor, Eden Bower, a beautiful singer, does her exercises in the nude. Fictional though this incident is, it conveys how social relations among the single men and women who lived in the rooming houses of Washington Square South inevitably had sexual undertones, if not overtones. Finally, as Hedger and Bower become friends and lovers, the focus is not so much on a love story but on the debate that arises between them over what an artist should value most: artistic integrity, to which Hedger is committed, or celebrity and commercial success, which Eden Bower seeks.

Integrity or popularity: the subject was a perennial one where artists gathered; only the places where they gathered changed. In 1900 two of the most popular artists' hangouts had been the Black Cat on Bleecker and Maria's at its second site, West Twelfth Street. By 1907, however, Maria Daprato had moved her hotel and restaurant again, this time out of the Village altogether, and the original Black Cat had closed. For artists and writers wanting a cheap meal, Mama Bertolotti's on West Third Street under the elevated line offered a "Fifteen Cent Lunch." Those who could afford a classier though still modestly priced Italian place had a variety of choices, one being Renganeschi's at 139 West Tenth Street. According to one man who dined there in 1907, "For forty cents you get the most complete dinner, with wine, that can be found in the city" (fig. 30).[47]

The artist John Sloan made several visits to Renganeschi's in 1909 and 1910. On one of those occasions he was joined by his distinguished artist friend Robert Henri and Henri's second wife, Marjorie Organ. She was a native of Ireland whose parents had brought their family to New York in 1899. The Organs had lived on Waverly Place, and Marjorie had attended St. Joseph's School on Washington Square, but in subsequent years the Organs had moved out of Greenwich Village. These small changes—an Irish family moving out of the neighborhood and an Italian restaurant, Renganischi's, opening for business just around the corner from that family's old home—reflected the larger demographic trends that would soon bring an

30. A forty-cent table d'hôte restaurant. The drawing's caption has the man in the right foreground whispering to his companion: "The food is bad, but there's brains here—BRAINS." From *New York World*, November 15, 1913.

end to Irish dominance in a part of the west Village that had once been an Irish preserve.[48]

Another artists' rendezvous in the Village was Gonfarone's, which, according to one chronicler of bohemian life "rose into prominence at the corner of Eighth and Macdougal Streets as a resort of scribes, artists, cranks, and lovers" after Maria's moved farther uptown. Here Stephen F. Whitman's fictional hero Felix sat, watching "the patrons round him, their feet twisted behind chair-legs, their elbows on the table, all arguing with gesticulations. Sometimes, there floated to him such phrases as: 'bad color scheme!' 'sophomoric treatment!' 'miserable drawing!' ' no atmosphere!' "[49]

Gonfarone's was a restaurant with an attached hotel, whose original owner was a widow named Caterina Gonfarone. She had recently made her longtime manager, Anacleto Sermolino, a full partner in the ownership and operation of the place. About the time she did so, in 1906 or 1907, the Committee of Fourteen had begun its inspections of all hotels. But Gonfarone's, which investigators described as a "legitimate hotel," never gave the committee cause for concern.[50]

Anacleto Sermolino's daughter Maria later recalled that "Madama" Gonfarone's started out as a tiny basement restaurant that initially attracted only Italians, and that even these customers were exclusively northern Italians like Madama and the Sermolino family. The energetic Anacleto soon talked Madama into moving the dining room upstairs, getting a liquor license, and expanding into several small neighboring houses on MacDougal and Eighth. Even though Madama worried about having to borrow money to pay for this expansion plan, Papa Sermolino (as Anacleto was called) made it work out. He pampered his customers, offered seven-course meals for fifty to sixty cents ("including a pint of California red wine; imported wine was ten cents extra"), and hired trios of musicians, at least one of whom had to be a singer, to provide music. "They were short on Beethoven and Bach," his daughter Maria remembered, "but long on Bellini, Rossini, Verdi and Puccini." Soon Gonfarone's was attracting a larger clientele, most of them non-Italians, many of them artists and writers who enjoyed the good food and the Old World ambience.[51]

Several sources of artist patrons were close at hand. Washington Square South was barely three blocks away, and diagonally across the street from Gonfarone's corner location was MacDougal Alley, a narrow, block-long lane behind the mansions on Washington Square North. Since the late 1880s the alleyway's low-lying buildings, which had once been stables and carriage houses for the elite's horses, carriages, and servants, had gradually been converted into studios and workshops for artists, most of whom were sculptors. A spirit of friendly collegiality prevailed within the MacDougal Alley artists' enclave, with well-established individuals encouraging the lesser-knowns. Chief among the alley's luminaries in 1910 was Daniel Chester French, a prolific sculptor whose numerous commissioned works included the Minute Man Memorial at Concord, Massachusetts, and the seated figure of Abraham Lincoln in the Lincoln Memorial in Washington, D.C. Toward the other end of the alley was the studio of James Earl Fraser, an artist and sculptor best known for *The End of the Trail* (1894), his statue of a weary mounted Native American warrior. Among the other artists in the MacDougal Alley colony was Gertrude Vanderbilt Whitney, a sometime student of Fraser's, who opened a studio there in 1907.[52]

In addition to being an aspiring sculptor, Whitney was an extremely well-to-do socialite who had inherited a fortune from her Vanderbilt connections and had further enhanced her wealth through marriage to Harry Payne Whitney, a financier and sportsman. Whitney's decision to establish a studio at 19 MacDougal Alley was prompted in part by a marital crisis. She had married Harry in 1896 in what—for her—had been a love match, and she was distraught when within only a few years he began having affairs with other women. Unfulfilled by her roles as a society matron and mother, Whitney in 1900 set out in earnest to become a sculptor. Over the next few years, as Harry's interests and amusements—raising and racing thoroughbreds, playing polo, yachting, and hunting—diverged ever more sharply from hers, she became increasingly determined to make something of herself independently of him and of the social roles expected of her. As she wrote in her journal in 1904, "I cannot be the sort of person which my life demands me to be—so why not try and be my own self." At this point she also recognized that her money and social position, far from hindering her in what she wanted to do, could enable her both to support herself as an artist and to have an influence as a patron of the arts.[53]

Whitney already had several connections with Greenwich Village, and these played a role in her decision to set up a studio there. Since 1903 she had served on Greenwich House's board of trustees, and for many years she not only gave Simkhovitch's settlement monetary gifts as large as or larger than those from any other benefactor, but assisted Greenwich House's programs by teaching art classes to the neighborhood children. Whitney also had ties with all three of the most important circles of Village artists—those connected with the Tenth Street Studio, MacDougal Alley, and the group known as The Eight.[54]

The Tenth Street Studio, located just east of Sixth Avenue on the side street whose name it bore, was a venerable institution that dated back to the mid–nineteenth century. It had been built and endowed by Emily Johnston de Forest's father and grandfather. Once the workplace of such distinguished tenants as Albert Bierstadt, Winslow Homer, and Augustus Saint-Gaudens, its last illustrious occupant was John La Farge, who died in 1910. Many years earlier, in 1898, Whitney had visited La Farge at his north Village studio and had come away deeply impressed both by the man and by the spare functionality of his workplace.[55]

Her connection with the MacDougal Alley circle also went back quite a few years. Not long after her visit with La Farge, she began to correspond with Daniel Chester French. She studied with James Earle Fraser and Andrew O'Connor, both of whom were sculptors with close ties to the Mac-Dougal Alley group. Her decision to become a neighbor of the MacDougal Alley artists was a natural outgrowth of these earlier relationships.

The third circle of Village artists with which Whitney soon developed ties were painters who were known collectively as The Eight. They acquired the name in 1907 as the result of a controversy that pitted the distinguished painter Robert Henri and his students against the conservative coterie that led the National Academy of Design, an organization whose exhibitions were considered the principal arbiter of artistic taste in New York City. Rejecting the emphasis on the pretty, uplifting, and often upper-class subject matter favored by traditionalists in the National Academy, Henri and his students chose to represent the grittier realities of daily life among ordinary city dwellers. Similarly, in matters of style, instead of the sharply defined lines and figures typical of the Academy's dominant faction, The Eight preferred briskly applied, more spontaneous brush strokes that they felt were more suitable for depicting the fast pace of life in a metropolis where continuous activity was the rule.[56]

Henri and his students had long felt that the Academy's traditionalists promoted orthodoxy and mediocrity rather than diversity and innovation, and when the jury selecting items for the Academy's spring 1907 show rejected paintings submitted by several of Henri's students and gave Henri's entries less than unanimous approval, the rivalry between the two factions became a matter for press comment. "The academy," Henri told a reporter, "rejects good work right and left and the result is that the exhibitions are dull. . . . There are many, many good painters in the country whose work is never seen on this account."[57]

Unwilling to take what he viewed as a slight to himself and his students, Henri joined seven members of his circle in organizing their own exhibit, which opened at the Macbeth Galleries on Fifth Avenue in February 1908. The insurgents, dubbed "The Eight" in press accounts, included two Villagers, William Glackens and Everett Shinn, and three Villagers-to-be, John Sloan, Ernest Lawson, and Maurice Prendergast. Sensational press reports—"New York's Art War and the Eight 'Rebels,'" and "8 Artists Secede from the Academy"—provided good publicity for the Macbeth Galleries show, although references to "war" and "secession" greatly overstated the magnitude of the break being made by Henri and his allies. Even as they sought ways to show their work independently of the Academy, most of The Eight also continued to submit paintings for the Academy's exhibits.[58]

As these events were unfolding, Gertrude Vanderbilt Whitney was asserting herself ever more confidently as an art patron and a sculptor. In

April 1907 she organized an art exhibition at the Colony Club, an exclusive social club founded in 1903 for wealthy New York women. In an era when American art was not greatly admired by the city's elite, it was striking to note that about a third of the pieces shown were by contemporary American painters with ties to the insurgents within the National Academy of Design. That this was no accident was confirmed in February 1908, when she bought four paintings—one each by Robert Henri, Ernest Lawson, George Luks, and Everett Shinn—during the Macbeth Galleries exhibit. In so doing Whitney was making a dramatic statement about herself and her view of contemporary art. To paraphrase an astute scholar's interpretation of Whitney's purchases, they were evidence of how she was distancing herself from the conventions of her upper-class New York circle and identifying herself with the more iconoclastic artists of MacDougal Alley and the Village.[59]

Two of The Eight were Villagers in 1908: William Glackens, who maintained a studio on Washington Square, and Everett Shinn, who had his home and studio west of the square at 112 Waverly Place. Three more of the insurgents—Ernest Lawson, John Sloan, and Maurice Prendergast—moved to the Village (and stayed for longer or shorter periods) over the next few years. Although great differences in temperament, politics, and even artistic style were evident among these five men and the rest of The Eight, they shared an appreciation of city life and in particular of life in New York City. All had migrated to New York City from somewhere else, most of them from Philadelphia, a move Glackens and George Luks made in 1896, Shinn in 1897, Henri in 1900, and Sloan in 1904. (Sloan had also spent the summer of 1897 in the city.) In every case their decision to move to New York reflected their ambition to make their mark in a burgeoning metropolis that was surpassing its American rivals—Boston, Philadelphia, and Chicago—and becoming a world-class city and the nation's unquestioned cultural capital. Simply put, New York had the tallest buildings, the largest population, the most new immigrants, and the most magazines and art galleries in the country.

Each of The Eight appreciated this urban environment and consciously pursued an esthetic that embraced city life in all its varieties. From the various studios he occupied on Washington Square, first at number 3 on the north side and later at number 50 on the south, William Glackens observed the passing parade of life and incorporated it into his art. Although many of his paintings, particularly portraits of friends and family, did not directly reflect the surrounding urban milieu, several important paintings and nearly all the illustrations he did for *Collier's* had city scenes as their subjects. Ordinary citizens are shown engaged in commonplace activities: shopping, playing, or just taking a stroll.

Implicit in Glackens's presentation of these images of daily life is his interpretation of them as positive expressions of the human spirit—an interpretation definitely not shared by his near neighbors, the patrician members of the Washington Square Association. Around the same time that the association was waging war on street vendors and pushcart merchants (1908–1911) and campaigning for orderly public behavior in Washington Square (1910–1912), Glackens was producing cover pictures for *Collier's* that presented in an amiable, indulgent spirit the behaviors that the Village gentry deplored and decried (fig. 31). *Patriots in the Making* (1907) shows a rowdy Fourth of July celebration in a working-class neighborhood; in *A Football Game* (1911) the neighborhood boys are turning a vacant lot into a dust bowl; and *Washington Square* (1913) depicts urchins, both boys and girls, roughhousing—throwing snowballs, fighting, and playing pranks—on the south side of the patricians' beloved park.[60]

John Sloan, though more radical than Glackens politically, shared his friend's interest in urban life. One of Sloan's favorite pastimes was roaming the city's streets in search of subject matter. His rambles often took him into the Village, which was barely half a mile from the West Twenty-third Street apartment he and his wife, Dolly, occupied until 1911. (They moved to East Twenty-second in 1911 and in 1912 to the Village, where he established his studio at 35 Sixth Avenue and they made their home at 61 Perry Street.) What caught his eye were images of the ebb and flow of daily life. The era's popular amusements are represented in *Carmine Theatre* (1912), a small movie house near his Sixth Avenue studio, and *Movies* (1913), a nighttime scene outside a similar neighborhood theater at night, where potential patrons are shown considering whether they want to see that evening's offering, *A Romance of the Harem*. In *Renganeschi's Saturday Night* (1912) Sloan depicts a restaurant scene of nicely dressed diners, with a tuxedoed waiter about to attend to a party of three young women, the central figure of which is a pretty blonde whose posture and animation suggest that she and her friends are shopgirls excitedly enjoying a night out. In his etching *Hell Hole* (1917) Sloan immortalized Tom Wallace's Golden Swan, one of those Sixth Avenue saloons that so troubled the Committee of Fourteen's investigators.[61]

As it happened, the Golden Swan was one of the Village dives that the Hudson Dusters patronized. Various Village artists and writers—Djuna Barnes, Dorothy Day, Charles Demuth, and Eugene O'Neill, most of them migrants to the Village during its post–1912 bohemian era—also frequented the saloon. They went there, in part, to rub shoulders with the gangsters and other "lowlife" types who were among its habitués. Unlike the moral reformers who viewed the criminal element with revulsion, the neighborhood's artists approached the Hell Hole scene with undisguised

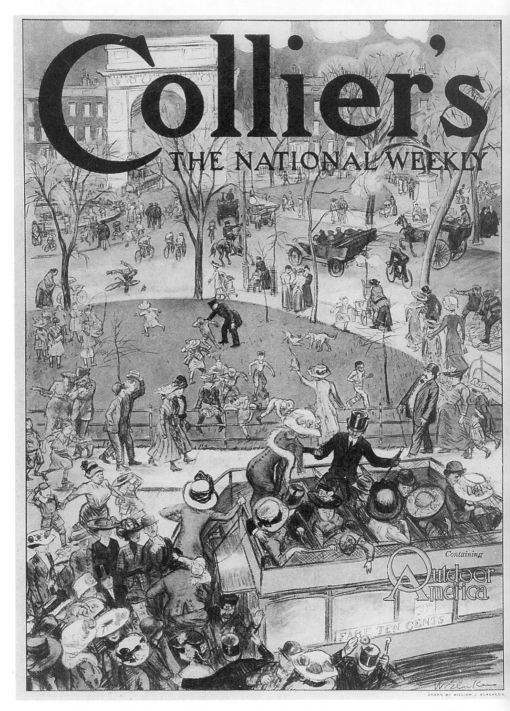

31. *A Spring Morning in Washington Square, New York*, an example of how William J. Glackens converted the view from his studio window into a magazine illustration. From *Collier's*, April 16, 1910.

interest. "Girl-painters and girl-writers," Albert Parry wrote in his *Garrets and Pretenders* (1933), "avid for local color, were unafraid to go to [the] Hell Hole and make friends with the toughs."[62]

One reason that Sloan and Glackens (and Shinn and Lawson as well) were successful interpreters of early twentieth-century city life is that they were not just observers but also participants. The most extensive evidence of their activities comes from a diary that John Sloan kept between 1906 and 1913. Entry after entry documents his enthusiastic pursuit of virtually every available kind of public entertainment. (Dancing was an exception.) He attended performances at the city's most popular vaudeville theaters, opera at Hammerstein's, a Wild West show at Madison Square Garden, baseball games between top-flight teams of black players, automobile races, and motion pictures of every type, both high and low quality. On one of several outings to Coney Island's amusement parks, he went on rides and, though he had never learned to dance well, he had fun watching the assembled crowds at a concert hall doing the "Stomach Dance," one of the latest fads.[63]

Masquerade dances were also the rage in 1910, and Glackens, who was more playful than Sloan, did his share of dancing at the costume balls sponsored by the Kit Kat Klub, an organization for magazine illustrators. Like Sloan, Glackens visited Coney Island and enjoyed the sights and sounds of ordinary New Yorkers at play. Occasionally, Glackens and his wife, Edith, along with several artist friends, got together at Everett and Florence Shinn's Village apartment and amused themselves by staging silly skits. For about a year in 1911–1912 this purely amateur activity took on semiprofessional status when Shinn named the group the Waverly Place Players and offered public performances at a small theater he built in back of his studio. The plays, with titles such as "Ethel Clayton, or Wronged from the Start," were parodies of old-fashioned melodramas and had much in common with a popular entertainment style of the time, the comedy acts offered by the city's cheap vaudeville theaters.[64]

Villagers in The Eight regularly dined with friends in a West Side commercial entertainment zone where streetwalkers plied their trade. During 1910 and 1911 the artists particularly favored two sites for their rendezvous: Mouquin's, a modestly priced French restaurant on West Twenty-eighth Street near Sixth Avenue, and Petitpas', a small bistro and boardinghouse run by three French sisters on West Twenty-ninth Street. Both places were less than a mile north of the Village in the so-called Tenderloin district that the Committee of Fourteen denounced as one of the worst vice zones in the city. Indeed, the Haymarket, a concert saloon widely regarded as a citadel of vice and a gathering place for prostitutes and gangsters, stood at West

Twenty-ninth Street and Sixth Avenue, barely a block from the artists' favorite haunts.

Sloan used scenes related to the city's illicit pleasures in his art and rendered them without placing a negative judgment on those who participated in them. His painting *The Haymarket* (1907) evokes both the allure of the dance hall and the response of respectable people, working-class and middle-class alike. Three women in elaborate white dresses, possibly prostitutes, are about to enter the dance hall, the promise of pleasure within suggested by the hall's glowing interior that can be glimpsed through the doorway; among the onlookers is a mother who is frowning at her daughter because the youngster is gazing back at the Haymarket's entrance with a look of curiosity and wonder. In his only Greenwich Village picture that touched a related subject, *The Women's Night Court: Before Her Makers and Her Judge* (1913), Sloan inverted the moral scheme to which the Committee of Fourteen and like-minded respectables adhered. He portrayed the individual being arraigned at Jefferson Market Court as a sweet-looking young woman in white surrounded by a group of men—a judge, two bailiffs, a court recorder, and others—whose hard eyes and hard-heartedness, suggested by their frowns and dark attire, contrast with her winsome softness (fig. 32).[65]

Sloan's interpretation of certain subjects, including *Night Court*, was influenced by a growing commitment to socialism that dated from 1908. In 1909 he began drawing political cartoons for the *New York Call*, a Socialist daily. The following year he and his wife, Dolly, joined the Socialist Party, and Sloan even made a token run for the New York State Assembly on the Socialist ticket. One of his drawings also appeared in the second issue of *The Masses*, a New York–based Socialist monthly magazine that commenced publishing in January 1911, but his primary commitment in this period remained to *The Call*, which had a large circulation among working-class radicals on the Lower East Side. *In Memoriam*, a front page illustration done in response to the Triangle fire of March 1911, was a powerful political statement, juxtaposing a skeletal figure of Death and a silk-hatted capitalist beside a black triangle labeled "Profit," "Rent," and "Interest," inside of which lay the burned body of a young woman worker (fig. 33).[66]

In actively supporting the Socialist Party and its publications, Sloan moved away from the political views held by most of The Eight and closer to the left-leaning Villagers who had founded the A Club cooperative housing association and writers' colony in 1906. After Sloan joined the party in 1910, the names of A Clubbers—Robert and Martha Bruère, Arthur Bullard, and Ernest Poole, all of whom were also party members—began appearing in Sloan's diary with some regularity. Just as Glackens and Sloan capitalized on the magazine revolution by doing illustrations for mass cir-

32. John Sloan's *The Women's Night Court: Before Her Makers and Her Judge*, illustration for *The Masses*, August 1913. Crayon on paper, 1913. Collection of the Whitney Museum of American Art, Purchase 36.38.

culation journals, the writers from the A Club circle found in the new magazine era a ready market for their manuscripts. Collectively, in a three-year period (1910–1912), the A Clubbers mentioned above and three other A Club veterans, Leroy and Miriam Finn Scott and Mary Heaton Vorse, produced seven books and 115 essays or stories in major magazines.[67]

Mary Heaton Vorse, the most prolific of all the A Club writers, returned to the Village in the fall of 1910 after a nine months' absence. Newly widowed, she rented rooms for herself, her two young children, and her aged father at 88 Grove Street. Never a joiner, she did not become a Socialist, but she shared the socially progressive, feminist views to which her A Club friends subscribed. Moreover, widowhood and the need to be the sole breadwinner for her family had helped her clarify her thinking about the place of women in American society.

Scarcely had Vorse settled at her new Village address than she learned about a public health crisis that touched her heart deeply. Most milk distributed in New York City in 1910 was tainted, unpasteurized, handled in unsanitary ways, and often watered down to increase volume and thus the

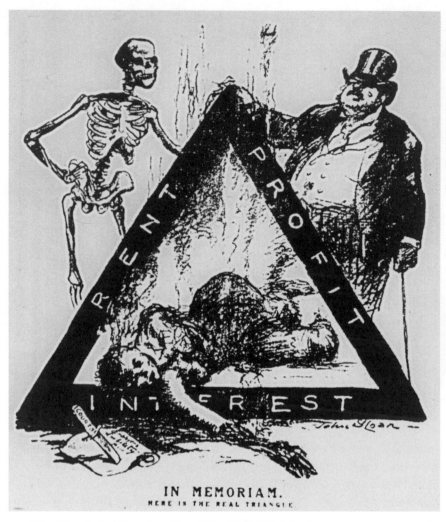

33. John Sloan's *In Memoriam*. From *New York Call*, March 27, 1911.

income of farmers paid by bulk weight. As a consequence, infant mortality rates were extremely high in the city, and fatalities traceable to impure milk always rose during the summer when poor-quality milk spoiled especially fast. Since 1892, Nathan Straus, a New York philanthropist, had funded milk stations throughout the city at which poor mothers could get milk free. He also advocated laws to require pasteurization and toured widely in the United States and Europe to promote that cause. But early in 1910, tired of being subjected to criticism that questioned his methods and his motives, Straus announced he was going to close his New York City milk stations at the end of that summer.

At this point Mrs. J. Borden Harriman, president of the Colony Club, stepped into the breach, proposing to establish a New York Milk Committee to run an expanded system of milk depots throughout the city. District leaders would be found to help organize branch milk stations in every neighborhood. In Greenwich Village the existing milk distribution depot was on MacDougal Street, and Vorse volunteered to be the Milk Committee's chairman for the district. She had previously investigated the impact of poverty on infant mortality rates in western Europe and had written that a "society that allowed children to die because their parents didn't make enough money seemed senseless and vicious." But she also took the issue personally; as a single mother she found it frightening to think of what might happen to her children if she couldn't support them adequately. "I was the sole support of my children," she wrote. "I saw myself poor and my own wanted and beloved children dying because I couldn't make enough money." With help from her old friend Mary Simkhovitch of Greenwich House, Vorse succeeded in keeping the local depot operating. Much to Vorse's satisfaction, a substantial drop in the city's infant mortality rate occurred in the years immediately after the new program was initiated.[68]

Vorse took an interest in every aspect of the Village and didn't mind living close to its Sixth Avenue vice zone. Luke O'Connor's Greenwich Avenue Raines Law hotel and saloon, whose unaccompanied female patrons so troubled the Committee of Fourteen's investigators, was located barely two blocks from Vorse's Grove Street apartment. One day a friend made a passing reference to the place, and Vorse jokingly replied: "You mean the Working Girl's Home?" The name stuck, becoming a part of Greenwich Village lore in her generation.[69]

In doing research for a magazine article titled "Picture Show Audiences" (1911), Vorse went to Lower East Side, Bowery, and Greenwich Village movie theaters (fig. 34). She conducted her Village investigation at a movie house that was located in the Village's Italian quarter near Bleecker Street and Our Lady of Pompei Church. Vorse was impressed with the friendly informality of the moviegoers, especially of several Italian mothers with their children who, upon learning that Vorse also had children, quizzed her on why she had not brought them along. The featured film was a melodrama about a cowboy who became a thief to provide for his dying wife, a plot that stimulated a noisy debate among those present about whether the cowboy's crimes were simply immoral or justified by his love for his wife. But to close the Village segment of her article, Vorse chose to describe one viewer's more private response, the reaction of a young innocent, "an eager

34. *Movies* by John Sloan, 1913. The Toledo Museum of Art, Museum Purchase Fund, 1940.16.

little girl of ten or eleven," for whom the images unfolding on the screen were so entrancing that she was literally spellbound: she "couldn't laugh, couldn't clap her hands with the others."[70]

Another Village story from about this time connects Vorse and her A Club friends to another of the era's allurements, the new dance styles of the 1910s. In 1910, Bobby Edwards, a musician newly arrived in the Village, convinced owner Paul Paglieri of Paglieri's restaurant on West Eleventh Street to sponsor after-dinner dances. When diners had finished eating, the floor would be cleared of tables and chairs, and the music would begin. According to one oft-told tale, A Clubbers—among whom Vorse, Arthur Bullard, and Leroy Scott were mentioned specifically—were the core group of a "merry crowd" of Tuesday night partygoers that danced the new dances and called themselves the "Crazy Cat Club."[71]

The Committee of Fourteen's early campaigns and The Eight's rebellion, like the history of Our Lady of Pompei, Little Africa, Greenwich House, Ascension Forum, A Club, the Washington Square Association, and the Women's Trade Union League prior to 1912, all belong to the latter days of the Sixth Village, the period immediately before Greenwich Village gained its reputation as America's bohemia. Of course, the years from 1898 to 1911 can be viewed both as the final phase of the Sixth Village and as a prelude to the Seventh. But before the thinking of individual Villagers and the public's perception of the neighborhood could be truly transformed, something more had to happen to trigger the change. For Mary Heaton Vorse that something, the event that gave her life a whole new dimension, was a huge strike by textile workers in Lawrence, Massachusetts.

In mid-January 1912, a spontaneous worker protest against wage cuts led to a walkout of more than twenty thousand Lawrence mill operatives, approximately half of whom were women and children. Having no significant prior ties with organized labor, the strikers in their hour of need accepted help from representatives of the Industrial Workers of the World (I.W.W.), a radical industrial union. Early in the strike the I.W.W.'s national leader, Big Bill Haywood, arrived in Lawrence to assist other I.W.W. organizers who were already on the scene. Some property damage had been done by workers during the strike's first few days, and this provided the pretext for the governor to send in the state militia. By then the strikers had adopted the tactic of nonviolent protest—picketing and massive street demonstrations—but the local police and the state militia responded harshly, and before the middle of February two workers had been killed, one shot, the other bayonetted.[72]

As these events unfolded, New York City social progressives, including many Villagers, became involved and organized parades, fundraisers, and public addresses in support of the Lawrence mill workers. When the strikers proposed to send some of their children out of town for the duration of the strike for their safety and to publicize their poverty, the workers' New York sympathizers welcomed the chance to help. On succeeding Sundays, February 10 and February 17, trains carrying more than a hundred children each arrived in Grand Central Station, where John Sloan's wife, Dolly, representing the Women's Committee of the Socialist Party, distributed food and warm clothing to the youngsters. Offers to house the Lawrence children were screened with an eye to placing as many as possible with working-class families and members of the Socialist Party. At least four Villagers—Inez Milholland, Percy Stickney Grant, Anne O'Hagan Shinn, and Martha B. Bruère—volunteered. Milholland and Grant were turned down as being too rich; what decisions were made on Shinn's and Bruère's offers is unknown.[73]

Another group of children, scheduled to leave Lawrence for Philadelphia on February 24, was prevented from departing by state militiamen, who handled the crowd of waiting mothers so roughly that two pregnant women had miscarriages. Shocked by this news, Mary Heaton Vorse and another Villager, Joe O'Brien (a Socialist and feminist who would soon become her husband), traveled to Lawrence together to see for themselves what was happening. At least two other Villagers, Ernest Poole and Lincoln Steffens, also made the pilgrimage to Lawrence.

The Villagers came away impressed by Haywood and his I.W.W. co-workers and inspired by the joyful spirit of the strikers, who sang almost constantly as they marched and picketed. The fact that women had played an increasingly large role in street demonstrations—the theory being that police and militia would hesitate to attack them for fear of attracting more negative press attention—was also cause for admiring comment among sympathetic Villagers. Two months into the strike, the mill owners, unable to recruit enough strikebreakers to keep the mills running at capacity and faced with a torrent of public outrage because of the mistreatment strikers had endured, finally capitulated and offered the workers a pay increase and time-and-a-quarter pay for overtime. On March 14, 1912, tens of thousands of Lawrence workers gathered and voted to accept the mill owners' offer. Then, as was often done at labor meetings in the period, the assembled throng joined in singing "The Internationale," a revolutionary Socialist anthem dating from the late nineteenth century.

Pro-labor Villagers were deeply affected by this chain of events. Mary Heaton Vorse recalled feeling that she had witnessed a battle between "the forces of Light and of Darkness," and the forces of light had won. This result was an eye-opener for Vorse and other socially progressive Villagers. If a group of previously unorganized workers, who had exceedingly diverse ethnic origins and whose ranks included many women and children, could defy and defeat the combined economic and political power of the mill owners, state and local officials, and many local small businessmen and religious leaders, then perhaps the first serious cracks had appeared in the old system. If so, then perhaps the looked-for transformation of American society would come sooner rather than later, and the time would quickly arrive when, as a line from "The Internationale" promised, "The earth shall rise on new foundations."[74]

6

Becoming Bohemia

Bᴇᴛᴡᴇᴇɴ 1914 ᴀɴᴅ 1916 several national magazines identified Greenwich Village as the "American Bohemia" and the "New World Latin Quarter." It had not always been so. The original meeting place for New York bohemians was Pfaff's, a German beer garden where Walt Whitman had held court in the late 1850s, and though its location on Broadway just north of Bleecker Street was not far from the Village, it was part of a Broadway–Bowery scene rather than within the Village orbit. Later on, in the 1890s and early 1900s, New York bohemians disagreed about which bistro or neighborhood truly represented bohemia. The Village had its adherents, notably Robert W. Chambers, a painter-illustrator who wrote about Maria's in *In the Quarter* (1894), and James L. Ford, the journalist whose *Bohemia Invaded* (1895) was set in a classic bohemian gathering place just south of Washington Square. But James L. Huneker, the art and music critic to whose circle Bert and Mary Heaton Vorse once belonged, and William Sidney Porter, the writer better known as O. Henry, both slighted the Village. Huneker and Porter sometimes met at West Side cafes outside the Village, usually at The Eight's favorite French restaurant, Mouquin's, but Huneker's primary loyalty was always to Lüchow's, a German restaurant at East Fourteenth Street and Irving Place, and O. Henry's preferred bohemian hangouts were even farther north on the East Side near Madison Square and Twenty-sixth Street.[1]

The geographically dispersed nature of early twentieth-century bohemianism was well documented in July 1907 when *The Bohemian* magazine published Charles F. Peters's article "When New York Dines A La Bohe'me." Although Peters mentioned a number of Village restaurants—Renganeschi's, Gonfarone's, and six small Italian places on or near Bleecker Street in the south Village, only a small portion of his article dealt with Village sites; fully three-quarters of the text was devoted to describing French, Italian, Hungarian, German, and even North African and Near Eastern bohemian places scattered through the city outside the Village's boundaries.[2]

Adding to the difficulty of defining the precise geography of New York bohemianism was the imprecision with which the words *bohemian* and *bohemia* were commonly used at the turn of the twentieth century. In his article Peters ventured no definition beyond saying that the bohemian was the "artist of life and the fool of trade." This contrast between a bourgeois class devoted to trade and moneymaking and bohemians who devoted themselves to art and life was a generally accepted starting point for describing the bohemian as a social type. Almost any kind of unconventional behavior—disregard for wealth and social status, smoking by women in public, informality in clothing, looser sexual mores—was regarded as a sign of incipient or actual bohemianism. That bohemian hangouts often had a European flavor—French, German, Italian, Hungarian, and the rest—was a reflection of the bohemian's affection for European culture, especially for Paris, home to the original Latin Quarter and Montmartre. Certain occupations related to the arts—writing, poetry, painting, sculpting, acting, and journalism—were also generally viewed as characteristically bohemian. However, even more important than one's devotion to the arts was the spirit with which one lived. A true bohemian was assumed in popular lore to be a free spirit: playful, expressive, spontaneous, unconventional, and individualistic. That inattention to practical matters of money and status might make one poor contributed to the stereotype of bohemians as starving artists.

Ironically, although Greenwich Village became widely identified as America's bohemia in the mid-1910s, many members of the founding generation, the group of artists and writers whose activities drew attention to the Village as a bohemian enclave, refused to apply the word *bohemian* to themselves. Mary Heaton Vorse, her A Club friends, and John Sloan, a leading figure in The Eight group, all explicitly rejected the term because it implied a dilettantism or lack of seriousness about art and life. Nevertheless, the bohemian label stuck because the founders of the Seventh Village, whether or not they were self-identified bohemians, fit popular preconceptions of what a bohemian should be. They had the right occupations, admired European culture, were interested in new and unorthodox ideas, and could be found drinking and dining at New York City's bohemian cafes and restaurants.[3]

The Seventh Village began to take form in late 1912, and 1913 was its first full year as a distinct phenomenon. So swift was its rise that by early 1915 the Village, which only three years earlier had usually been portrayed in the public press in its Sixth Village guise as a mixed-class, mixed-ethnic neighborhood, was with increasing frequency being described as a bohemian republic or city-state. Still, the transformation of the neighborhood into the Seventh or Bohemian Village, though it happened very quickly, was not all of a piece. The first or founding phase, 1912–1916, was a period of intense intellectual and artistic creativity led by a small group of Villagers connected with *The Masses*, Mabel Dodge's salon, the Liberal Club, and the Provincetown Players. But this in-group, "our crowd" phase of Seventh Village history did not last long. Even before the founders' cohesion and intensity began to diminish in 1916, the publicity their activities had generated led a larger group of newcomers to migrate to the Village. Some of the newcomers came to emulate the Seventh Villagers, others to gawk at them, and more than a few to try to profit from marketing bohemianism to tourists and pretenders. It was this second phase of the Seventh Village's history, the selling-of-bohemia or "faux bohemia" period, that solidified the Village's popular reputation as a playground for unconventional spirits. By 1917, much to the dismay of the Seventh Village's founders, bohemianism for bohemianism's sake had triumphed over political and cultural substance within America's Montmartre.

THE SEVENTH VILLAGERS

Inspired by the conviction that the old order's hold over art and society was weakening, Village artists and writers began to explore fresh ways of bringing a new order into being. The mostly informal network of friendships that had characterized the Village artists' community before 1912 was now strengthened and extended through institutions run by the Seventh Village's founders: a revitalized journal, *The Masses*; a salon hosted by Mabel Dodge; two gathering places on MacDougal Street—the Liberal Club and Polly's Restaurant—where the core group met and socialized; annual costume balls for fun and fundraising; and a summer outpost in Provincetown that became the birthplace of the Provincetown Players. Since the Seventh Villagers and their varied activities have been the subject of dozens of biographies, histories, and analytical essays, only a brief description is needed here to delineate the timing and main features of this short-lived but potent attempt to transform American cultural and political life (map 5).[4]

The Seventh Village began to take shape in the fall of 1912 when *The Masses* was reorganized as a writers' and artists' collective. Founded in 1911 by Piet Vlag, an East Side Socialist and advocate of worker cooperatives, *The Masses* in its original phase had a narrow and orthodox editorial line and, except for artwork by John Sloan and Art Young, a drab appearance. The journal's poor public reception discouraged Vlag, and publication was suspended in August 1912. But John Sloan, Mary Heaton Vorse, and several other *Masses* writers and artists refused to let the magazine die altogether. They invited Max Eastman to become editor and put out a redesigned magazine starting in December.[5]

The revitalized *Masses* was the first joint project launched by the core group of artists and writers whose activities set the tone for the Seventh Village in its founding phase. Under Eastman *The Masses* was owned and run collectively by its contributing members. Their goals, as outlined in the early issues during the Eastman era, were to promote a cultural and political revolution and to do so in a lively, iconoclastic way. Editorial sessions with twenty or more participants in attendance, each with one vote, lasted for hours and occasionally bruised a writer's feelings, but the gatherings also generated a strong sense of camaraderie and common purpose among the Seventh Village's founders. An open, everything-is-possible spirit prevailed. Nominally a Socialist journal, *The Masses* featured an eclectic and often contradictory mix of viewpoints: Marxist, anarchist, feminist, Freudian, labor unionist, pagan, and bohemian. The journal's artists, led initially by John Sloan, were delighted to have an outlet for artwork that commercial magazines wouldn't touch—a subject pointedly addressed in December 1912 with a two-page illustration of a magazine editor prostituting his staff to the wishes of a bloated figure representing fat-cat advertisers. Some of the women's submissions—Helen Hoyt's poem about menstruation and Elizabeth Grieg's cartoon that sympathetically depicted an unwed mother—would have been impossible to place in more conventional magazines.[6]

Membership in the *Masses* collective was constantly augmented by new recruits. John Reed, the journalist and aspiring poet, and Mabel Dodge, a well-to-do woman looking for outlets for her considerable wealth and talents, were two such individuals who joined the *Masses* circle early in 1913. They almost immediately came to play major roles in three events—the Armory Show, the Paterson Strike Pageant, and the establishment of Dodge's Fifth Avenue salon—that greatly enhanced the reputation of the Seventh Villagers as movers and shakers.

Dodge returned to the United States in November 1912 after eight years

—Blackmer—

MAP 5. The Seventh Village, 1912–1918

1. Mabel Dodge's Salon ....23 Fifth Avenue
2. Provincetown Playhouse..................139 MacDougal Street
3. Liberal Club and Polly's ....137 MacDougal Street
4. Webster Hall....................................119 East Eleventh Street
5. Bruno's Garret..................................58 Washington Square South
6. Seventh Avenue Extension ....Greenwich Avenue to Varick Street
7. Sheridan Square
8. Hudson Park
9. Public School 95 ....Clarkson Street

in Florence, Italy. She rented the second-floor apartment in a mansion located at 23 Fifth Avenue and promptly redecorated the place in white. She
also persuaded her amiable husband, Edwin Dodge, to move out to rooms
at the Brevoort, the pleasant French hotel and artists' rendezvous only a
block away. Mabel was full of energy but initially she was without direction.
Although she had previously hosted a salon at her villa in Florence, it was
not until Lincoln Steffens suggested that her talent for bringing people
together for conversation made her ideally suited to host a salon in New
York that she decided to use her Fifth Avenue apartment for that purpose.
Hutch Hapgood, who shared her quasi-mystical, questing spirit, helped her
find interesting people to invite, and early in 1913 Dodge's "Evenings" got
under way.[7]

Her timing was perfect. Talk and more talk about new ideas and more
new ideas was the order of the day. As she wrote in retrospect, "it seems as
though everywhere, in that year of 1913, barriers went down and people
reached each other who had never been in touch before." So on Wednesday
evenings (or at other times on Thursdays) Dodge opened the rooms of her
Fifth Avenue apartment to a kaleidoscopic array of guests of every ideological hue—"Socialists, Trade-Unionists, Anarchists, Suffragists, Poets, Lawyers, Murderers, 'Old Friends,' Psychoanalysts, I.W.W.'s, Single Taxers,
Birth Controlists, Newspapermen, Artists, Modern-Artists, Clubwomen,
Woman's-place-is-in-the-home Women, Clergymen, and just plain men"
(fig. 35). At the height of their success, most of Dodge's Evenings were
organized around a topic or special guest, such as A. A. Brill on psychoanalysis, "Big Bill" Haywood on the I.W.W., Emma Goldman on anarchism, or
two blacks performing African American dances. Convinced that a radical
shift in consciousness was in progress, Dodge believed that bringing
cutting-edge thinkers and doers together would hasten the coming transformation.[8]

Several months before Dodge's Evenings entered their peak period in the
fall of 1913, she had become involved in two other activities that served
as defining events in the Seventh Village's first full year. The first of these,
the International Exhibition of Modern Art (better known as the Armory
Show) was not, strictly speaking, a Village event, although it is often treated
as such. The connection is made because the Armory Show reflected a spirit
of rebellion against traditional values, an interest in exploring new ideas,
and a desire to educate Americans regarding emerging cultural trends, all
of which were prominent features of the Seventh Village milieu.

Among the more particular links between the Village and the Armory
Show was the fact that its chief organizers, Arthur B. Davies (one of The
Eight) and Walter Kuhn, were Robert Henri's students; Davies in particular

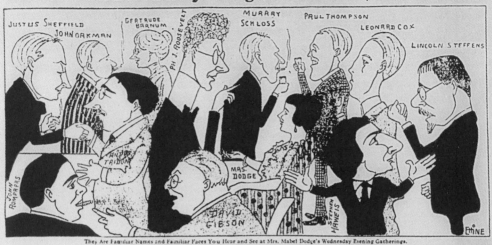

with Parlor Socialists and Others
At a Wednesday Night Soiree on Fifth

They Are Familiar Names and Familiar Faces You Hear and See at Mrs. Mabel Dodge's Wednesday Evening Gatherings.

35. A cartoonist's depiction of a Wednesday evening gathering at Mabel Dodge's Fifth Avenue salon. From *New York World*, March 29, 1914.

had learned a great deal about organizing an exhibition from The Eight's Macbeth Galleries venture in 1908 and the much larger Exhibition of Independent Artists in 1910. Moreover, Village sculptors and painters were well represented in the Armory Show's American section, and Mabel Dodge made a significant contribution to publicizing the exhibit in the month before it opened on February 17, 1913.

Unfortunately for the American progressives—a term that characterized The Eight and most of Henri's students—avant-garde European artists stole the Armory Show. Whether they were the objects of outrage or applause, it was the Cubists (George Braque and Pablo Picasso), the Fauvists (Henri Matisse, Georges Rouault, and Raoul Dufy), and Marcel Duchamp's "Nude Descending a Staircase" that, as Milton Brown has written, "shattered the even complacency of American art." By virtually every measure, the exhibition was a stunning success.[9]

The Armory Show had only recently closed (mid-March 1913) when another event, a massive strike in Paterson, New Jersey, captured the Seventh Villagers' imagination. The strike had begun in February, when approximately twenty-five thousand workers walked out of Paterson mills to protest changes in work rules. The walkout and the conditions in the mills, which accounted for nearly 60 percent of silk production in the United States, bore some resemblance to the situation in Lawrence in 1912. Once again, leading I.W.W. organizers Big Bill Haywood and Elizabeth Gurley Flynn joined the fray, counseling the strikers to hold firm against piecemeal settlements. But the strike went on, and by mid-April there was no sign that the mill owners would give in.

At this point a number of Villagers became deeply involved in the conflict. Despite their class and educational differences from the I.W.W. leadership, many Villagers were attracted to the Wobblies by their radical rhetoric and their affinity for the grand gesture. The one-eyed Haywood, veteran of many bitter labor struggles in the West, had already achieved folk hero status with Villagers who hoped that a decisive blow to the capitalist class system would be quickly followed by a new, democratic industrial order. Paterson looked enough like Lawrence, where the I.W.W. (with some help from its middle-class allies) had won a huge victory, that the Villagers were eager to help promote yet another working-class success.

The fact that Haywood had a mistress, Bea Shostak, a schoolteacher who lived in Greenwich Village, and that he frequented Dodge's salon contributed to the emergence of what became the Paterson Strike Pageant. One evening in late April, Mabel Dodge, Hutch Hapgood, John Reed, and others visited Haywood at Shostak's apartment near Washington Square. When Haywood complained that the Paterson strike was stalled because New York City newspapers were not giving much coverage to it, Dodge suggested producing a public pageant to raise funds and publicize the strikers' cause. John Reed volunteered to organize the pageant, and in mid-May Haywood presented the plan for the pageant to Paterson workers.

Three weeks of feverish work followed, with Reed rehearsing strikers in New Jersey while Mary Heaton Vorse, Mabel Dodge, Lincoln Steffens, Hutch Hapgood, and Jessie Ashley either raised funds or provided newspaper coverage. Reed's Harvard classmate Robert Edmond Jones designed a large stage set, and John Sloan organized its construction. Dozens of other Villagers contributed to the cause. On the scheduled day, Saturday, June 7, more than a thousand Paterson workers took the ferry from Hoboken to the Lackawana Pier in the Village, marched up Christopher Street and over to Fifth Avenue, and continued from there to the old Madison Square Garden on East Twenty-sixth Street, where they went through one last rehearsal. The site was resplendent in red—huge red banners in the hall, ushers wearing red bow ties or red hair ribbons, and red lights spelling out "I.W.W." on the Garden's celebrated tower, designed by Stanford White. The pageant itself was a triumph; the huge worker contingent enacted scenes from their strike and an overflow audience of perhaps fifteen thousand joined them in songs, jeered actors playing the police, and wept when the funeral of a slain worker was reenacted (fig. 36).

The aftermath was less happy. Heavy costs and too many free admissions produced losses rather than the hoped-for gains to finance the strike. In addition, the strike leadership, having underestimated the ability of Paterson mill owners to shift production to newer mills in Pennsylvania, was unable to force the owners to capitulate. Defeated, the strikers—those who weren't blacklisted—straggled back to work. Grand gestures such as Haywood's no-compromise strategy and the Villagers' pageant had failed to bring victory. Bitter recriminations followed; the I.W.W. firebrand Elizabeth Gurley Flynn charged that the pageant's failure financially had demoralized the strikers, causing them to lose heart and abandon their fight. The link between working-class and Village radicals, always at best, in one historian's words, a "fragile bridge," was damaged but not destroyed, as cooperation between the two groups during the unemployment crisis of 1913–1914 would prove.[10]

Despite the pageant's failure to produce a successful end to the Paterson strike, morale among Villagers in the the *Masses*-Dodge salon circle remained high. In the fall of 1913 they widened their group's social sphere beyond gatherings in homes, at editorial meetings, and at Dodge's salon by establishing two more hangouts where the *Masses* crowd and their friends socialized. The two new places, Polly's Restaurant and the rooms of a reorganized Liberal Club, shared the same MacDougal Street address, with Polly's occupying the basement and the Liberal Club just upstairs.

Polly's Restaurant was a joint project among three Village anarchists— Polly Holladay, her brother Louis Holladay, and Hippolyte Havel, Polly's sometime lover. Havel claimed to have come up with the idea for a Village bistro where radicals could eat together and talk revolution. Often cited as the purest example of the Seventh Villager type, Havel amazed and delighted his compatriots with his ability to be more outrageous than anyone else. He gained notoriety by addressing patrons of the restaurant as "bourgeois pigs," an insult that never failed to please those in search of authentic radical ambience. Havel served as cook and waiter, and Polly handled finances and flirted with customers. When discovered by the press in early 1914, the restaurant was still called simply "The Basement," but it went down in Village history as "Polly's," the first of several restaurants she was to run and, more important, the first of many Village bistros to be run by a self-identified bohemian owner for a bohemian crowd.[11]

The Liberal Club story is more complex. Founded about 1907, the club was a debating society for socially progressive New Yorkers. Although dur-

36. Paterson Strike Pageant poster, by Robert Edmond Jones. Tamiment Institute Library, New York University.

ing the 1910–1912 period its meetings were held in the Gramercy Park area, Villagers—Lincoln Steffens, Hutch Hapgood, and Percy Stickney Grant—played leading roles as officers or charter members. The club's monthly meetings followed a format in which a member or guest speaker presented a general proposition—in February 1910 Steffens took as his theme "there is good in good people," for example—and then defended the stated position against all challengers.[12]

In the summer of 1913, however, various internal conflicts led these kid-glove radicals to split irrevocably, a division that became public in September when the president, Reverend Percy Stickney Grant, resigned along with most of the other officers. The immediate cause seems to have been a controversy over sexual morality. One member, Henrietta Rodman, a city schoolteacher who had battled resourcefully with the city Board of Education over discrimination against married women teachers (especially those who became pregnant), secretly married a man who allegedly had a common-law wife. Rodman's campaign on behalf of teachers did not trouble moderate Liberal Club members. But they objected strenuously when it seemed that Rodman and her supporters (described in newspaper reports as "ultra-liberal" Greenwich Villagers, although several of them did not live in the Village) also expected the organization to take a tolerant attitude toward the practice of free love, the convention-defying lifestyle to which Rodman subscribed. Rodman's defenders said that club officials had no business condemning her on a matter of private morality, but divisions over this point proved irreconcilable, and the Rodman faction relocated itself to club rooms on MacDougal Street, thus initiating a new era in which the Liberal Club became closely associated with the *Masses* crowd.[13]

Like many women in the *Masses* and new Liberal Club circle, Rodman was a women's rights activist. A Socialist, free love advocate, and feminist, she repeatedly made headlines during the 1913–1915 period. Her high-profile war with the Board of Education, which finally resulted in her suspension from teaching, ultimately forced the board to relax its prohibition on women teachers returning to the job after having a baby. A radical feminist as well as an advocate of women's suffrage, Rodman insisted that suffrage would not be a significant achievement unless women voters adopted more socially progressive views than men. By wearing sandals, smoking in public, keeping her maiden name, and campaigning for legalizing the distribution of birth control information, Rodman challenged many other conventions of her time. She founded a Feminist Alliance that advocated a radical new scheme of cooperative housing for married professional women proposed by Charlotte Perkins Gilman, another leading feminist of the day. This feminist apartment house program would have allowed women to pursue their careers while experts hired for the purpose provided child care, cooking, house cleaning, and laundry services for the residents.[14]

Rodman was joined by other Village radicals in the public pursuit of these causes—hearings with the Board of Education, rallies for birth control that resulted in the arrest of several friends, and massive vote-for-women marches from Washington Square up Fifth Avenue in 1913 and 1914. Two feminist mass meetings held at Cooper Union under the auspices of the Peoples' Institute in February 1914 provide a useful short list of Villagers seeking to liberate women from public and private constraints on their personal development. Marie Jenney Howe, whose husband, Fred Howe, was the director of People's Institute, chaired both meetings.

At the first meeting on February 17th, twelve men and women each gave ten-minute talks on the subject "What Feminism Means to Me." *The Masses* was well represented by the magazine's editor, Max Eastman, and its associate editor, Floyd Dell, a writer and Liberal Club member recently arrived in the Village from Chicago. Henrietta Rodman, Crystal Eastman, and Frances Perkins were among the women Villagers on the panel. Three nights later, the seven speakers were all women. Their topic, "Breaking into the Human Race," was explained by Howe. "We're sick of being specialized to sex," she said. "We intend simply to be ourselves, not just our little female selves, but our whole, big, human selves." This goal would be achieved, the speakers argued, when women were granted the right to work at the jobs they wanted, to keep their maiden names when they married, to establish unions and other organizations to further their interests, and to ignore mainstream fashion styles.[15]

Six of the seven women who spoke at the second mass meeting belonged to Heterodoxy, a Greenwich Village women's organization that had been founded by Marie Jenney Howe in the winter of 1912–1913. Heterodoxy's members gathered for lunch every other Saturday and adhered to a strict rule of secrecy in regard to the meetings' proceedings. For this reason Heterodoxy does not figure in the public history of the Seventh Village or in the public's perception of the Village as a bohemian enclave. Nevertheless, Heterodoxy made an essential contribution to the Seventh Village milieu. The Heterodites supported each other in pursuing a radical feminist perspective that involved a "shift away from a strictly political and legal definition of emancipation to a new and more modern understanding of the psychological and spiritual dimensions of liberation." This greatly expanded feminist agenda underlay and energized the Seventh Villagers' support of women's sexual expression, pursuit of male-female psychological intimacy, and encouragement of women Villagers who sought to blend careers and marriage—positions that distinguished the Villagers' version of cultural radicalism from both the mainstream suffragist platform and the standard Socialist politics of the time.[16]

During the unemployment crisis of 1913–1914 members of the Seventh Villagers' inner circle once again, as they had at Paterson, energetically allied themselves with working-class protesters. An economic downturn that started in fall 1913 soon produced conditions in New York City worse than any since 1907–1908. As early as December city-run lodging houses could not meet the demand for sleeping space, and less than a month later the new year began on a solemn note for the working-class New Yorkers who lined up by the hundreds outside of Fleischmann's, a Village bakery that distributed leftover baked goods free of charge to all comers every evening at midnight. By February 1914 between 350,000 and 500,000 New York City workers were unemployed, and perhaps one-third of them also homeless.[17]

In late February Frank Tannenbaum, twenty years old, unemployed, a member of the I.W.W., and a protégé of Emma Goldman, called on jobless workers to join him in a direct action plan that involved marching into the city's wealthier churches and demanding food and shelter. The first such "church raid" took place on Friday, February 27, and received front-page coverage from the city's newspapers—exactly the publicity that Tannenbaum had hoped to attract. Over the next three nights, Tannenbaum's army of the unemployed descended on other churches located near Lower Manhattan's working-class districts. On the evening of Sunday, March 1, the raiders targeted the elegant First Presbyterian Church on Fifth Avenue in the north Village. The startled worshipers, once they overcame their surprise, treated the invaders quite generously.[18]

Two other Village churches, St. Luke's Episcopal on Hudson Street and Percy Stickney Grant's Church of the Ascension on Fifth Avenue, soon announced policies of opening their doors to the homeless and, in Ascension's case, serving their unemployed guests coffee and sandwiches in the parish hall. But many New York church leaders were far less compassionate, as the marchers found when they brought their protest to St. Alphonsus Catholic Church on the corner of West Broadway and Canal (the very southernmost edge of the Village) on the night of March 5, 1914. Not only were the raiders' appeals for food and shelter summarily rejected, but police were summoned and almost two hundred marchers arrested (fig. 37). Although most of the detainees received jail sentences of sixty days or less, the presiding judge, determined to set a stern precedent in the case of their ringleader, sentenced Tannenbaum to a year in Sing Sing.[19]

Village radicals and reformers showed their support for the city's unemployed in diverse ways. As mentioned earlier, several important Village churches offered Christian hospitality and aid. Some individuals, notably

Calling the Christian Bluff

37. *Calling the Christian Bluff,* John Sloan's drawing of Frank Tannenbaum's church raiders being driven off by the police. From *The Masses,* April 1914. Tamiment Institute Library, New York University.

Mabel Dodge and Frances Perkins, invited groups of unemployed men and women to their homes to discuss the plight of New York's workers. Pro-labor Villagers also organized themselves as the International Workers' Defense Conference (also known as the Labor Defense Conference). The group's officers included Jessie Ashley, Big Bill Haywood (of the I.W.W.), and Mary Heaton Vorse's husband, Joe O'Brien, and many well-known Seventh Villagers—Mabel Dodge, Frances Perkins, Frederick Howe, Lincoln Steffens, and Hutch Hapgood, among others—lent time and money to its efforts. The workers' middle- and upper-class allies gave unemployed workers legal and material assistance, defended the protesters' right to free speech, and tried to prevent the brutal police assaults on demonstrators that became commonplace at the height of the crisis.[20]

During March and April 1914, Mary Heaton Vorse's rented house on West Eleventh Street in the Village served as the I.W.W. command center from which many initiatives on behalf of the unemployed were launched.

As she was swept up in dealing with crisis after crisis, Vorse experienced a deep sense of camaraderie with her working-class friends. Though she had felt a powerful bond with workers earlier during the Lawrence strike of 1912, at that time she and O'Brien had been, as she put it, "spectators" viewing the workers' struggle from the outside. 1914 was different. "Now," she wrote, "suddenly we were on the inside, part of the movement, . . . feeling that their struggle and ours was single and indivisible."[21]

Vorse also played a crucial role in another of the Seventh Villagers' most important achievements, the founding of the Provincetown Players in 1915. Vorse had bought a small house in Provincetown, Massachusetts, in 1907, and her enthusiastic reports about this little Cape Cod community gradually enticed her Village friends to spend part or all of their summers there also. In 1914, 1915, and 1916, at the height of the Seventh Village's most creative period, a veritable mass exodus of friends from the *Masses* and Liberal Club circle summered at Provincetown. Of the first such summertime retreat, one participant wrote: "We were as a new family." In 1914 alone, this "family" included, among others, Mary Heaton Vorse and Joe O'Brien, Max Eastman and Ida Rauh, Hutch Hapgood and Neith Boyce, three mid-westerners, Floyd Dell, Susan Glaspell, and her husband, George Cram "Jig" Cook (all three of them writers who had become members of the Seventh Villager crowd in 1913), and Polly Holladay and Hippolyte Havel, who set up a temporary Provincetown branch of Polly's Restaurant for the duration of the summer.[22]

Much the same group, with a few additions—Mabel Dodge and Maurice Sterne, her artist-lover and future husband, and Leo Stein, her old friend from Paris and Florence—headed back to Provincetown for the 1915 summer season. One July evening at a small gathering, someone raised a topic of interest to all present: the sad state of American theater. Soon after moving to its new MacDougal Street location, the Liberal Club had begun to put on amateur theatricals at its club rooms, the usual fare being silly one-acters about Village life written by Floyd Dell and others. By February 1915 their interest in drama had led some Liberal Club members to form the Washington Square Players, which staged more serious plays at an uptown theater. But the Players had refused to produce "Suppressed Desires," a satire that Jig Cook and Susan Glaspell had written about the Villagers' fascination with psychoanalysis, on the grounds that the subject matter was too specialized to appeal to a general audience. Cook now proposed that the vacationing Villagers perform the play for themselves in Provincetown. Neith Boyce also offered her script called "Constancy," and the two plays were performed on July 15, 1915, at the cottage Boyce and Hapgood were renting.[23]

One thing led to another, though the animating spirit behind these developments was neither so completely spontaneous nor totally amateurish as legend would have it. Counting in their circle an able set designer, Robert Edmond Jones, two future Pulitzer Prize winning playwrights, Susan Glaspell and Eugene O'Neill (a recruit who joined in 1916, the second Provincetown season), and other men and women who had already embarked on successful careers as authors of fiction and nonfiction works, the vacationing Villagers could draw on a deep pool of artistic talent. Moreover, a significant core group had some familiarity with the emergent European avant-garde theater of the time and the ethnic theaters found on New York's Lower East Side, and many had also contributed to shaping two culturally insurrectionist events in 1913, the Armory Show and the Paterson Strike Pageant. In other words, they were primed to attack the sterile commercialism and conventionality of Broadway theater, and they had the talent to make good on their challenge.

Their project quickly gained momentum. In addition to Boyce's "Constancy" and Cook and Glaspell's "Suppressed Desires," two other one-act plays were staged at Provincetown in 1915, one of them Wilbur Daniel Steele's "Contemporaries," an allegory based on the Tannenbaum church raids. The following summer the company organized itself as the Provincetown Players and rented space on the town's wharf where it staged more plays, including, on July 28th, Eugene O'Neill's "Bound East for Cardiff." That fall they took their experimental theater to Greenwich Village and opened a small playhouse in a building next door to the Liberal Club on MacDougal Street. Over the company's relatively brief life, two Provincetown summers and six seasons on MacDougal Street, the group's artistic output was impressive: nearly one hundred plays by no less than forty-seven writers. The company's ensemble approach, its practice of privileging the interpretative views of directors and writers over those of actors, its innovative set designs, and its commitment to plays that had serious social and political content all contributed to making the Provincetown Players, in the words of Adele Heller, "one of the most valuable of the early experimental theatres that helped to establish American drama as a serious art form."[24]

By November 1916, when the Provincetown Players opened their first New York season, the Village countercultural scene was greatly changed from what it had been barely four years earlier. When the the *Masses*–Liberal Club circle had begun to take shape in 1912–1913, its members' commitment to cultural and political transformation had distinguished them from dilettantish bohemianism. That distinctive trait was still evident in 1916, culturally in the experimentalism of the Provincetown Players and politically in the militance of, for example, Ida Rauh and Jessie Ashley, who contrived to get themselves arrested for passing out birth control pamphlets at Union Square in order to trigger a judicial test of New York's ban on distributing such literature. But by 1916 the committed radicalism of the *Masses* core group was becoming less typical of the Seventh Village counter-cultural community than another, more familiar type of bohemianism devoted to wine, sex, and song. Even though the lines between the two types of Village bohemians—those committed to political and cultural activism, and those who simply dropped out of bourgeois society with no intention of trying to transform it—were by no means absolute, the growing prominence from 1915 onward of the latter kind of bohemianism had significant consequences inside Greenwich Village.[25]

Publicity generated by the Seventh Villagers' most visible activities—the revitalized *Masses*, the Armory Show, the Paterson Strike Pageant, and the Liberal Club's schism—made Village radicalism seem exciting and attractive. As early as spring 1914, New York newspapers ran articles on Dodge's salon and about Liberal Club members dining at Polly's basement restaurant. The tone of these articles, especially those in the *New York World*'s Metropolitan section, a lively, attractively illustrated feature of the Sunday *World*, was light-hearted and amusing. "Revelling with Parlor Socialists and Others At a Wednesday Night Soiree on Fifth Avenue" ran the headline of the story about "Mrs. Mabel Dodge's Wednesday Evening Gatherings." When you dine on MacDougal Street with members of the Liberal Club, the *World* announced, "You Are Served Socialism with Soup, Music with Meat, Politics with Pie and Advanced Thoughts on New Ideas with Your Coffee." It sounded like a lot of fun and certainly didn't seem to require serious political commitment.[26]

In December 1914 *The Masses* sponsored its first masquerade ball. Announced as the "Futurist Ball" (*futurism* was a term used for almost any avant-garde style of art or literature, e.g., cubist painting or imagist poetry), the dance was held uptown at Leslie Hall, on Broadway and Eighty-third Street. Again, metropolitan dailies covered the event with upbeat headlines—"What a Wild, Arty Cut Up Night for the Insurgent Devil-May-Cares!"—and pictures of the radicals in bizarre costumes. Two months later, in February 1915, the Liberal Club held its own costume ball, an Arabian Nights theme affair at Webster Hall on East Eleventh, soon to be the primary location for Village dances. These early balls were mainly for members of the Seventh Village's core group, and the masquerade format was in no way an innovation, since costume balls had been popular with New Yorkers for many years. The fact that a dance craze swept the city in the 1910s simply provided another reason for organizing balls. In 1913, for

38. An advertisement for the Socialist Party's annual ball, 1914. From *New York Call*, March 20, 1914.

instance, the Socialist Press Club held a costume ball in January, and the Jewish *Forward* featured a "Mask March" at its February ball. By early 1914 the number of organizations holding such dances was on the upswing, as indicated by columns of the Socialist *New York Call* that carried announcements of no fewer than three masquerade balls scheduled for a single two-week period (fig. 38).[27]

The Seventh Villagers soon gave their costume balls a special bohemian twist. In 1916, the Liberal Club announced that its February Webster Hall dance would be a "Pagan Rout." From that time onward sponsors of Village dances emphasized that their dances were in the tradition of Parisian Latin Quarter baccanalia. A major goal of having dances was to raise money, and the sponsors frankly set out to attract paying customers by playing on the reputation of artists and writers as being sexually liberated. One sponsor promised an "Art Models' Frolic" with the Village's "prettiest girls . . . in laughs and lingerie," and reports about another ball said that many models came, "some *au naturel.*" By 1917, if not earlier, Village balls were attracting few actual Villagers, and the dances' main purpose had become selling bohemia to tourists. Members of the older Seventh Village group bemoaned this development, but, as some recognized, they had been the first to use dances as fundraisers.[28]

One individual who began selling bohemia early in the Seventh Village's history was Guido Bruno. Bruno, whose birth name was Curt Kisch, arrived in New York from Chicago in late 1913. He settled his family in Yonkers and began to explore Village bohemianism. Sometime in 1914 he opened a small second-story shop called Bruno's Garret on Washington Square South, the "garret" being a reference to the popular bohemian image of a starving artist living in an attic room. The shop's location, directly across the street from the Fifth Avenue bus line's Washington Square stop, was shrewdly chosen to attract the attention of uptown New Yorkers and tourists as they arrived in the Village. Bruno was half huckster and half sincere patron of avant-garde art, and he demonstrated his commitment to the latter by adopting young artists and writers as his protégés, among them the imagist poet Alfred Kreymborg, the artist Clara Tice, and the writer Djuna Barnes. But his main activity was offering visitors to the neighborhood a romanticized version of Village bohemianism. "Greenwich Village!" he wrote. "A republic in the air! A gathering of constantly changing men and women."[29]

In 1915, Bruno began publishing works by his favorite artists, sponsoring art exhibits at the garret, and issuing a small magazine he named *Bruno's Weekly.* Some articles carried information on representatives of the old Village, especially Washington Square North patricians like Emily Johnston de Forest, but the primary focus was on the bohemian Seventh Villagers. Hippolyte Havel, revered by his friends in the *Masses* crowd as a model anarchist, wrote a piece for an August 1915 issue of *Bruno's Weekly* that became a classic, if not *the* classic, statement of the Seventh Village's credo. "When I speak of Greenwich Village," Havel wrote, "I have no geographical conception in view. The term Greenwich Village is to me a spiritual zone of mind." The net effect of Bruno's first year as the chief publicist for Village bohemianism was that when major New York dailies did features on the neighborhood—for example, the *New York Tribune's* piece in November 1914, "Who's Who in New York Bohemia," and the *New York Sun's* article a month later, "Everybody Is Doing Something in Bohemia"—the individuals and sites chosen were associated with Bruno's bohemian Village rather than with the neighborhood's political radicals.[30]

One telling phrase in the *Tribune's* "Who's Who in New York Bohemia" suggests how the self-conscious and faux bohemian newcomers tended to live in the Village but not really be of it. Before 1914 most Village artists and writers had frequented neighborhood saloons and restaurants that were owned by middle-class Italian, French, and Irish ethnics. The new Villagers were different. As the *Tribune* reporter put it, "If Greenwich Village ever did gaze entranced upon the surroundings of Americanized Italy, its eyes are turned away now. For Greenwich Village is eating all to itself in little cubby holes."[31]

The transformation of the radical Village into a bohemian Village progressed swiftly from 1915 to 1918. A host of small Village publications— the *Pagan* and the *Ink Pot* in 1916 and the *Greenwich Village Spectator* and the *Quill* in 1917—emerged and took on the role that *Bruno's Weekly* had once performed alone, publishing stories about Village characters and advertising the shops, restaurants, and galleries about which tourists or newcomers would want to know. With few exceptions the bohemian Village press advertised the "little cubby holes"—tearooms, restaurants, arts and crafts shops, bookstores—that were owned and operated by self-conscious bohemians.

The marketing of bohemia reached new heights during 1917. A host of Village eccentrics energetically exploited the tourist trade: the stick-thin Tiny Tim peddling his "Soul Candy," Mme. Cluette of the Art Mecca offering to show visitors a "Soul Light Shrine" of "Hindoo Origin" in the shop's basement, and the waif-like Sonja the Cigarette Girl, who specialized in selling cigarettes to women, promising "no criticism or hard looks." The Seventh Village also acquired an unofficial photographer, Jessie Tarbox Beals, who began to chronicle the local bohemian scene in earnest in 1916 and then in April 1917 opened a shop, the Village Art Gallery, at 6½ Sheridan Square, where she sold her pictures of New York's Left Bank and some of its better-known habitués. As a service to visitors who needed help locating the Seventh Village's most outré sites, Adele Kennedy, a sandal-shod young woman with bobbed hair, undertook to offer guided tours of artists' studios, gift shops, and tearooms to all who, as she explained to a reporter, came "primed for thrills, anxious to be shocked," and hoping to see some bohemian "freaks." An alternative to employing Adele's services was to turn to a full-length guidebook to the best of Greenwich Village bohemia that Anna Alice Chapin published in 1917.[32]

The brevity of the Seventh Village's lifespan is in no way surprising. Its history followed a course quite typical of many cultural and political insurgencies. A group of creative individuals had come together purposefully and for a time were afire with enthusiasm for liberation and transformation. Drawn by news of exciting things being done, others came to the Village to join the movement, their numbers and varied motivations diluting the communal intensity that had characterized the founders' inner circle. Before too long, the coalition of individualists who had launched the revolution began to unravel.

This process began as early as 1916, when John Sloan and several other artists seceded from *The Masses* staff in protest over editorial captions they felt inappropriately politicized their art. One cause or another soon removed other key figures from the inner circle. In 1916, Inez Milholland died of exhaustion in the midst of a strenuous national speaking tour for women's suffrage. In 1917, Mabel Dodge went off to Taos, and by that time John Reed was already spending more time in Russia than in the Village.

American entrance into World War I in April 1917 proved much more damaging to the Seventh Village spirit than did individual defections and absences. The tolerance for diverse views that had allowed for harmonious coexistence among individuals from different political and artistic camps broke down as Villagers divided for or against the war. Village magazines of the commercialized bohemia type generally rallied to the flag, and the artists of MacDougal Alley, led by Gertrude Vanderbilt Whitney, organized a four-day "Alley Festa" in June 1917, which raised about $60,000 for the Red Cross and other war relief agencies and produced more than $500,000 in Liberty Bond sales. Army recruiting stations in the Washington Square area did a booming business, but so too did the nearby office of an anti-war organization, the Bureau of Legal Advice. Founded in May 1917 by a coalition of liberals and Socialists that included several radicals with Village ties (Jessie Ashley served as treasurer and Charles Recht as one of its lawyers), the Bureau opened an office at 70 Fifth Avenue to offer free legal counseling to draft resisters and conscientious objectors.[33]

Villagers opposed to the war did not escape unscathed from a retaliatory campaign that the federal government launched to repress anti-war sentiment. The most famous case in point involved *The Masses*. In mid-1917, federal authorities, angered by the magazine's opposition to the war, refused to allow it to be shipped through the U.S. mail, causing the magazine to cease publication and leading, in 1918, to two trials of *The Masses*'s editors for conspiracy to obstruct enlistment. Split juries in both trials failed to convict, thus giving advocates of a free press a belated, if somewhat pyrrhic, victory, but the climate of super-patriotism and repression that prevailed in the country during the war proved inhospitable to the Seventh Villagers' spirit of joyful iconoclasm. By July 1918, the demoralized condition of the Village bohemians was all too apparent from a *New York Times* report that the Liberal Club was bankrupt and on its last legs as an organization.[34]

On the night of January 23, 1917, John Sloan, Marcel Duchamp, and four friends ascended a staircase inside Washington Arch, hung red balloons and Chinese lanterns from the top of the monument, and declared Greenwich Village a free and independent republic. The symbolism was playful but not without a point for historians seeking to understand the legacy of the Seventh Village. Like a skyrocket, it had risen high and had lit the sky with a series of brilliant bursts—the revitalized *Masses*, Dodge's salon, the Armory Show, and the Paterson Strike Pageant—and, after only a slight pause, secondary explosions followed: the Liberal Club schism, Polly's Restaurant, Provincetown summers, and the founding of the Provincetown Players.[35]

The initial bursts of light soon ended, but their afterimage lingered. Although the core group of Seventh Villagers had fragmented, many of its leading members continued to pursue radical political causes and artistic innovations in the 1920s. A new generation of artists and writers came to the Village, drawn by its reputation as a special gathering place for individuals engaged in testing the boundaries of conventional thought and behavior. In much the same way, many participants in the Village's later incarnations—the Beat Village of the 1950s, the countercultural Village of the 1960s, and the gay and lesbian Village of the 1970s and eighties—were aware of and attracted by the neighborhood's reputation as a pre–World War I bohemian enclave and can, therefore, be counted as spiritual heirs of the Seventh Villagers' grand rebellion.[36]

THE NEIGHBORHOOD, 1913–1918

Although the image of the Village as a republic of free spirits won wide popular acceptance during the mid-1910s, it reflected only a tiny sliver of Village life between 1913 and 1918. The vast majority of Villagers were not bohemians, and for them the most important changes in the neighborhood in the mid-1910s were not due to the emergence of a bohemian enclave so much as to shifts in the neighborhood's ethnic composition and developments in local housing and transportation conditions. This is not to suggest that the nonbohemian Villagers were unified in what they thought constituted a social neighborhood. On that subject, they differed greatly among themselves, and therein lies a key to understanding how the Village functioned as a social community for the diverse groups who lived in it in the early twentieth century.

A useful starting point for describing who lived in the Village between 1913 and 1918, the heyday of the Seventh Village, is to recognize that despite constant shifts in the Village's ethnic composition, several long-standing demographic trends continued into the 1910s. In 1910, a majority of Villagers were still either foreign-born or the children of immigrants. Federal census figures for the year show that the Village had a population of 124,603, more than 55,000 of whom were foreign-born and nearly 48,000 more of whom were native-born children of immigrants. The Italian presence in the Village had continued to grow relative to that of other ethnic groups. By 1910, Italians outnumbered both of the Village's two other large ethnic groups, the Irish and old stock Protestants (which were present in roughly equal numbers), by more than two to one. Between 1910 and 1920, the local Italian population grew slightly, while the Irish and old stock Protestants lost ground. In the same ten-year period the number of German-born Villagers, which in 1910 had stood at 3,733 (compared with 11,047 Irish-born Villagers), dropped precipitously, by approximately 50 percent.[37]

The African American community, which for at least four decades had been characterized by constant turnover but by relatively stable total numbers (varying from 1,200 to 1,600), also shrank significantly in the 1910s. In the south and west Village areas where most black Villagers had long lived, the African American population fell from nearly 1,300 in 1910 to fewer than 600 in 1920. Summarizing the consequences of this demographic change in a dramatic manner, one investigator asserted that by 1920 only "three Negro blocks" remained of an enclave that had once been much larger.[38]

One such block, the narrow lane known as Gay Street, had among its residents a family that had persisted in the Village for more than two decades despite the comings and goings of many individual African Americans and the overall shrinkage of the neighborhood's black population. This family, the Morgan J. Austins (mentioned in chapter 1 as residents of MacDougal Street in 1900 and Minetta Lane in 1910), lived at 9 Gay Street in 1920. Morgan had died and at least one of his sons (Artie) had joined the uptown migration of black New Yorkers, moving to a boarding house on West 113th Street. But Annie, the family's Irish American matriarch, three of her mixed-race children, and six of her grandchildren remained Villagers. They were part of a sixteen-person household that occupied a three-story brick row house. Reading between the lines of the census, which shows that the family shared its small rented house with three adult male boarders (two Italians and a West Indian black) and that Annie's son, daughter, and son-in-law were employed, respectively, as a chauffeur, store saleslady, and truck driver, it appears that the Austins were still following their long-standing practice of turning to each other for social and financial support.[39]

The broad demographic shifts in the Village were accompanied by losses of significant individuals in various Village constituencies. Among the west Village Irish, for instance, an older generation of men and women who had immigrated to the United States before the American Civil War was passing from the scene. The death of individuals like William ("Billy") Walker of St. Luke's Place (in 1916) and Thomas Kennedy of 41 Christopher Street (in 1918) deprived St. Joseph's parish and Tammany's reform wing of stalwart supporters and, along with the migration of Irish Villagers to other parts of the city, went far to explain why Irish county societies, whose core members had long been drawn from among men of the Walker–Kennedy generation, lost strength in the Village after World War I.[40]

Death and the passage of time also weakened the ranks of north Village patricians. Families like the Johnston–de Forest clan stayed in their ancestral homes, but the Old New York element of Washington Square North suffered a major loss when Serena Rhinelander died in 1914. The next year the Rhinelander mansion was sold, and the contrast between Old New York society and that of the new century was vividly illustrated in October 1915 just after the mansion's new owner, a wealthy suffragist, moved in. According to a Village weekly, "lovers of the old order of things were much amazed to wake up last Saturday morning and behold the windows of the prim and ultra-conservative Serena Rhinelander home aglow with yellow suffragist slogans and banners in all its windows."[41]

Three developments had a particularly important influence on the Village's physical environment between 1913 and 1918. These were the construction of the Seventh Avenue subway line, the movement to remodel old tenements and run-down houses and turn them into middle-class properties, and the passage of the Zoning Act of 1916.

Physically, the most drastic change in the Village was caused by the Seventh Avenue extension, which required the destruction of the better part of ten blocks of mostly residential buildings between Greenwich Avenue and Varick Street. "The Cut," as it was called locally, temporarily divided the far western part of the Village from the rest by the deep trench in which the Seventh Avenue subway lines were laid, and the project also caused a significant loss of housing stock in that part of the neighborhood. (Although the extension of Sixth Avenue south of Carmine Street in the mid-1920s affected a somewhat smaller area, the project again forced Villagers to adjust to many changes in the neighborhood. Two of the largest changes were the removal of the Sixth Avenue Elevated line and the construction of Our Lady of Pompei's present-day church on Carmine Street, a move required because the parish's old church on Bleecker was demolished to clear a path for the new section of Sixth Avenue.)

The prospect of the Seventh Avenue subway opening its station at Sheridan Square had a noticeable effect in the Village even before regular service commenced in July 1918. The ancient horsecars—small buses drawn by one or two horses that once had criss-crossed the neighborhood in great numbers—had been gradually going out of service, and the final trip of the Fourth Street line, the last to operate in the Village, took place in July 1917. Even more significant, the expectation that the new subway's arrival would make the west Village more accessible to commuters and tourists stimulated local real estate entrepreneurs to begin remodeling old homes into studio apartments.

No Village entrepreneur promoted the remodeling business with greater enthusiasm or success than Vincent Pepe. Born in Italy in April 1876, Pepe had been only eleven when his parents brought him to the United States. A brother, Michael, had immigrated to New York earlier in the 1880s. The Pepe brothers were representative of the younger Italian Villagers, both those born in Italy and those born in New York, whose careers did not depend mainly on serving the needs of an insulated immigrant community. Just before the turn of the century the Pepe brothers formed a real estate firm that initially specialized in managing rental properties but gradually expanded into real estate development. By the mid-1910s its primary business was renovating old Village buildings into studio apartments, an enterprise that Vincent Pepe, the more active partner in the firm by World War I, publicized with articles in local publications touting his projects as producing "Real Estate Progress in Our Community." Widely recognized as the man to see if you wanted to rent an apartment in the neighborhood, he was identified in one small bohemian-run publication simply as "Vincent Pepe, the Village Landlord."[42]

Pepe and other real estate agents were not alone in their efforts to promote the Village's attractiveness as a middle-class residential neighborhood in the mid-1910s. Two important civic organizations, the Greenwich Village Improvement Society (G.V.I.S.) and the People's Institute, cooperated to initiate similar promotional campaigns in 1914. The G.V.I.S., founded by Mary Simkhovitch in 1903 with the goal of improving city services and

intergroup relations in the neighborhood, had remained largely a paper organization until 1913 when, with Simkhovitch as its president, it began several years of very intense activity. People's Institute, operating out of its
home base at Cooper Union, had specialized for fifteen years in sponsoring
free educational programs to a mainly Lower East Side working-class clientele. In 1914, however, the new director of People's Institute, Frederick
Howe (who with his wife, Marie Jenney Howe, the founder of Heterodoxy,
had recently moved to West Twelfth Street in the Village), urged his board
to approve new programs, one of which was a cooperative venture with the
Greenwich Village Improvement Society. Both Howe and one of Howe's
high-ranking assistants, John Collier (who was a participant in the Liberal
Club–Dodge salon circle), had become convinced that the best way to prevent the social fragmentation that was widespread in large industrial cities
was to promote community spirit at the neighborhood level. Toward that
end, Howe and Collier established a People's Institute Greenwich–Chelsea
Committee and offered financial and staff assistance to the G.V.I.S., the
neighborhood association active in nearby Greenwich Village.[43]

One of the first fruits of cooperation between the G.V.I.S. and People's
Institute was the publication in 1914 of a sixteen-page pamphlet titled
"How Would You Like to Open a Door Like This—Ten Minutes After You
'Punch the Clock?' " This frankly promotional pamphlet, 20,000 copies of
which were printed for distribution throughout the city, carried the message that the Village had something for everyone. In the north Village near
Fifth Avenue wealthy families could find "spacious old-fashioned elevator
apartments" or "quaint red brick houses" with ten to twelve rooms that
could be rented for $1,200 to $2,400 a year. But near Washington Square
South or west of Sixth Avenue over to Hudson Street, four to seven rooms
could be rented for as little as $25 and no more than $70 a month. And
many examples of the "big handsome solid-looking house, with high ceil-
ings and square rooms" were also available in the Village. All these rental
properties, the authors continued, were close to the city's major transportation hubs: only eight minutes from Penn Station, ten by ferry from Jersey
City, and ten or less from Cunard, White Star, and Anchor line docks where
one could board a ship for Europe. Boats to Coney Island and Rockaway
Beach could be reached in less than fifteen minutes, and commuters who
worked anywhere in Manhattan from Midtown to the Battery could be
home in fifteen minutes.[44]

From the picture on the cover of the People's Institute–G.V.I.S. pamphlet (a handsome house door) and the pamphlet's content it was clear that
its authors were intent on promoting the Village as a pleasant residential
neighborhood. That the pamphlet's middle-class sponsors favored a neigh-

borhood of this sort was no surprise. All the local advocacy groups that had campaigned to improve public services in the Village—the G.V.I.S., the People's Institute Greenwich–Chelsea Committee, and the Washington Square Association—wanted to preserve and enhance the status of the Village's core section as a neighborhood of middle- or upper-class houses and small businesses. Moreover, the leaders of these civic organizations agreed that statutory restrictions on commercial and industrial construction would go far toward securing the Village's long-term future as an attractive residential district.

Between 1913 and 1916, everything fell into place to facilitate passage of the appropriate zoning restrictions. In 1913 the state legislature authorized the city Board of Estimate and Apportionment to establish a comprehensive zoning plan for all five city boroughs. That very fall the victory of two Fusion (i.e., anti-Tammany) candidates, John Purroy Mitchel as mayor and George McAneny as president of the Board of Aldermen, opened the way to the passage, after a long and complicated process, of the Zoning Act of 1916. On the day (May 27, 1916) that the Board of Estimate's hearings dealt specifically with the Village, Vincent Pepe and William Spinney (a Greenwich House social worker), representing the Greenwich Village Improvement Society, testified in favor of making the Village's core area a residential and small business zone in which building heights would be limited and from which large manufacturing establishments would be excluded. Although a number of real estate developers opposed these restrictions, the G.V.I.S. got most of what it wanted, and the heart of the Village between Houston and West Thirteenth from Hudson Street over to West Broadway (a Seventh Avenue corridor excepted) was designated as a residential and business zone.[45]

The events of 1913–1918 ensured that the Village would not, as patrician and middle-class residents had feared only ten years earlier, suffer the fate that had befallen most of Manhattan south of Fourteenth Street, which had been taken over by slum housing and commercial or industrial buildings. The north Village gentry and middle-class west Villagers, by staying in their homes despite the expansion of tenements and factories nearby, had achieved a holding action that kept their parts of the neighborhood residential in character until that status was written into law in the Zoning Act of 1916. At that point in the late 1910s, the arrival of the Seventh Avenue subway encouraged entrepreneurs to add to the neighborhood's housing stock through refurbishing old homes or constructing new apartment buildings.

By 1918, therefore, the survival of certain features of the Village's nineteenth-century physical environment—its quaint street patterns and low-rise residences—was assured, and even the neighborhood's geographical borders remained fairly well defined, distinct from nearby districts. However, the ten years from 1908 to 1918 had brought many developments that placed the neighborhood's social fabric under great strain: the growth of the Italian population, the tensions that arose over the neighborhood's public spaces, the conflicts between laborers and factory owners in the garment industry, the moral reformers' efforts to control the behavior of disorderly Villagers, and the emergence of the bohemian Village.

Despite these strains and the heterogeneity of the Village's population, the word *neighborhood* did have a social meaning for many Villagers—though the particular meaning it had varied from group to group. For example, the self-defined bohemians and cultural radicals whose activities the public found so captivating between 1913 and 1918 had a distinctive view of neighborhood and social community. Hippolyte Havel's well-known definition of the Village as "a spiritual zone of mind" idealized a kind of neighborhood not tied to geographical boundaries. Havel in fact made it quite clear that most residents of Greenwich Village lacked the freedom of spirit and radical unconventionality needed to be considered true Villagers. Nevertheless, Greenwich Village as a geographical entity was not without importance to the bohemian residents, since it was a place in which a cultural radical could find a dense concentration of like-minded individuals for inspiration.[46]

At first glance it might seem that the middle-class New Yorkers targeted by Village real estate promoters had little in common with Havel's "true" Villagers, since the middle-class New Yorkers who rented the neighborhood's refurbished houses and recently constructed apartment buildings were drawn to the Village because of its material features—nice homes, excellent transportation, and good schools—rather than to the pursuit of the spiritual values with which Havel's true Villagers were said to be imbued. However, as the historian Caroline Ware found, bohemian Villagers and middle-class newcomers shared one very important attitude toward community. Both valued the Village for its reputed tolerance of individual differences and in fact thought that neighborliness at its best consisted principally of a reciprocal arrangement in which neighbors did not meddle in one another's private affairs. This spirit of "rampant individualism," as Ware called it, meant that neither the newcomers nor the bohemians made any attempt to bridge the social gulf between themselves and the Catholic, immigrant, and working-class residents of the neighborhood.[47]

Clues to how those Catholic, immigrant, and working-class Villagers viewed their neighborhood can be gleaned from data that Ware and her research team gathered during interviews with old-time Villagers in the early 1930s. Ware's researchers asked sixty Irish Villagers, most of them residents of west Village blocks near Jones Street (where the offices used by Ware were located), questions about what neighborhood life had been like "before the war."[48]

Several of Ware's informants asserted that their part of the Village had been "a genuine neighborhood" before World War I. According to these old-timers, around the turn of the century (but possibly a bit earlier) members of the neighborhood's largest ethnic groups—Irish, Germans, and old stock Protestants—had enjoyed friendly relations. "Each block," they said, "was more or less like a big family," in which casual socializing took the form of "back-and-forth visiting," and residents felt so confident about neighborhood safety that they didn't lock the front doors of their houses. These old residents, Ware reported, believed that the prewar Village had been "a social as well as a geographical unit." But in the postwar period many Irish families moved out of the west Village and relations with the Italians who replaced them varied, Ware wrote, "from violent antagonism to indifference." The arrival of bohemian and middle-class Villagers served only to further undermine any sense of neighborly solidarity.[49]

But what, precisely, had broken down? The neighborly paradise whose loss Ware's Irish informants bemoaned had always excluded many local residents from its charmed circle. African Americans, though present in substantial numbers in the west Village during the era when neighborliness supposedly prevailed, were not members of the Irish old-timers' social networks. Similarly, Italian newcomers were viewed by Irish Villagers as intruders rather than neighbors. In fact, even Irish informants who spoke of the friendly relations that existed between Irish Villagers and their German and "American" neighbors also spoke with pride of the many west Village saloons that "you couldn't walk in[to] unless you were Irish." On close examination, therefore, it's clear that the social intimacy remembered so fondly by the Irish old-timers was achieved by excluding everyone who did not belong to a relatively homogeneous group of insiders. This pattern, of course, is quite consistent with the preponderance of evidence from the period which indicates that the Village as a whole was always more a constellation of smaller social communities—the patrician north Village, the Irish west Village, and so on—than a single social unit, and that even when Villagers from different ethnic groups were neighbors, as they often were in nearly every section of the Village, they usually remained strangers to one another socially.[50]

Well aware of the fragmenting effect that ethnic and class diversity had on social community in the Village, Mary Simkhovitch of Greenwich House made combatting social fragmentation a central goal of her long career in the neighborhood. What she hoped to create was a more inclusive form of neighborhood and neighborliness. From her very earliest years at Greenwich House she had sought to promote harmonious working relations across ethnic lines by inviting representatives of a wide variety of ethnic and religious groups to be members of Greenwich House's board of trustees and officers of the Greenwich Village Improvement Society. Her goal, she said, was to foster "community spirit," the chief sign of which would be the coming together of "all groups" locally in a spirit of "mutual respect, sympathy, and cooperation." This, she emphasized, did not require a process of homogenization that would eliminate ethnic differences but rather an appreciation of the unique contribution that every group of Villagers made to the neighborhood.[51]

After making a good start toward learning about and responding to the neighborhood's needs during the first ten years (1902–1912) of the settlement's existence, Simkhovitch and her Greenwich House staff accelerated the pace of their community spirit-building activities during the next five years. From 1913 to 1917, Simkhovitch often turned to members of the Greenwich Village Improvement Society to spearhead her campaign for neighborhood improvements. In 1914, the same year that the G.V.I.S. cooperated with People's Institute to publish their promotional pamphlet, they also prepared a survey of the quality of local street lighting, street pavement, and playgrounds and lobbied municipal authorities for improvements. Simkhovitch and her allies also campaigned successfully for passage of the Zoning Act of 1916 and won approval from the city to keep selected local public schools open after school hours to serve as community social centers. Under this program two schools, P.S. 41 on Greenwich Avenue and P.S. 95 on Clarkson Street, became available to the general public in the late afternoon and evening for such activities as basketball games, dances, and community meetings.[52]

Old Home Week, a five-day neighborhood festival held in May 1913 and sponsored by the Greenwich Village Improvement Society, was a particularly ambitious undertaking launched in pursuit of Simkhovitch's goal of promoting neighborhood-wide civic spirit. A featured event of the Old Home Week program consisted of speeches by elderly past and present residents of the Village who reminisced about the neighborhood as they had known it forty or more years earlier (fig. 39). Two distinguished old-time Villagers, Robert W. de Forest of Washington Square North, who had grown up on Charles Street, and Everett P. Wheeler, an eminent lawyer whose childhood home had been on Grove Street, spoke at the opening day ceremonies. Later in the festival, lesser-known Villagers were introduced and asked to share their memories of former times. These individuals included Euphemia M. Olcott, a resident of the north Village since 1844,

39. A scene from a historical pageant performed in Hudson Park under the auspices of Greenwich House. From Greenwich House, *Annual Report,* 1912.

two venerable retired firemen (Jimmie Winters, age ninety, and Dan Mott, eighty three), and Colonel J. Frank Supplee, the oldest member of the local National Guard unit. Elected officials—Alderman Henry Curran, Borough President George McAneny, State Assemblyman James ("Jimmy") Walker, and Congressman Jefferson M. Levy—each took a turn at the speaker's podium at various points during the week.[53]

Old Home Week's other events included a parade of Village organizations, a band concert, prayer meetings at many local churches, a dramatized presentation by Greenwich House school children of Longfellow's "Hiawatha," and a closing dinner at Public School 95. Most of the week's programs emphasized the Village's past, and several speakers and newspaper accounts suggested that Greenwich Village was unique among the city's neighborhoods in being able to mount a celebration of its history in which so many speakers could be found who had firsthand memories of earlier times. But the festival did not just look backward. By evoking the past as a reference point, it also addressed contemporary concerns about the lack of continuity and cohesion that several commentators felt had become typical of life in the city's neighborhoods.[54]

At least two speakers, Professor Charles S. Baldwin of Columbia University and the lawyer Everett P. Wheeler, asserted that in some respects the present Village was a better place to live than it had been, fond memories though they had of their childhood years in the neighborhood. Baldwin's reasons for making this point bore directly on the goal of inclusiveness that underlay the festival planners' efforts. He noted that many Irish names appeared on the Old Home Week program and observed that this was a welcome departure from the values of an earlier era, when Protestant Villagers had been wont to say, "We must keep the village American," meaning that Irish immigrants were not welcome there.[55]

Diversity was honored in various ways. Numerous Irish speakers and old-timers participated in key events throughout the week. The Italian-born realtor Vincent Pepe made an invaluable contribution as the planning committee's treasurer, and Old Home Week's organizers actively sought to involve other Italian Villagers through invitations sent to every Italian church and religious society in the neighborhood. Nevertheless, Old Home Week's inclusiveness had its limits. All the major addresses on the topic of the Village's past were given by Protestants of western European background. Black Villagers, despite their long-standing presence in the neighborhood, were given no visible role to play in scheduled events, although a Greenwich House staff member on the planning committee did make an effort to have a letter from a black woman resident of the Minettas included among a series of letters to the editor that the *New York World* published about Old Home Week.[56]

These decisions by the celebration's organizers conform to a general pattern evident in the community festivals, pageants, and reunions that enjoyed wide popularity throughout the United States in the decades before World War I. In contrast with the approach of the Village radicals, who less than a month after Old Home Week staged the Paterson Strike Pageant, a central theme of which was class conflict between factory workers and their employers, mainstream progressives like Mary Simkhovitch generally sought, as the historian David Glassberg has observed, to emphasize social cohesion. Most contemporary community celebrations portrayed old stock Protestants as the founders of American towns and cities that then "cheerfully welcomed 'later' immigrant groups" and their "colorful" ways, a historical approach intended to offer "a tangible demonstration of how disparate ethnic groups could unite into one community." But as Glassberg adds, "blacks and Asians were generally absent from the pageant portrait of the community and its history"—a statement that applies equally well to Greenwich Village's Old Home Week, which offered a version of the neighborhood's past without any reference to blacks or black historical consciousness (fig. 40).[57]

The following May, 1914, a second neighborhood festival, this one called

40. Some faces in the crowd of Villagers watching a Greenwich House pageant. From Greenwich House, *Annual Report*, 1912.

the Village Fair, was sponsored by Greenwich House in cooperation with the Greenwich Village Improvement Association. As Greenwich House's headworker and the G.V.I.S.'s president, Simkhovitch issued a press statement declaring that the occasion was being held to promote "the general happiness of the neighborhood." Toward that end, a full array of entertainments was scheduled. George McAneny, now president of the Board of Aldermen, and State Assemblyman Jimmy Walker once again gave opening-day speeches. The next few days' activities included a Village parade, a beauty contest for Village babies, an old-timers' reunion dinner, two dances, social events at local public schools, a half marathon race, and exhibits of Italian women's needlework and a marionette show by the Italian drama club at Richmond Hill House (formerly West Side Branch settlement house).[58]

An innovative feature of the Village Fair was a farm exhibit in Hudson Park across the street from Jimmy Walker's old home on St. Luke's Place. The display of farm animals—a pig, eight goats, some chickens and ducks, and a milk cow—made a particularly big hit with festival-goers. City children who had never heard barnyard sounds shrieked with delight every time the pig grunted. Newspaper reporters had great fun describing the difficult time organizers had finding a suitable cow (a Long Island farmer came to

41. Dancers at a Village ball held at a Hudson River recreation pier under Greenwich House sponsorship. From Greenwich House, *Annual Report*, 1915.

the rescue and loaned them one named "Annie"), then the trouble they had getting someone to volunteer to milk Annie, and finally the test of wills between the out-of-practice volunteer and an uncooperative Annie during the milking demonstration. Overall, the festival accomplished Simkhovitch's goal of promoting "general happiness." The only slightly sour note was struck during the closing night's dance, at which, according to a newspaper report, conflicts arose between attendees who wanted to do old-fashioned barn dances and members of a younger set who clamored for the latest dance fad, the tango (fig. 41).[59]

Besides hoping that Old Home Week and the Village Fair would be fun for everyone who attended, the events' organizers attempted to foster neighborliness by drawing many different types of Villagers into festival activities. After compiling a list of all the neighborhood's religious organizations, the fair's sponsors made sure that each received publicity about forthcoming events, including the possibility of hosting activities at their churches. Similarly, all political viewpoints were welcomed. Tammany district leader Charles Culkin was invited to suggest names of old residents, and he responded by sending a list culled from his carefully maintained files. Republican Alderman Curran, Tammany Democratic Assemblyman Walker, and Independent Democrat McAneny were featured speakers. Robert W. de Forest represented patrician Villagers, and Italian traditions were recognized through the exhibits held at Richmond Hill House. Two

Italian cherubs won the boys' and girls' baby beauty contests, and Public School 95, a large (2,600-pupil) grammar school, 98 percent of whose students were Italian, was chosen as the site for many Village Fair events.[60]

That ethnic lines were in fact crossed as a result of Simkhovitch's efforts to promote community spirit is most easily documented by examples of cooperation between Village settlement workers and the leaders of the local Italian community who were members or supporters of the Greenwich Village Improvement Society. During Old Home Week in 1913, the G.V.I.S. logo appeared on festival invitations and programs, but Simkhovitch and her Greenwich House staff did most of the real work of organizing and running the five-day affair. In 1914, however, much more of the basic legwork for the Village Fair was done by G.V.I.S. members other than Simkhovitch, with Vincent Pepe, the festival's energetic treasurer, carrying the heaviest workload. Pepe's commitment to the festival was just one more example, along with his role as the "Village Landlord," of the way his public activities now extended well beyond the bounds of the Italian immigrant community.

Father Antonio Demo was another Italian immigrant whose connections with individuals and organizations outside the south Village Italian enclave expanded steadily from 1908 to 1918. Barely able to speak English in 1899 when he arrived in the Village to become pastor of Our Lady of Pompei, Demo initially had little need for English because at first he had little contact with anyone outside his immigrant flock. Gradually, however, this insular position vis-à-vis the surrounding non-Italian community broke down, in part because he was called on to represent the interests of his Italian-speaking parishioners to various municipal and private legal or social welfare agencies, and also because he was invited with increasing frequency to advise civic organizations regarding the needs and preferences of Italian Villagers.

A careful student of Demo's wide contacts with institutions outside the Italian immigrant community has suggested that his behavior in this regard was "most unusual" for Italian Catholic clergymen before World War I. Those contacts increased in the 1910s and took an ever-wider variety of forms. In 1910 the librarian of the local public library asked Demo to suggest appropriate titles for Italian readers, and from 1913 onward Village public school principals frequently contacted him about problems involving students whose parents belonged to his parish. An important moment that signaled his increasingly open attitude toward contacts from outside the Italian immigrant community came in 1911, when he allowed members of the Women's Trade Union League of New York, many of whom were middle- or upper-class Protestants, to distribute pro-union leaflets outside of Our Lady of Pompei during memorial masses for victims of the Triangle fire.[61]

In the mid-1910s Demo also carried on an extensive correspondence with administrators working for the Greenwich District of the Charity Organization Society. These exchanges concerned cases of Italian individuals and families in need of social or economic assistance. For several years Demo served, along with a number of school principals and social workers, as a member of a committee sponsored by an organization known as the School and Civil League, whose mission it was to promote a knowledge of American institutions in Village schools. He frequently received invitations to participate in programs run by the Village's two main social settlements, Greenwich House and Richmond Hill House. When an officer of the Greenwich Village Improvement Society wrote urging him to support the G.V.I.S., Demo responded by making a small monetary donation to the group's work. By the mid-1910s Demo's civic activities were a practical example of Mary Simkhovitch's conviction that the process of building community in a modern urban neighborhood did not require social intimacy or cultural homogeneity so much as it did mutual respect and pragmatic cooperation among the various subgroups who lived in the area.[62]

Simkhovitch's efforts to promote her ideal of neighborhood enjoyed considerable success during the five-year period from 1913 to 1918. By 1917, if not earlier, it was clear that she had accomplished many of her objectives. A new grammar school (P.S. 95) had opened on Clarkson Street, and along with P.S. 41 on Greenwich Avenue it had been designated as a neighborhood social center. A public bath house for which Simkhovitch had long lobbied had been built in Hudson Park. The neighborhood's recreation facilities had been augmented by the conversion of the Barrow Street pier into a recreation site. The publicity that the Committee on Congestion had given earlier to the need for urban planning had helped create the political climate in which the Zoning Act of 1916 became law.

By January 1917, when Greenwich House moved its main facility from Jones Street to larger quarters on Barrow Street, Simkhovitch's priorities were shifting to matters beyond the confines of Greenwich Village. She had been elected president of the National Federation of Settlements in 1916, and the entrance of the United States into World War I in April 1917 inevitably distracted her and other many Villagers from a focus on local concerns. Not that Simkhovitch's work in the neighborhood was finished. She did not retire from her position as Greenwich House's head resident until 1946, when she was seventy-nine years old. But by 1917 the formative period of her career in neighborhood social work was definitely coming to a close.

One idealized description of urban neighborhoods portrays them as tight-knit social communities. The individuals and families who reside in such neighborhoods are said to benefit from participating in extended social networks that provide their members with a sense of belonging and identity, offering them a refuge in the otherwise impersonal, fragmented, competitive world of modern industrial society. Whether or not this portrait is accurate for American urban neighborhoods in general—it has been suggested, for example, that many such model neighborhoods were, in fact, the products of nostalgia, in which the neighborhood of one's youth is remembered as a better place in a better time—it is clear that Greenwich Villagers as a whole never shared a social community of the ideal type between 1898 and 1918.[63]

Much too much ethnic, class, and cultural diversity existed in the Village to support neighborhood-wide social intimacy. Although on some occasions, most of which occurred between 1908 and 1915, an impressive amount of communication and cooperation did take place across ethnic and class lines, these moments were the products of very special circumstances prompted either by the impact of a traumatic event (most notably the Triangle fire) or the efforts of middle-class social progressives committed to reaching out to their working-class neighbors. Major examples of this latter kind of cross-class, cross-ethnic interchange include the alliance between middle-class members of the Women's Trade Union League and garment workers, the Church of the Ascension's sponsorship of Ascension Forum, and Mary Simkhovitch's many attempts to foster neighborliness through such initiatives as the Greenwich Village Improvement Society, community festivals, and neighborhood social centers.

More typically, however, feelings of social community and neighborliness in Greenwich Village existed only among smaller networks of Villagers who shared ties based on membership in a particular ethnic group, church, social club, or political organization or who lived in close proximity on a specific block or section of a block. Outside of these more intimate social networks, except under unusual circumstances, Villagers of different types for the most part had little social intercourse with one another, and even the Village's smaller social communities were constantly buffeted by changes in the ethnic, physical, and political character of the neighborhood. The period from 1898 to 1918 was a time of ongoing transformation that left few, if any, Villagers untouched.

These latter days of the Sixth Village—years when a roiling mix of creeds, colors, classes, and nationalities shared the neighborhood—bequeathed a twofold legacy to its successors. The first, widely acknowledged by historians and Village residents alike, is the Sixth Village's contribution as the location in which the Seventh Villagers came together as a group and from which they then launched their grand rebellion, thereby creating the Village's reputation as an enclave of free spirits whose unconventional ways are tolerated, even honored, by their neighbors. This reputation, which led to the famous image of the Village as America's Montmartre, put down its first roots in a Sixth Village milieu; once established, it continued to inspire emulation by succeeding generations of Villagers.

By contrast, the second legacy of the Sixth Village era, the example it represents of a mixed-class, mixed-ethnic neighborhood, has scarcely been recognized at all. An obvious reason for this neglect is that at first glance the Sixth Village has always seemed to be the drab older sister to its vivacious bohemian younger sibling. In addition, because a number of other late nineteenth-century wards in lower Manhattan had diverse populations, the Village-as-multicultural-neighborhood phenomenon may seem to lack the uniqueness that attaches to the Village-as-America's-bohemia.[64]

Whatever the cause for the Sixth Village's relative obscurity, its special qualities are significant and merit close attention. A striking degree of awareness of their neighborhood as a distinct social and geographical entity existed among Villagers at the turn of the twentieth century, as indicated by the fact that it was there that the city's first neighborhood association, the Greenwich Village Improvement Society, was established in 1903. Moreover, from the first the society's leaders made it their goal to foster a spirit of inclusiveness that would transcend the narrow ethnic and class boundaries that so often defined "neighborhood" in other parts of the city. From the vantage point of yet another century's turning, therefore, at a time when the populations of many American cities are exceedingly diverse, the cosmopolitan makeup of the pre–World War I Village and the plethora of Villages that existed inside its borders—the African American, Irish, and Italian Villages, and the cross-ethnic, cross-class Village networks spon-sored by the Women's Trade Union League, the Church of the Ascension, and Greenwich House—can serve as positive examples of the potential for cultural vitality that exists in a heterogeneous society of the sort that may well be "the future of us all."[65]

NOTES

Introduction

1. Floyd Dell, *Love in Greenwich Village*, 16. The names and spellings used here are Dell's. Recent scholars offer variations: Steven Watson, *Strange Bedfellows*, 123, and Rick Beard and Leslie Cohen Berlowitz, eds., *Greenwich Village*, 55.
2. As of 1900 no consensus existed regarding the location of the Village's southern boundary. Some contemporaries placed it at Houston; others said Charlton or Canal.
3. Dell, *Love in Greenwich Village*, 14.
4. Two phases: Watson, *Strange Bedfellows*, 123. American quarter: Thomas A. Janvier, "Greenwich Village," 356–57, and Janvier, *In Old New York*, 148. Foreign-born population: Caroline F. Ware, *Greenwich Village, 1920–1930*, 11.
5. Many Seventh Villagers wrote memoirs and, like Dell, most—e.g., Hutchins Hapgood, *A Victorian in the Modern World*, and Max Eastman, *Enjoyment of Living*—implicitly adopted the rise-of-bohemia framework. For treatments of the pre–World War I Village by the next generation of observers see Albert Parry, *Garrets and Pretenders*, and Allen Churchill, *The Improper Bohemians*. Three recent studies place the Seventh Village rebels in broader contexts: Watson, *Strange Bedfellows;* Adele Heller and Lois Rudnick, eds., *1915, The Cultural Moment;* and Christine Stansell, *American Moderns*.
6. Ware, *Greenwich Village*, 93. See pp. 81–105 for Ware's comparison of the pre- and postwar Village.

1. Neighbors and Strangers

1. Hapgood, *Types from City Streets*, 9. By 1905 a successor "Chat Noir" was doing business at 551 West Broadway, just around the corner from the original Black Cat.

2. On African American Villagers prior to the Civil War see Thelma Wills Foote, "Cross-roads or Settlement?" in Beard and Berlowitz, eds., *Greenwich Village: Culture and Counterculture,* 120–33. The history of the term "Little Africa" is outlined by Sule Greg C. Wilson, "Little Africa," in Kenneth T. Jackson, ed., *The Encylopedia of New York City,* 685.

3. Jacob Riis, *How the Other Half Lives,* 157.

4. Ibid., 161–62.

5. "Stephen Crane in Minetta Lane," in Fredson Bowers, ed., *Stephen Crane: Tales, Sketches, and Reports,* 400–404.

6. Ibid., 403, 405.

7. *U.S. Census: New York* (1900), reel 1082, E. D. 52, pp. 24B–25A.

8. Louise Bolard More, *Wage-Earners' Budgets,* 16–21.

9. *U.S. Census: New York* (1910), reel 1030, E. D. 809, p. 9A.

10. *U.S. Census: New York* (1900), reel 1082, E. D. 52. For data on lot size, building use, and building height see the *Sanborn Fire Insurance Maps: New York* (1904; microfilm ed., 1983), reel 55, vol. 3, map 6.

11. *U.S. Census: New York* (1900), reel 1082, E. D. 52, pp. 14B–15B.

12. The term "Richmond Negro": William F. Ogburn, "The Richmond Negro in New York City," Great Migration's communal and familial features: Joe William Trotter Jr., ed., *The Great Migration in Historical Perspective.*

13. The three studies by Giddings students: William F. Ogburn, cited in note 12 above; Ernest Jasper Hopper, "A Northern Negro Group", and Seymour Paul, "A Group of Virginia Negroes in New York City."

14. Ogburn, "The Richmond Negro in New York City," 47, and Paul, "A Group of Virginia Negroes in New York City," 26–47.

15. There are discrepancies in the census reports of Mary Clayton's childbearing history. The 1900 census, reel 1085, E. D. 52, p. 15B, reports that she had eighteen children; the 1910 census, reel 1030, E. D. 809, p. 9A, gives the figure of twelve.

16. For the number of nineteenth-century black Villagers see Lucille Genevieve Lomax, "A Social History of the Negro Population in the Section of New York City known as Greenwich Village," 31–41.

17. Adam Clayton Powell Jr., *Adam by Adam,* 46. On the late nineteenth-century history of the church see *New York Times,* Oct. 28, 1890, p. 8; Nov. 15, 1890, p. 3; Feb. 27, 1893, p. 8; and Oct. 23, 1896, p. 3. See also three typescript manuscripts from the Schomburg Center for Research in Black Culture: Ellen Terry, "Abyssinian Baptist Church," (11 pp., dated June 13, 1938), Waring Cuney, "Activity of the Churches during the Depression" (3 pp., dated Aug. 31, 1939), and Sydney H. French, "The Abyssinian Baptist Church" (8 pp., dated Jan. 9, 1940)—all from the Federal Writers' Project Negroes of New York files. Adam Clayton Powell Sr., *Against the Tide,* adds a few details.

18. *New York Times,* Oct. 2, 1896, p. 16.

19. Ogburn, "The Richmond Negro in New York City," 58, 64.

20. Ibid., 42.

21. Paul, "A Group of Virginia Negroes in New York City," 49; Hopper, "A Northern Negro Group," 36; and *New York Times,* Oct. 13, 1896, p. 2.

22. Ogburn, "The Richmond Negro in New York City," 39–40; and *New York Times,* Apr. 29, 1889, 11.

23. *New York Tribune,* Nov. 27, 1889, p. 5.

24. Ogburn, "The Richmond Negro in New York City," 21. The estimate of Chase's income

is based on figures for another A. M. E. sexton in Hopper, "A Northern Negro Group," 31. See also income tables in More, *Wage-Earners' Budgets*, 16–21.

25. Contemporary observer: Mary White Ovington, *Half a Man*, 34. Writing in 1930, Lomax, "A Social History of the Negro Population," 92, said that Italians pushed blacks out, although her tables 3a, 3b, and 4 (following p. 92) show black persistence. Similarly, Edwin G. Burrows and Mike Wallace, in *Gotham*, 993, 1123–24, after correctly noting that black Villagers began leaving in the 1860s, state that Italians pushed the "remaining blacks" out in the 1890s, when in fact (according to Caroline Ware: Census Summary folder, box 51, Caroline Ware Papers, F.D.R. Library) more than five hundred blacks lived in the Minetta area alone as late as 1910. The city directory for 1903–1904 shows the Abyssinian Baptists and Zion A. M. E. still in the Village, but the 1904–1905 directory places Mother Zion on West 89th St. and the Abyssinian Baptists on West 40th St. The Baptists left first: the *Sanborn Fire Insurance Map: New York* (1904), reel 55, vol. 3 index, lists Zion A. M. E. at 166 Waverly, the Abyssinian Baptists' former address.

26. Ovington, *Half a Man*, 34–35.

27. Silvano Tomasi, *Piety and Power*, 15–17.

28. Mary Elizabeth Brown, *From Italian Villages to Greenwich Village*, and Donald Tricarico, *The Italians of Greenwich Village*, 12.

29. Tricarico, *Italians of Greenwich Village*, 13.

30. *New York Tribune*, Mar. 6, 1895, p. 4; *New York Times*, Apr. 29, 1895, p. 2.

31. Brown, *From Italian Villages to Greenwich Village*, 17, 22–24.

32. *Il Progresso Italo-Americano*, May 10, 1898, p. 2.

33. Ibid.

34. Social worker: More, *Wage-Earners' Budgets*, 11. According to Tricarico, *The Italians of Greenwich Village*, 6, the six-to-one ratio applies to the years 1899–1910. Tomasi, *Piety and Power*, 16–17, notes that over a longer period, 1876–1930, the southerners' lead slips to four to one.

35. Tricarico, *The Italians of Greenwich Village*, 5–7, says that the earliest south Village Italian residents were northerners, often Genovese. For a useful map, "Location of Italian Colonies in New York City with Sources of Emigration in Italy," see Robert E. Park and Herbert A. Miller, *Old World Traits Transplanted*, 242.

36. Baptismal records: Brown, *From Italian Villages to Greenwich Village*, 16. Pio Parolin, "Autobiography," p. 41 of the Italian version, Father Pio Parolin Papers, Center for Migration Studies. Marriage registration figures: Patrizia Salvetti, "Una parrocchia italiana di New York e i suoi fedeli," 50–52.

37. Tricarico, *The Italians of Greenwich Village*, 14.

38. Mary Elizabeth Brown, "A Case Study of the Italian Laymen and Parish Life at Our Lady of Pompei, Greenwich Village, New York City," in Frank J. Cavaioli, Angela Danzi, and Salvatore J. LaGumina, eds., *Italian Americans and Their Public and Private Life*, 94–102. Also consulted: census, city directory, and parish records, the latter found in the "Records of Our Lady of Pompei," Center for Migration Studies.

39. *New York Times*, May 31, 1896, p. 32. Also spelled Fugazi.

40. On Fugazy see Victor R. Greene, *American Immigrant Leaders, 1800–1910*, 122–28.

41. On Scalabrini's arrival see *New York Times*, Aug. 4, 1901, p. 5. The *New York Times*, Aug. 11, 1901, p. 8, also reported his visit to the Bleecker Street offices of the Saint Raphael Society, an immigrant aid society under Scalabrini's direction with close ties to Our Lady of Pompei.

42. All Italian men over the age of twenty-one had to do mandatory military service. Brown, *From Italian Villages to Greenwich Village*, 21–22, 28–29.

43. Maria Sermolino, *Papa's Table d'Hôte*, 27.

44. Undated letter from Zaboglio to his superior, Bishop Scalabrini, quoted in Stephen Michael Di Giovanni, "Michael Augustine Corrigan and the Italian Immigrants," 373. For more details about Leary see ibid., 365, 372, and *New York Times*, Apr. 27, 1919, p. 22.

45. Marie's patrons: Parry, *Garrets and Pretenders* 91–95, and James L. Ford, *Forty-odd Years in the Literary Shop*, 206–207. Social service agencies and Italian immigrants: Lilian Brandt, *The Charity Organization Society of the City of New York, 1882–1907*, 160, and Robert A. Woods and Albert J. Kennedy, eds., *Handbook of Settlements*, 221.

46. Miss Leary and Father Demo: Brown, *From Italian Villages to Greenwich Village*, 32. Judson Church's outreach: Anthony F. Mauriello, "Our Lady of Pompei, New York City: Its First Twenty-five Years" (Typescript dated May 11, 1967), copy in Records of Our Lady of Pompei, series V, box 25, folder 291.

47. Simkhovitch, *Neighborhood*, 107.

48. Ware, *Greenwich Village*, 203–204, divides the newer arrivals into two subgroups, but their economic status was so similar that I combined them here.

49. Gene Fowler, *Beau James*, 21.

50. *U.S. Census: New York* (1900), reel 1082, E. D. 56, p. 14 and E. D. 58, pp. 13A–13B.

51. Quotation: Hamilton Fish Armstrong, *Those Days*, 62–63. *U.S. Census: New York* (1900), reel 1082, E. D. 56, pp. 14–15A; E. D. 57, pp. 1A–1B and 11B–12A; and E. D. 58, pp. 9A–12B.

52. John T. Ridge, "Irish County Societies in New York, 1880–1914," in Ronald H. Bayor and Timothy J. Meagher, eds., *The New York Irish*, 296. On County Clare Street and the County Antrim colony see Ware, *Greenwich Village*, 204, 639.

53. On County Clare organizations see *The Irish-American*, Jan. 25, 1902, p. 4; July 12, 1902, p. 5; Oct. 23, 1909, p. 4; Nov. 13, 1909, p. 8; Dec. 18, 1909, pp. 7–8, and Jan. 8, 1910, p. 2. My thanks to John T. Ridge for bringing William Crowley's cigar business to my attention.

54. Jones Street saloons: Simkhovitch, *Neighborhood*, 90.

55. Old-time Democrat's statement: Fowler, *Beau James*, 14. Ware, *Greenwich Village*, 204, quotes the unwritten rule.

56. Burrows and Wallace, *Gotham*, 828.

57. Robert D. Cross, *The Emergence of Liberal Catholicism in America*, 27.

58. For the diary of a priest who participated in Farrell's discussion group see Nelson J. Callahan, ed., *Diary of Richard L. Burtsell, Priest of New York*. Farrell, Burtsell, and Accademia: Florence D. Cohalan, *A Popular History of the Archdiocese of New York*, 121.

59. Simkhovitch, *Neighborhood*, 171–72.

60. On Father O'Flynn see *The Catholic News*, Aug. 25, 1906, p. 1, and Sept. 1, 1906, p. 2. The Boys' Club is described in *The Irish-American*, Jan. 11, 1902, p. 5.

61. For an analysis of Seth Low–era battles between municipal reformers and machine politicians see Kenneth Finegold, *Experts and Politicians*, 35–44. Oliver E. Allen, *The Tiger*, 170–205, offers a lively account of the Croker regime.

62. *New York Times*, Apr. 8, 1962, p. 87, and June 28, 1905, p. 3; *U.S. Census: New York*: (1880), reel 7, E. D. 231, p. 14; (1900), reel 1087, E. D. 145, p. 5; (1910), reel 1006, E. D. 164, p. 11A; and (1920), reel 1189, E. D. 233, p. 11.

63. *New York Times*, Apr. 8, 1962, p. 87.

64. Henry H. Curran, *Pillar to Post*, 129.

65. "Milk punch" quotation: Fowler, *Beau James*, 14. Simkhovitch mentions her friendship with Walker in *Neighborhood*, 170–71. On Voorhis: *New York Times*, Feb. 6, 1932, p. 15.
66. *New York Times*, May 16, 1913, p. 13.
67. For a list of New York City polling places in 1897 see *New York Times*, Oct. 8, 1897, p. 15.
68. Despite some factual errors, two old biographies, Louis J. Gribetz and Joseph Kane, *Jimmie Walker*, and Fowler, *Beau James*, remain the best sources of information on his career before 1909. George Walsh, *Gentleman Jimmy Walker*, 12–22, draws heavily on these accounts in describing Walker's early life.
69. *Tammany Times*, Sept. 30, 1901, p. 15. On commercial entertainments and working-class New Yorkers see Daniel Czitrom, "Underworlds and Underdogs," 536–58, and Kathy Peiss, *Cheap Amusements*.
70. Curran, *Pillar to Post*, 114.
71. Ibid., 115.
72. Tammany's response to the changing times: Thomas M. Henderson, *Tammany Hall and the New Immigrants*, and Robert F. Wesser, *A Response to Progressivism*.

2. For Their Mutual Benefit

1. The historian quotation: Alan F. Davis, *Spearheads for Reform*, 6–7. The constitution quoted here is the University Settlement Society's: Woods and Kennedy, eds., *Handbook of Settlements*, 228. For general background on the settlement movement see Davis, *Spearheads*, Mina Carson, *Settlement Folk*, and Robyn Muncy, *Creating a Female Dominion in American Reform, 1890–1935*.
2. "Headworker's Reports, March 1900 and October 1900," Series 4: Headworkers' Subject and Correspondence File, reel 6, microfilm ed., University Settlement Society of New York City Papers; hereafter cited as Univ.S.Soc. Papers.
3. University Settlement Society of New York, *Report for the Year, 1900*, 17.
4. James B. Reynolds, "The Settlement and Municipal Reform," in Isabel Barrows, ed., *Proceedings of the National Conference of Charities and Correction*, 142; and "Headworker's Report, March 1900," reel 6, Univ.S.Soc. Papers.
5. Thomas's words as quoted in the University Settlement Society of New York, *Report for the Year, 1900*, 18–20.
6. James B. Reynolds to Mary K. Simkhovitch, Mar. 13, 1901, reel 6, Univ.S.Soc. Papers.
7. *New York World*, May 15, 1901, p. 1.
8. The quotations are from ibid., and an undated *New York Sun* clipping in reel 6, Univ.S.Soc. Papers. See also *New York Evening Journal*, May 15, 1901, p. 8; *New York Times*, same date, p. 5; and *New York Tribune*, same date, p. 1.
9. Mary K. Simkhovitch, *Neighborhood*, 92.
10. University Settlement Society of New York, *Year Book* (1901), 64–67.
11. Ibid., 64; and Richmond Hill House report for 1907, quoted in Woods and Kennedy; eds., *Handbook of Settlements*, 221.
12. University Settlement Society of New York, *Year Book* (1901), 66–67. See Carson, *Settlement Folk*, 52, on the slum dwellers' generally greater receptivity to "organized, regularly scheduled, and resident-led activities" over "simple sociability."
13. On this group see James Boylan, *Revolutionary Lives*, and Robert D. Reynolds Jr., "The Millionaire Socialists." For Finn, who married Scott in 1904, see "Who's Who Section," reel 22, Univ.S.Soc. Papers.

14. Davis, *Spearheads for Reform*, 33–34.

15. Jeremy P. Felt, *Hostages of Fortune*, 38–62, 220. See reel 2, Univ.S.Soc. Papers, for Hunter's May 19, 1903 child labor campaign report.

16. See Richmond Hill House's introductory announcement, dated August 25, 1903, in box 4, James Graham Phelps Stokes Papers.

17. Robert Hunter to V. Everit Macy, Aug. 9, 1902, reel 6, Univ. S. Soc. Papers.

18. Simkhovitch, *Neighborhood*, 60. Simkhovitch's *Neighborhood* (1938) and her *Here Is God's Plenty* (1949) are invaluable primary sources on her life and thought. For a scholarly treatment see Domenica Maria Barbuto, " 'The Matrix of Understanding.' "

19. Simkhovitch, *Neighborhood*, 11–59, on her early career.

20. Ibid., 88.

21. Henry N. Hyde and Emerson G. Taylor, eds., *Quindecennial Record, Class of Eighteen Hundred and Ninety-five, Yale College*, 116.

22. Jones Street's buildings: *Sanborn Fire Insurance Maps: New York* (1904; microfilm ed., 1983), reel 55, vol. 3, map 5.

23. Population and nationality data from *U.S. Census: New York* (1900), reel 1085, E. V. 99.

24. Simkhovitch, *Neighborhood*, 112–13, 116–17, 138; Greenwich House, *Second Annual Report* (1904), 7–8. For microfilm copies of this and other *Annual Reports:* Greenwich House Papers. See also Mary White Ovington, *The Walls Came Tumbling Down*, 13.

25. Simkhovitch, *Neighborhood*, 90.

26. Greenwich House, *First Annual Report* (1903), 5. For the visitor's observations: *New York Times*, Aug. 16, 1903, p. 10.

27. The Greenwich House men no sooner moved out of number 88 in September 1903 than Robert Hunter, having resigned as University Settlement's headworker and married J. G. Phelps Stokes's sister Caroline, moved in. While the Hunters were still in residence, Caroline's unmarried sister, Helen Stokes, rented 90 Grove Street from Blum. (She later bought it and eventually purchased number 88 also, leasing the space she didn't need in the houses to social progressives in her circle, including her brother, J. G. Phelps Stokes, and his wife, Rose Pastor Stokes.) These houses: Henry Hope Reed Jr., "Discover New York," *New York Herald Tribune*.

28. Simkhovitch, *Neighborhood*, 95.

29. Miriam Finn Scott's statement in "Who's Who Section," Reel 22, Univ.S.Soc. Papers.

30. Simkhovitch, *Neighboorhood*, 95–96.

31. Ibid., 36.

32. Greenwich House, *First Annual Report*, 3.

33. The quotation is from ibid., 8.

34. More, *Wage-Earners' Budgets*, 11–12.

35. Ibid., 6, 29, 136.

36. Ibid., 12.

37. Ibid., 152–201.

38. Ibid., 190–95.

39. Ibid., 191–92.

40. Ibid., 190–93.

41. Ibid., 167–71.

42. Ibid., 170.

43. Ibid., 171–75.

44. Ibid., 172, 174–75.

45. Ibid., 30, 156–59.

46. Ibid., 156, 158.
47. Ibid., 159; and Elsa Herzfeld, *A West Side Rookery*, 22.
48. Herzfeld, *A West Side Rookery*, 21–23. Anna Schumacher is called Mrs. Fisher throughout.
49. Ibid., 5. The privy's outdoor location is mentioned by Simkhovitch, *Here Is God's Plenty*, 33.
50. Herzfeld, *A West Side Rookery*, 9.
51. Ibid., 9–11; and *U.S. Census: New York* (1900), reel 1085, E. D. 100, pp. 4A–4B.

3. The Patrician Response

1. Henry James, *The American Scene*, 4, 87–95.
2. Neith Boyce, "Autobiography," series III, box 30, folder 914, p. 129; Hapgood Family Papers.
3. *New York Tribune*, May 1, 1889, p. 8.
4. *New York Times*, May 31, 1890, p. 1; May 5, 1895, p. 3.
5. Ibid., May 31, 1890, p. 1.
6. Ibid., May 5, 1895, p. 3.
7. Sidney Ratner, ed., *New Light on the Great American Fortunes*, 51.
8. Terry Miller, *Greenwich Village and How It Got That Way*, 225. For background on the People's Institute see Robert B. Fisher, "The People's Institute of New York City, 1897–1934."
9. For information on these households see *U.S. Census: New York* (1900), reel 1085, E. D. 106, pp. 15B, 16A, 18B.
10. On the "new immigrants": Maxine Schwartz Seller, ed., *Immigrant Women*, 83, 87. See also Twelfth Census of the United States, 1900, "Special Reports: Occupations", 646.
11. Richard Watson Gilder and *The Century*: Arthur John, *The Best Years of the Century*, ix–xi, 1–4; and Henry F. May, *The End of American Innocence*, 52–79.
12. Mary Heaton Vorse, "Village Story," box 33, Mary Heaton Vorse Papers.
13. On some Mugwumps as social progressives: Gerald W. McFarland, *Mugwumps, Morals, and Politics, 1884–1920*, 107–23.
14. Michael G. Kammen, "Richard Watson Gilder and the New York Tenement House Commission of 1894," 364–82. On the Trinity furor: *New York Times* Dec. 9, 1894, p. 1; Dec. 13, 1894, p. 3; Dec. 14, 1894, p. 2; Dec. 24, 1894, p. 8.
15. James A. Hijiya, "Four Ways of Looking at a Philanthropist: A Study of Robert Weeks de Forest," 404–18.
16. On John Taylor Johnston and the Metropolitan Museum of Art: Calvin Tomkins, *Merchants and Masterpieces*. After her father's death Emily Johnston de Forest became a major benefactor of the museum, a role described by Kathleen D. McCarthy, *Women's Culture*, 120–21.
17. Emily Johnston de Forest, *John Johnston of New York, Merchant*, 154.
18. Armstrong, *Those Days*, 62–63.
19. Facts about these individuals and their households was drawn from census and directory sources and the *Greenwich Village Historic District Designation Report*, 1:52–59, 142–49.
20. The best single source on de Forest is still Hijiya, "Four Ways of Looking at a Philanthropist," cited above in number 15.
21. Brandt, *The Charity Organization Society of the City of New York*, 157.

22. For the quotation see Hijiya, "Four Ways of Looking at a Philanthropist," 413–14. C.O.S. *Annual Reports* from the 1880s show that de Forest served on district committees from 1884 to 1888. See series I, box 192, Charity Organization Society files, Community Service Society Papers.

23. Greenwich Village housing data: Robert W. de Forest and Lawrence Veiller, eds., *The Tenement House Problem*, 1:194, 200–201, 205.

24. Richard Plunz, *A History of Housing in New York City*, 48. Plunz also notes (pp. 84–85, 125–26) less positive results. A vigorous case that for the poorest of the poor the law's benefits "proved to be largely illusory" is made by Anthony Jackson, *A Place Called Home*, 135–56. An essay by Jenna Weissman Joselit, "The Landlord as Czar," in Ronald Lawson, ed., *The Tenant Movement in New York City, 1904–1984*, describes the angry response of Lower East Side tenement dwellers to rising rents, 1904–1914 (pp. 40–49).

25. Lowell's comment: "Fortieth Anniversary [of Robert W. de Forest's] Presidency of the Charity Organization Society, January 10, 1928," series I, box 96, p. 46, C.O.S. files, Community Service Society Papers. Scholarly treatments of Low's decision and de Forest's and Veiller's responses differ. See Hijiya, "Four Ways of Looking at a Philanthropist," 415; Roy Lubove, *The Progressives and the Slums*, 153–54; Gerald Kurland, *Seth Low*, 145–46; and Davis, *Spearheads for Reform*, 183.

26. *New York Times*, Dec. 7, 1901, p. 1.

27. De Forest and Veiller, eds., *The Tenement House Problem*, 1:201. For housing trends see Ware, *Greenwich Village*, chart 1, opp. p. 12.

28. James W. Kennedy, *The Unknown Worshipper*, 80, 88.

29. There is a chapter on Grant in Kennedy, *The Unknown Worshipper*, 77–90. For examples of his harping on the free pew situation see Church of the Ascension, *Year Book* (1905), p. 3; (1906), p. 3; (1911), p. 3; and (1913), p. 8—all published in the stated years by Ascension Press of New York. Copies at New York Public Library.

30. Church of the Ascension, *Year Book* (1907), 5.

31. Grant used the word "inclusion" in ibid., 5. Elsewhere he seemed to prefer the word "catholicity," as for example in the 1908 *Year Book*, 5–6.

32. The quoted words, in the order they appear in the text, are from *World's Work* (July 1905), 6414; *New York Tribune* (Jan. 21, 1905); *New York Mail* (Jan. 5, 1899)—all found in "Scrapbooks," box 37, People's Institute Papers, New York Public Library. See also Fisher, "The People's Institute of New York City."

33. *Christian Herald* (Jan. 29, 1902), clipping in box 37, People's Institute Papers, New York Public Library. Another collection, small but useful: People's Institute Papers, Cooper Union for Science and Art.

34. Church of the Ascension, *Year Book* (1908), 88.

35. Ibid., 85.

36. *New York Times*, April 9, 1910, part 2, p. 191, a review of Irvine's autobiography, *From the Bottom Up* (1909). For more on Irvine see *New York Sun*, Nov. 23, 1913, part 4, p. 4, and Kathryn J. Oberdeck, *The Evangelist and the Impresario*, 237–49, which cover his career at the Church of the Ascension. Oberdeck notes (p. 403) that some of Irvine's papers, including copies of sermons from the Church of the Ascension period, have been deposited at the Huntington Library, San Marino, Calif., where "they await archival organization."

37. Church of the Ascension, *Year Book* (1908), 82.

38. Ibid., 82, 85, 87; Kennedy, *The Unknown Worshipper*, 84.

39. Madge C. Jenison, "The Church and the Social Unrest," *Outlook* 89 (May 16, 1908): 114.

40. Church of the Ascension, *Year Book* (1908), 5–6, 85.
41. Ibid., 82, 86.
42. Church of the Ascension, *Year Book* (1909), 4, 69–70.
43. For a complete list of vestrymen see Kennedy, *The Unknown Worshipper*, 166–73, and Church of the Ascension, *Year Book* (1910), 4.
44. *New York Times*, June 25, 1910, p. 1, which misspelled Fieldman's name.
45. Ibid. For the pre-1913 Liberal Club: Lincoln Steffens to his mother, Feb. 7, 1910, in Ella Winter and Granville Hicks, eds., *The Letters of Lincoln Steffens*, 1:237–38.
46. *New York Times*, June 27, 1910, p. 2.
47. Church of the Ascension, *Year Book* (1910), 5–6.
48. *New York Times*, Nov. 10, 1910, p. 5; and Bruce St. John, ed., *John Sloan's New York Scene*, 475.
49. Church of the Ascension, *Year Book* (1908), 6.
50. *New York Times*, June 27, 1910, p. 2.
51. These individuals were identified through standard biographical sources: *Dictionary of American Biography*, *Who Was Who*, and *Who's Who in New York*.
52. Washington Square Association *Bulletin* (hereafter cited as WSA *Bulletin*), no. 1 (Feb. 19, 1907): 1, and no. 4 (Dec. 31, 1907): 1. Copies at New York Public Library.
53. Ibid., no. 3 (May 15, 1907): 6.
54. Ibid., no. 8 (Oct. 31, 1908): 2.
55. J. Owen Grundy, "No. 8 Former Home of Mayors," *The Villager* (July 29, 1948), clipping in a Grundy scrapbook, "Greenwich Village–Washington Square."
56. *U.S. Census: New York* (1910), reel 1061, E. D. 826, p. 11B, for Mastrino; ibid., reel 1030, E. D. 808, p. 1A, for Gordon.
57. See WSA *Bulletin*, no. 10 (Mar. 25, 1909): 6–12, 17–18, 20–24; and no. 13 (Jan. 1, 1910): 3, 5.
58. Ibid., no. 10 (Mar. 25, 1909): 11–12, 20–21.
59. Ibid., no. 11 (June 17, 1909): 6.
60. Ibid., no. 11 (June 17, 1909): 12–13; no. 13 (Jan. 1, 1910): 3; and no. 14 (Feb. 28, 1910): 5–6, 11.
61. Curran, *Pillar to Post*, 134.
62. Armstrong, *Those Days*, 59.
63. WSA *Bulletin*, no. 10 (Mar. 25, 1909): 21–22; no. 11 (June 17, 1909): 2, 11; no. 13 (Jan. 1, 1910): 5; and no. 15 (Oct. 1, 1910): 14–16.
64. Curran, *Pillar to Post*, 116, 118–26, 130–31.
65. Ibid., 132–34.
66. Ibid., 134–36, and WSA *Bulletin*, no. 22 (Dec. 17, 1913): 21; and no. 19 (Dec. 30, 1911): 10–11.
67. WSA *Bulletin*, no. 17 (Apr. 29, 1911): 10.
68. Ibid., no. 15 (Oct. 1, 1910): 8; no. 17 (Apr. 29, 1911): 16; no. 18 (Sept. 30, 1911): 4, 12; no. 20 (Mar. 30, 1912): 9.
69. Ibid., no. 11 (June 17, 1909): 8.
70. Ibid., no. 20 (Mar. 30, 1912): 4–5; no. 21 (Dec. 17, 1912): 4; and no. 18 (Sept. 30, 1911): 2, 9, 12–13. On Stover: *New York Times*, Mar. 23, 1911, p. 6; and Apr. 26, 1929, p. 25.
71. WSA *Bulletin*, no. 17 (Apr. 29, 1911): 10.
72. Paul Boyer, *Urban Masses and Moral Order in America, 1820–1920*, 235–51. The quotation is from p. 240. For related material on Central Park see Roy Rosenzweig and Elizabeth Blackmar, *The Park and the People*, 392–94, 412–16, 423–25.

73. WSA *Bulletin*, no. 20 (Mar. 30, 1912): 18–19.

74. Ibid., 19–23.

75. Ibid., no. 21 (Dec. 17, 1912): 4; no. 23 (Feb. 28, 1914): 1, 4, 9, 18–19; and no. 24 (July 14, 1914): 1–5, 11–12, 17, 19.

76. Ibid., no. 20 (Mar. 30, 1912): 1.

4. ALLIES

1. On Boyce and Hapgood see the Hapgood Family Papers. See also three items by Ellen Kay Trimberger on the Boyce-Hapgood marriage: Trimberger, ed., *Intimate Warriors;* Trimberger, "The New Woman and the New Sexuality," in Heller and Rudnick, eds., *1915, The Cultural Moment;* and Trimberger, "Feminism, Men, and Modern Love," in Ann Snitow, Cristine Stansell, and Sharon Thompson, eds., *Powers of Desire*, 131–52.

2. For N.Y.U. and women law students see Phyllis Eckhaus, "Restless Women," 1996–2013. Women and the legal profession ca. 1900: Karen Berger Morello, *The Invisible Bar;* and Virginia G. Drachman, *Women Lawyers and the Origins of Professional Identity in America.*

3. Doty and Rauh: Madeleine Z. Doty, "Autobiography," box 2, folder 32, Madeleine Z. Doty Papers.

4. Printed sources on Vorse include her autobiography, *A Footnote to Folly;* Dee Garrison, ed., *Rebel Pen;* and Dee Garrison, *Mary Heaton Vorse.* The major manuscript collection is the Mary Heaton Vorse Papers, Wayne State University. Vorse's oral history memoir, "The Reminiscences of Mary H. Vorse," (Columbia University), is strongest on her later years.

5. Vorse, *A Footnote to Folly*, p. 32; and *New York Tribune*, Feb. 11, 1906, sec. 4, p. 4, in which the group is called "A Club." See also James Boylan, *Revolutionary Lives.*

6. *New York Tribune*, Feb. 11, 1906, sec. 4, p. 4.

7. Ibid. See also *New York Tribune*, Feb. 8, 1906, p. 2; *New York Evening Journal*, Feb. 7, 1906, p. 5; and Feb. 8, 1906, p. 9.

8. Ernest Poole, *The Bridge*, 113–76. English Walling to Anna Strunsky, from Paris, undated 1905, in series I, box 15, Anna Strunsky Walling Papers, Yale University; or reel 32292, microfilm ed., Anna Strunsky Walling Papers, Tamiment Institute Library.

9. Brubaker in Anna Strunsky Walling et. al., *William English Walling*, 39; Walling to Strunsky, undated 1905, series I, box 15, Anna Strunsky Walling Papers, Yale; and *New York World*, June 16, 1908, p. 1.

10. Filia Holtzman, "A Mission that Failed," 227–37. See also Reynolds Jr., "The Millionaire Socialists," 15–25; Poole, *The Bridge*, 172–74; Doty, "Autobiography," ch. 3, pp. 3–4; and Ernest Poole, "Maxim Gorki in New York," 79–80.

11. On the NYWTUL see Nancy Schrom Dye, *As Equals and as Sisters.*

12. Max Horn, *The Intercollegiate Socialist Society, 1905–1921*, 1–15, 235–36.

13. Charles Flint Kellogg, *NAACP: A History of the National Association for the Advancement of Colored People*, 9–16, 97.

14. 1912 Socialist Party platform: Henry Steele Commager, ed., *Documents of American History* (6th ed., 1958), 249–53.

15. Teller quotation: *New York Tribune*, Feb. 11, 1906, sec. 4, p. 4. Vorse, *A Footnote to Folly*, 34.

16. On the Pooles: Truman Frederick Keefer, *Ernest Poole*, 35. The marriage of Graham and Rose Pastor Stokes, another Protestant-Jewish couple in the University Settlement Soci-

ety group, received even more intense newspaper attention: box 75, J. G. P. Stokes Papers. See also Patrick Renshaw, "Rose of the World," 415–23.

17. *The Reader's Guide to Periodical Literature* listed many items by A Clubbers, 1906–10: Martha Bensley (4), Howard Brubaker (1), Robert Bruère (9), Arthur Bullard (4), Madeleine Z. Doty (1), Miriam Finn Scott (4), Hamilton Holt (7), Ernest Poole (30), Leroy Scott (17), Charlotte Teller (2), Mary Heaton Vorse (50), English Walling (13), Walter Weyl (11), Bertha Poole Weyl (7).

18. Poole, *The Bridge*, 171; Vorse, *A Footnote to Folly*, 32–33.

19. Garrison, *Vorse*, 38; Walter Weyl to Mary Heaton Vorse, June 26, 1907, Vorse Papers, WSU.

20. Doty, "Autobiography," ch. 2, pp. 2–3.

21. Ibid., ch. 3, pp. 1–4.

22. Doty, "Autobiography," ch. 3; and Eastman to Mother, Sept. 30, Oct. 1, and Oct. 17, 1906, box 6, folder 168, Crystal Eastman Papers.

23. Eastman to Mother, Feb. 18, 1905, box 6, folder 168, Eastman Papers.

24. Eastman to Mother, Dec. 5, 1906, ibid.

25. Crystal to Max, n.d., [Dec. 1906]; to Mother, Feb. 12, 1907, ibid.

26. Doty, "Autobiography," ch. 3, p. 4.

27. *New York Times*, Jan. 12, 1907, Saturday Review of Books section, p. 16; Doty, "Autobiography," ch. 3, p. 7.

28. "Love is everything": Anna Strunsky Walling, "David Graham Phillips, The Last Years of His Life," 20; see also a Phillips letter (1910) quoted in Louis Filler, *Voice of Democracy, A Critical Biography of David Graham Phillips*, 145. "Love and sex": Doty, "Autobiography," ch. 3, p. 7.

29. Doty, "Autobiography," ch. 3, pp. 8, 10; and David Graham Phillips to Doty, June 27, 1907, box I, folder 12, in ibid. Doty saved fifty-five of Phillips's letters to her.

30. *Charities and the Commons* was renamed *Survey* in 1909. On Kellogg see Clarke Chambers, *Paul U. Kellogg and the Survey*.

31. Eastman to Mother, June 3, 1907, box 6, folder 169, and Crystal to Max Eastman, "Friday," typescript 1909–5 [n.d., 1909], box 6, folder 171, Eastman Papers.

32. Simkhovitch's statements: Greenwich House, *First Annual Report* (1903), 1; *Fifth Annual Report* (1906), 7; and *Eighth Annual Report* (1909), 17–18.

33. Greenwich House, *Tenth Annual Report* (1911), 14; and *Eighth Annual Report* (1909), 16.

34. Charity Organization Society, *Twenty-sixth Annual Report* (for year ending Sept. 1908), 29–33 copy in box 193, C.O.S. files. Simkhovitch, *Neighborhood*, 145.

35. Simkhovitch, *Neighborhood*, 160. *New York Times* coverage of the exhibit and conference: Mar. 1, p. 5; Mar. 11, p. 3; Mar. 12, p. 2; Mar. 14, p. 3; and Mar. 15, p. 5—all in 1909.

36. Simkhovitch, *Neighborhood*, 90, 160, and Simkhovitch, *Here Is God's Plenty*, 101.

37. On Woerishoffer: Roderick W. Nash, "Carola Woerishoffer," in Edward T. James, ed., *Notable American Women*, 4:539–40; *Carola Woerishoffer*; and Greenwich House, *Tenth Annual Report* (1911), 4–7.

38. Ida Tarbell, as quoted in *Carola Woerishoffer*, p. 5.

39. Sue Ainslie Clark and Edith Wyatt, "Women Laundry Workers in New York," 404.

40. Greenwich House, *Tenth Annual Report* (1911), 4–6.

41. Doty, "Autobiography," ch. 3, pp. 13, 19.

42. On Forel: Bram Dijkstra, *Idols of Perversity: Fantasies of Feminine Evil in Fin-de-Siècle Culture* (1986), 216. See Doty, "Autobiography," ch. 3, pp. 19, 20, where she rendered the title of Forel's book as "Sex and Psychology."

43. Ibid., ch. 3, p. 20.

44. *New York Herald*, April 24, 1910, reprinted in Blanche Wiesen Cook, ed., *Crystal Eastman on Women and Revolution*, 358–66; and Max Eastman, *Enjoyment of Living*, 340.

45. Eastman's *Enjoyment of Living*, 319–84, gives a detailed account of these events, but one marred by his air of studied superiority to Milholland and Rauh.

46. Vorse, *A Footnote to Folly*, 38.

47. Pauline Newman, "The Triangle Shirtwaist Factory," in Joan Morrison and Charlotte Fox Zabusky, eds., *American Mosaic*, 9–14. Newman worked for the company from 1901 to 1909.

48. Transcript I:30, N.Y.C. Immigrant Women, CUNY American Social History Project.

49. Accounts of the strike: Dye, *As Equals and Sisters*, 88–94; Meredith Tax, *The Rising of the Women*, 205–40; Philip S. Foner, *Women and the American Labor Movement*, 133–67.

50. For the WTUL's list of eleven major activities undertaken on behalf of the strikers see Tax, *The Rising of the Women*, 228.

51. *New York World*, Dec. 4, 1909, p. 18.

52. See "College Girls as Pickets in a Strike," *New York Times*, Dec. 19, 1909, Magazine Section, p. 5. On individuals: Milholland in Eastman, *Enjoyment of Living*, 319; Woerishoffer in *Carola Woerishoffer*, 21–23; Bruère in Martha Bensley Bruère, "The Triangle Fire," 137; Weyl in *New York Times*, Dec. 4, 1909, p. 20; Vorse in Vorse, *A Footnote to Folly*, 33. The *New York Call*, Nov. 24, 1909, p. 2, reports that arrests of Triangle strikers dropped from 146 in the four weeks before NYWTUL women began picketing to only three in the next seven weeks, indicating that A Clubbers joined the picket lines before Vorse left for North Africa in late October 1909.

53. Michael McGerr, "Political Style and Women's Power, 1830–1930," 864–85.

54. *New York Times*, May 22, 1910, p. 11; May 4, 1913, p. 1.

55. *New York Times*, Dec. 19, 1909, Magazine Section, p. 5.

56. On tensions in the NYWTUL-worker coalition: Tax, *The Rising of the Women*, 226–27, 229–31, and Dye, *As Equals and Sisters*, 110–21, 134–37. Dye and Tax also find much to praise, as does Mari Jo Buhle, *Women and American Socialism, 1870–1920*, 189–90. For divisions among second-wave feminists see Rachel Blau DuPlessis and Ann Snitow, eds., *The Feminist Memoir Project*, 8–21.

57. Vorse, *A Footnote to Folly*, 39.

58. Leon Stein, *The Triangle Fire*, 211.

59. Bruère, "The Triangle Fire," 137.

60. Ernest Poole, "My Street," 188.

61. These names come from newspaper reports; the "Registry of Masses," no. 4, in series XII, box 46, pp. 478–94, Records of Our Lady of Pompei: and Brown, *From Italian Villages to Greenwich Village*, 40–41.

62. *New York Times*, Apr. 27, 1911, p. 6.

63. Frances Perkins, "The Reminiscences of Frances Perkins," 90–114, 215–17; Czitrom, "Underworlds and Underdogs," 553–56.

64. Crystal Eastman, "A Year's Work-Accidents and Their Costs," 1143–74, and "Work-Accidents and Employer's Liability," 788–94; and More, *Wage-Earners' Budgets* (1907). For an investigator with close ties to Richmond Hill House: Mary Van Kleeck, *Artificial Flower Makers*, and the Mary Van Kleeck Papers.

5. VALUE CONFLICTS

1. Simkhovitch, *Neighborhood*, 90.
2. Greenwich House, *Third Annual Report* (1904), 5.
3. Charles W. Gardner, *The Doctor and the Devil*, 58; and *New York Herald*, Jan. 5, 1892, p. 8. For the social context of male sexual practice in turn-of-the-century New York: George Chauncey Jr., *Gay New York*, 37–41, 67–68. Chauncey says (p. 68) that "slide" was a slang term denoting a place where men in women's attire solicited male customers.
4. *New York Times*, Mar. 1, 1903, p. 10.
5. N.Y.C. Committee of Fourteen, *The Social Evil in New York City*, table XI, pp. 210–11. For the geography of Manhattan brothels, 1880–1889 and 1900–1909, see the maps in Timothy J. Gilfoyle, *City of Eros*, 200–201.
6. Committee of 14, *The Social Evil in New York City*, xi–xxxiii. For statistics on Raines Law hotels in 1905: George J. Kneeland, *Commercialized Prostitution in New York City*, 34.
7. The list is in *The Social Evil in New York City*, 43.
8. On Whitin see *New York Times*, July 20, 1926, p. 19. New York City directories (1907–1908, 1910–11) listed his address as 501 West 113th. Several undercover reports by "F. H. Whitin, Investigator": box 28, Committee of Fourteen Papers, New York Public Library (hereafter cited as Com.14 Papers, NYPL).
9. For a scholarly account of this sordid affair see Paul R. Baker, *Stanny*, 321–98. For the views of a great-granddaughter of White's: Suzannah Lessard, *The Architect of Desire*, 277–304.
10. Raines Law sandwiches at O'Connor's: Mary Heaton Vorse, "Village Story" or "The Villager," box 33, Vorse Papers, WSU. For the committee's file on "5 Greenwich Avenue, Luke O'Connor, licensee," see box 46, Com.14 Papers, NYPL.
11. From midnight to 5:15 A.M. the interval between trains on the Sixth Avenue Elevated was fifteen minutes: *Appleton's Dictionary of Greater New York*, 90.
12. Willoughby C. Waterman, *Prostitution and Its Repression in New York City, 1900–1931*, 103. Clinton Place Hotel file in box 47, Com.14 Papers, NYPL.
13. On Cadigan's: card file, box 47; investigator's reports, Jan. 5, 1907, box 28; Com.14, *Bulletin #15* (Dec. 23, 1907) and *Bulletin #16* (Feb. 10, 1908) in box 86; Com.14 Papers, NYPL.
14. Curtin's: card files, box 47; investigator's report, box 28—both in ibid.
15. On Wallace's Golden Swan, see box 47, ibid. Thomas J. Wallace's obituary: *New York Times*, March 16, 1922, p. 17. In the 1910s, the Golden Swan was the leading example of a Village saloon where there was interracial mixing across class lines. For the evolution of this phenomenon in the 1920s: Kevin J. Mumford, *Interzones*, 133–56.
16. This account and the one on the West Side Cafe draw on notes made by various inspectors on various evenings in the early 1910s. A few minor changes in punctuation and spelling have been made to avoid an excessive use of *sic*. On the Green Cup Cafe: investigators' notes for Aug. 26 and Sept. 16, 1911, Feb. 6 and May 23, 1912, Apr. 26, 1913, and Oct. 29, 191[5?], in box 28, Com.14 Papers, NYPL. A 1912 survey of the going rates at 140 brothels (Kneeland, *Commercialized Prostitution in New York City*, 4–5) broke them down as follows: 20 "fifty-cent houses," 80 "one-dollar houses," 6 at two dollars, and 34 charging five to ten dollars.
17. West Side Cafe quotations here and in the next two paragraphs: investigator's reports, Aug. 26, 1911, Feb. 6, 1912, and May 191[2?], in box 28, Com.14 Papers, NYPL.

18. *U.S. Census: New York* (1910), reel 1030, E. D. 809, p. 19A. For the committee's campaign against Seiderman (also spelled Saiderman, Seidman, Saideman) and his successor: file for 6 Carmine St., box 44, Com.14 Papers, NYPL.

19. Minetta park plan: See Simkhovitch's letters to George McAneny and E. P. Goodrich in Mar. 1912, unprocessed box 6 (1911–13), Greenwich House Papers. Simkhovitch noted some successes in the Minetta Lane–Minetta Street crackdown in Greenwich House, *Eleventh Annual Report* (1913), 6–7. Gilfoyle, *City of Eros*, maps X and XI, pp. 201–202, show a significant drop in the number of Minetta-area brothels in the 1910s.

20. *The Social Evil in New York City*, xxxii.

21. More, *Wage-Earners' Budgets*, 94–97. Theater statistics: Lary May, *Screening Out the Past*, 35, 44. The quoted words: *The Social Evil in New York City*, xiv, 54–55.

22. More, *Wage-Earners' Budgets*, 94–97.

23. *The Social Evil in New York City*, 53.

24. Margaret M. Hanway to Father Antonio Demo, April 19, 1910, series I, box 1, Records of Our Lady of Pompei. The census gives the family name as Farcella: *U.S. Census: New York* (1910), reel 1005, E. D. 126, p. 12A. The Gazzola (not her real name) quotation: transcript II:25–26, N.Y.C. Immigrant Women, CUNY American Social History Project.

25. Lewis A. Erenberg, *Steppin' Out*, 154. On middle- and working-class crosscurrents see Peiss, *Cheap Amusements*, 182–84.

26. Greenwich House, *Tenth Annual Report* (1911), 13. Similar efforts by the People's Institute and University Settlement met with similar responses (boredom or disorder) from their working-class clientele. See Peiss, *Cheap Amusements*, 180–83.

27. Otho G. Cartwright, *Boyhood and Lawlessness*, 40–47, 141–42.

28. Simkhovitch on the neighborhood's boy gangs: Greenwich House, *Eleventh Annual Report* (1913), 13.

29. This description of the Village crime rate draws on the *New York World*, July 3, 1898, p. 20; and robbery statistics compiled in 1899 by state investigators: New York State Assembly, *Report of the Special [Mazet] Committee of the Assembly Appointed to Investigate the Public Offices and Departments of the City of New York and the Counties Therein Included*, 4:4303.

30. The standard account of the Hudson Dusters, still useful despite many errors: Herbert Asbury, *The Gangs of New York*, 256–60. See also Luc Sante, *Low Life*, 225–26.

31. *New York Times*, Mar. 1, 1903, p. 10. See also ibid., Aug. 7, 1911, p. 1.

32. Asbury, *The Gangs of New York*, 256–57.

33. *New York World*, Dec. 6, 1914, Metropolitan Section, p. 4.

34. Ashbury, *The Gangs of New York*, 365–66; and *New York World*, May 13, 1915, pp. 1, 24, for Dopey Benny's alliance with the Dusters. On Dopey Benny see also Albert Fried, *The Rise and Fall of the Jewish Gangster in America*, 32–36, 82–85.

35. *New York Call*, Sept. 17, 1913, p. 1; and *New York Times*, Sept. 17, 1913, p. 1; Nov. 4, 1913, p. 1.

36. Asbury, *The Gangs of New York*, 258, describes the O'Sullivan affair but gets many details wrong. Arrests of Dusters: *New York World*, Nov. 5, 1913, p. 20; *New York Times*, Mar. 12, 1915, p. 5.

37. *New York World*, Dec. 26, 1914, p. 5; and *New York Times*, Dec. 26, 1914, p. 1. For part of the poem: Asbury, *The Gangs of New York*, 259.

38. Baff murder: *New York Times*, Nov. 25, 1914, p. 1; and Nov. 26, 1914, p. 6, the first of many reports. The Costello incident: *New York Times*, March 12, 1915, p. 5.

39. *New York Times*, March 5, 1916, p. 17, Sept. 8, 1918, p. 14, Aug. 2, 1919, p. 18; Aug. 3, 1919, p. 15.

40. Hapgood, *Types from City Streets*, 9.

41. Arthur Bartlett Maurice, *New York in Fiction*, 95. Maurice revisited these sites in 1916, reporting the results in *The New York of the Novelists*.

42. William Dean Howells, *A Hazard of New Fortunes*, 43; and David Graham Phillips, *The Great God Success*, 34–35.

43. Gender, age, and occupational data from *U.S. Census: New York* (1910), reel 1030, E. D. 808, pp. 7B, 11B, 12A, 13A.

44. For the quotation and valuable statistical information: Frank Luther Mott, *A History of American Magazines*, 4:8, 20–21, according to Mott, *McClure's* had substantial revenue from advertising but still lagged *Collier's* in 1905. See also Richard Ohmann, *Selling Culture*, 81–109.

45. Elizabeth Shepley Sergeant, *Willa Cather*, 33, 36. See also Sergeant, "Toilers of the Tenements," 231–48.

46. Sarah Orne Jewett to Willa Cather, Dec. 13, 1908, Anne Fields, ed., *Letters of Sarah Orne Jewett*, 249.

47. Both Mama Bertolotti's and Renganeschi's, the latter unnamed, are described in Charles F. Peters, "When New York Dines A La Bohe'me," 77–85. The Black Cat's history is difficult to untangle. A few sources treat the West Broadway version as the original, but two contemporaneous sources contradict this, Madeleine Doty's "Autobiography," ch. 2, p. 4, and Guido Bruno, who wrote in 1915 (*Bruno Chap Books*, vol. 1, special number on "Anarchists," pp. 6–7) that the original Black Cat on Bleecker "closed long ago."

48. On Marjorie Organ before her marriage to Henri: Bennard B. Perlman, *Robert Henri*, 85–86.

49. Parry, *Garrets and Pretenders* (1933), 258; and Stephen French Whitman, *Predestined*, 241.

50. Box 46, Com.14 Papers, NYPL.

51. Sermolino, *Papa's Table d'Hôte* (1952), 40, 81, 84, 87, 91, 126, 135. Anacleto Sermolino's obituary: *New York Times*, Jan. 16, 1937, p. 15.

52. On Whitney and the MacDougal Alley artists: Avis Berman, *Rebels on Eighth Street*, 75–77.

53. Whitney's journal, quoted in B. H. Friedman, *Gertrude Vanderbilt Whitney*, 223.

54. For Whitney's ties with the settlement see Greenwich House *Annual Reports*, Greenwich House Papers.

55. Anne Blaugrund, "The Tenth Street Studio Building, A Roster, 1857–1895," 64–71.

56. There are many books on The Eight. Two recent studies provide a starting point from which to work back in the literature: Elizabeth Milroy, *Painters of a New Century*, and Rebecca Zurier, Robert W. Snyder, and Virginia M. Mecklenburg, *Metropolitan Lives*.

57. *New York Sun*, Apr. 12, 1907, p. 1. See also "The Henri Hurrah," 4.

58. For a sampling of headlines and for more information on The Eight: Bennard B. Perlman, ed., *Revolutionaries of Realism*, 140, and Perlman's earlier book, *The Immortal Eight*, 170.

59. Berman, *Rebels on Eighth Street*, 92. For the importance of these and other Whitney purchases of paintings by American "progressives" see a letter Arthur B. Davies wrote her, as quoted in Friedman, *Gertrude Vanderbilt Whitney*, 240.

60. For these illustrations see Zurier et al., *Metropolitan Lives*, 122, 133, 140.

61. Reproductions: ibid., 94, 169, 172, 180. Sloan's "Hell Hole" etching and other Village scenes: David Scott, *John Sloan*, 75, 87, 117, 122, 162, 169–70, 172, 185. See also John Loughery, *John Sloan*, 91–111, 143–68.

62. Parry, *Garrets and Pretenders*, 269.

63. For an edition of Sloan's diary see St. John, ed., *John Sloan's New York Scene*.

64. For Glackens and Shinn's Waverly Place Players, synopses of several skits, and pictures of William and Edith Glackens and Everett and Flossie Shinn in performance see Ira Glackens, *William Glackens and the Ashcan Group*, 140–45.

65. Robert W. Snyder and Rebecca Zurier place *The Haymarket* and other pictures by The Eight in the urban milieu of the time: Zurier et al., *Metropolitan Lives*, 156–71.

66. *New York Call*, Mar. 27, 1911, p. 1. See also Patricia Hills, "John Sloan's Images of Working-Class Women," 157–96, which includes a reproduction of Sloan's "In Memoriam."

67. On the Bruères: Bert Vorse to Mary Heaton Vorse, April [1910], box 52, Vorse Papers, WSU. The count of the A Clubbers' magazine articles is based on *The Reader's Guide to Periodical Literature*, which covered major journals only.

68. Vorse, *Footnote to Folly*, 39. *New York Times* articles on the milk campaign in 1910: Mar. 14, p. 12; Aug. 17, p. 4; Aug. 25, p. 4; Sept. 1, p. 5; Sept. 18, p. 6; Sept. 28, p. 6; Oct. 25, p. 5; Nov. 19, p. 10.

69. Vorse, "Village Story," or "The Villager," box 33, Vorse Papers, WSU. See also Garrison, *Mary Heaton Vorse*, 48–49.

70. Vorse, "Picture Show Audiences," 441–47.

71. An early source on the A Clubbers and the Crazy Cat Club is Djuna Barnes, "Greenwich Village as It Is," *Pearson's Magazine* (Oct. 1916), reprinted in Alyce Barry, ed., *Djuna Barnes*, 223–32. See Djuna Barnes, *Greenwich Village as It Is*, 13, for the incident itself. Barnes places it in 1906, all right for the A Club but unlikely for Edwards. 1910 works better: Parry, *Garrets and Pretenders*, 267–68; and Bert Vorse to Mary Heaton Vorse, April 23, [1910], box 52, Vorse Papers, WSU.

72. The strike and its aftermath: Tax, *The Rising of the Women*, 241–320.

73. *New York Times*, Feb. 11, 1912, p. 1.

74. Vorse, *A Footnote to Folly*, 13.

6. Becoming Bohemia

1. The Village as bohemia: "Greenwich Village," 239–41; and "Disillusioned by 'Bohemia'?," 688–93. For Chambers, Ford, Huneker, and O. Henry see Parry, *Garrets and Pretenders*, 92–93, 258–60. The bistro called "Garibaldi's" in James L. Ford's *Bohemia Invaded* (1895) may be based on the original MacDougal Street Maria's. Maria's and other bohemian hangouts are mentioned in Ford's *Forty-odd Years in the Literary Shop*, 206–7

2. Peters, "When New York Dines A La Bohe'me," 77–85.

3. Examples of Villagers who rejected the term *bohemian*: Mary Heaton Vorse, "The Forerunners," typescript, box 20, Vorse Papers, WSU; *New York Tribune*, Feb. 11, 1906, sec. 4, p. 4; and John, ed., *John Sloan's New York Scene*, 301.

4. Two vivid recent overviews of the Seventh Village: Watson, *Strange Bedfellows*; and Christine Stansell, *American Moderns*.

5. On *The Masses* see Leslie Fishbein, *Rebels in Bohemia*; Rebecca Zurier, *Art for "The Masses"*; and Margaret C. Jones, *Heretics and Hellraisers*.

6. Jones, *Heretics and Hellraisers*, 6–7.
7. See Watson, *Strange Bedfellows*, 85–96; Robert M. Crunden, *American Salons*, 383–408; and Arthur Frank Wertheim, *The New York Little Renaissance, 1908–1917*, 63.
8. See Lois Palken Rudnick, *Mabel Dodge Luhan*. The quotations: Mabel Dodge Luhan, *Movers and Shakers*, 39, 83. A dismissive (and largely unconvincing) portrait of Dodge is Christopher Lasch, "Mabel Dodge Luhan: Sex as Politics" in his *The New Radicalism in America*, 104–40.
9. Milton W. Brown, "The Armory Show and Its Aftermath," in Adele Heller and Lois Rudnick, eds., *1915, The Cultural Moment*, 172. See also Martin Green, *New York 1913*; and Milton W. Brown, *The Story of the Armory Show*.
10. Steve Golin, *The Fragile Bridge*. See also Green, *New York 1913*; and Anne Huber Tripp, *The I.W.W. and the Paterson Silk Strike of 1913*.
11. *New York World*, Apr. 12, 1914, Metropolitan Section, p. 1.
12. 1907 founding: Watson, *Strange Bedfellows*, 397. Winter and Hicks, eds., *The Letters of Lincoln Steffens* (1938), 1:237–38.
13. *New York Times*, Sept. 12, 1913, p. 7. See also Keith N. Richwine, "The Liberal Club."
14. For Rodman's activities see June Sochen, *The New Woman*; and Sandra Adickes, *To Be Young Was Very Heaven*. The feminist apartment house scheme: Dolores Hayden, *The Grand Domestic Revolution*, 182–205. Newspaper items on Rodman: *New York Times*, Mar. 19, 1913, p. 8, and Apr. 5, sec. IV, p. 4, and Apr. 22, p. 12, in 1914; *New York Call*, Apr. 13, 1914, p. 1; and *New York Tribune*, Dec. 27, 1914, p. 9.
15. *New York Times*, Feb. 21, 1914, p. 18.
16. Kate E. Wittenstein, "The Heterodoxy Club and American Feminism, 1912–1930," 113. Both Wittenstein (pp. 12, 22) and Judith Schwarz, *Radical Feminists of Heterodoxy*, 17, say that Heterodoxy was founded in 1912 with twenty-five charter members, details based on Inez Haynes Irwin, "Adventures of Yesterday," 413–14, Inez Haynes Irwin Papers. But according to another original member, Edna Kenton, Heterodoxy was founded in January 1913 and had seventeen charter members. See Edna Kenton to Mabel Dodge Luhan, March 25, 1936, Edna Kenton Papers.
17. *New York Call*, Dec. 5, 1913, p. 1; Jan. 1, 1914, p. 4; and Feb. 3, 1914, p. 1. General background: Paul T. Ringenbach, *Tramps and Reformers, 1873–1916* 161–65; and Franklin Folsom, *Impatient Armies of the Poor*, 204–209. See also Donald A. Ritchie, "The Gary Committee," 327–35.
18. *New York Times*, Feb. 28, 1914, p. 1; Mar. 1, 1914, p. 1; Mar. 2, 1914, p. 1; Mar. 3, 1914, pp. 1, 6, 8; and Mar. 4, 1914, p. 1. See also John Haynes Holmes, "Tannenbaum in the Large," 94–95.
19. *New York Tribune*, Mar. 1, 1914, p. 2; *New York Call*, Mar. 4, 1914, p. 1; *New York Times*, Mar. 5, 1914, pp. 1, 8; Mar. 9, 1914, p. 4; Mar. 28, 1914, p. 1. See also "The Church and the Unemployed," *The Masses* 5 (Apr. 1914): 6–8; and Max Eastman, "The Tannenbaum Crime," *The Masses* 5 (May 1914): 10–13.
20. For a third version of the name, "International Defense League": *New York Call*, Mar. 19, 1914, p. 1. More details: *New York Times*, Mar. 12, 1914, p. 1; Perkins, "The Reminiscences of Frances Perkins," 307–309; and Vorse, *Footnote to Folly*, 56–64.
21. Vorse, *Footnote to Folly*, 61.
22. Susan Glaspell, *The Road to the Temple*, 236.
23. See Adele Heller, "The New Theatre," in Heller and Rudnick, eds., *1915, The Cultural Moment*, 217–32.
24. Ibid., 229–31.

25. For criticism of the "faker" type of bohemian see Ralph I. Bartholomew, *Souvenir Book of Greenwich Village*, 29–30.

26. *New York World*, Mar. 29, 1914, Metropolitan Section, p. 1; and Apr. 12, 1914, Metropolitan Section, p. 1.

27. *New York Tribune*, Dec. 26, 1914, p. 12; *New York World*, Dec. 27, 1914, Metropolitan Section, p. 2; and *New York Call*, Dec. 26, 1914, p. 2. Examples of costume balls held before the *Masses* and Liberal Club dances: *New York Call*, Mar. 9, 1912, p. 4; Mar. 18, 1912, p. 1, Apr. 24, 1912, p. 4; Jan. 17, 1913, p. 3; Feb. 8, 1913, p. 4; Jan. 16, 1914, p. 3; Jan. 17, 1914, p. 3.

28. *Bruno's Weekly* 2 (Feb. 5, 1916): 439–40 and (Feb. 26, 1916): 516. *The Quill* 1 (Nov. 1917): 24; *Greenwich Village Spectator* 1 (Oct. 1917): 2, 7; (Dec. 1917): 2; (Jan. 1918): 3; and (Feb. 1918): 1. For a *mea culpa*: Floyd Dell, "The Fall of Greenwich Village" in his *Love in Greenwich Village*, 298–99. On commercialized bohemianism see Jerrold Seigel, *Bohemian Paris*.

29. *Bruno's Weekly* 1 (July 26, 1915): 20. On Bruno see Arnold I. Kisch, *The Romantic Ghost of Greenwich Village*.

30. *Bruno's Weekly* 1 (Aug. 14, 1915): 34; *New York Tribune*, Nov. 14, 1915, sec. 4, p. 3; *New York Sun*, Dec. 5, 1915, sec. 5, p. 6.

31. *New York Tribune*, Nov. 14, 1915, sec. 4, p. 5.

32. Advertisements for Tiny Tim, Mme. Cluette, and Sonja: *Greenwich Village Spectator* 1 (July 1917): 2; and (Aug. 1917): 7; and *The Quill* 1 (Dec. 1, 1917): 26. For Beals photographs and written items: Jessie Tarbox Beals Papers. On Adele: *New York Times*, Oct. 7, 1917, sec. 7, p. 15. See also Anna Alice Chapin, *Greenwich Village*.

33. Friedman, *Gertrude Vanderbilt Whitney*, 390. The *New York Times* covered the Alley Festa every day from June 7 to 13, 1917. For a new bohemia magazine's support for the war effort see *The Quill* 3 (Sept. 1918): 4, 26–27. On the Bureau of Legal Advice: Frances H. Early, *A World without War*, 19–30, 62–64.

34. *New York Times*, July 25, 1918, p. 11. For more on the war's impact: Wertheim, *The New York Little Renaissance*, 215–41.

35. Churchill, *The Improper Bohemians*, 155–57.

36. On the Village's political and artistic vanguard in the 1920s: Daniel Aaron, "Disturbers of the Peace," and Blanche Wiesen Cook, "The Radical Women of Greenwich Village," both in Beard and Berlowitz, eds., *Greenwich Village: Culture and Counterculture*, 229–57.

37. Village population figures vary depending on the area included. I've used the Greenwich Village Improvement Society, "Report to the Board of Estimate and Apportionment, New York City" (typescript, June 1914), 3–4, copy at New York Public Library. See also Ware, *Greenwich Village*, graph opp. p. 38.

38. The quotation: Ware, *Greenwich Village*, 127. Using census figures from six south and west Village sanitary districts, Ware's research team reported the numbers for "Negroes and other coloreds" as 1,275 in 1910 and 572 in 1920 (Census Summary file, box 51, Caroline Ware Papers, F.D.R. Library).

39. For the Austins: *U.S. Census: New York* (1920), reel 1202, E. D. 719, p. 1.

40. Ware, *Greenwich Village*, 206. After World War I the County Clare Men's Society moved its meetings out of the Village.

41. *Bruno's Weekly* 1 (Oct. 30, 1915): 158.

42. Vincent Pepe, "Real Estate Progress in Our Community," 4–7; and Egmont Arens, *The Little Book of Greenwich Village*, 22. On Pepe: *New York Times*, June 6, 1935, p. 2; *U.S. Census: New York* (1900), reel 1082, E. D. 51, p. 12; and (1910), reel 1004, E. D. 109,

p. 4A. The *New York Times*, Apr. 15, 1917, sec. 4, p. 5, reported that the Seventh Avenue subway would spark a Village building boom.

43. "Board of Trustees Minutes," Jan. 26, 1914, Feb. 16, and May 18, 1914, People's Institute Papers. See also Fisher, "The People's Institute of New York City, 1897–1934," 271–79, 303; and John Collier, *From Every Zenith*, 79–82.

44. People's Institute, "How Would You Like to Open a Door Like This—Ten Minutes After You 'Punch the Clock?' " (1914).

45. *New York Times*, Mar. 28, 1916, p. 22; and S. J. Makielski Jr., *The Politics of Zoning*, 9–10, 19–21. A map of Village zones based on the 1916 law: Ware, *Greenwich Village*, 478.

46. Havel, "The Spirit of the Village," 34.

47. Ware, *Greenwich Village*, 106, 424.

48. Ibid., 439. Ware saved more than four boxes of raw data related to her Greenwich Village research but did not preserve the questionnaires compiled for Irish Villagers. However, the responses of Italian Villagers may be found in the "Questionnaire Summaries" file, box 52, Ware Papers.

49. Ware, *Greenwich Village*, 82, 99–100, 104. See also her section "Two Social Worlds" (105–26).

50. Ibid., 212.

51. Greenwich House, *Fourteenth Annual Report* (1915), 14.

52. On the public school social center movement see Barbuto, " 'The Matrix of Understanding,' " 170–76.

53. *New York Times*, May 20, 1913, p. 3; May 21, 1913, p. 11; and May 25, 1913, p. 8; and "The Spectator," *The Outlook* 104 (June 7, 1913): 300–303.

54. See Anne O'Hagan Shinn, "Where Barrow Street and Bleecker Meet," 24.

55. *New York Times*, May 20, 1913, p. 3.

56. Lindsay Denison to Elizabeth F. Thorne, May 21, 1913, box 1, file 11, Greenwich House Papers. Denison said the letter would be published, but the item is not clearly identifiable among the Old Home Week letters in the microfilmed editions of the *New York World*.

57. David Glassberg, *American Historical Pageantry*, 128–33.

58. *New York Evening Post*, May 27, 1914, a clipping in the Village Fair file, Greenwich House Papers.

59. "Too Much Tango for Old Greenwich in Barn Dance," clipping from an unidentified newspaper in ibid.

60. Charles W. Culkin to Mary K. Simkhovitch, May 10, 1913, Old Home Week file, ibid. *New York World*, May 27, 1914, p. 22; and May 30, 1914, p. 7; *New York Tribune*, May 28, 1914, p. 5; and *New York Times*, May 29, 1914, p. 9; and May 30, 1914, p. 21.

61. Mary Elizabeth Brown, "Italian Immigrant Catholic Clergy and an Exception to the Rule," 43.

62. Ibid., 46–51. For examples of Demo's correspondence with non-Italian individuals and agencies: series I, box 2, folders 13–18, and series I, box 10, folder 108, Records of Our Lady of Pompei.

63. On scholarship about New York City neighborhoods see Kenneth A. Scherzer, *The Unbounded Community*, 1–15.

64. On ethnically mixed wards: Frederick M. Binder and David M. Reimers, *All the Nations under Heaven*, 104–105.

65. Roger Sanjek, *The Future of Us All*, 367–93.

BIBLIOGRAPHY

Manuscripts and Unpublished Oral History Memoirs

Beals, Jessie Tarbox. Papers. Schlesinger Library, Radcliffe College.
Charity Organization Society. Files. Community Service Society Papers, Columbia University.
Committee of Fourteen. Papers. Manuscripts Division, New York Public Library.
Doty, Madeleine Z. Papers. Sophia Smith Collection, Smith College.
Eastman, Crystal. Papers. Schlesinger Library, Radcliffe Institute, Harvard University.
Federal Writers' Project, Negroes of New York Series. Schomberg Center for Research in Black Culture, New York City.
Greenwich House. Papers. Tamiment Institute Library, New York University.
Hapgood Family Papers. Yale Collection of American Literature, Beinecke Rare Book and Manuscript Library.
Irwin, Inez Haynes. Papers. Schlesinger Library, Radcliffe College.
Kenton, Edna. Papers. Columbia University.
New York City Immigrant Women. Oral History Collection. CUNY Social History Project, Tamiment Institute Library, New York University.
Our Lady of Pompei. Records. Center for Migration Studies, Staten Island, New York.
Parolin, Pio. Papers. Center for Migration Studies, Staten Island, New York.
People's Institute. Collection. Cooper Union for Science and Art, New York City.
People's Institute. Papers. Manuscripts Division, New York Public Library.

Perkins, Frances. Reminiscences. Oral History Collection, Columbia University.
Stokes, J. G. P. Stokes. Papers. Columbia University.
Stokes, James Graham Phelps. Papers. Manuscripts and Archives, Yale University.
University Settlement Society of New York City. Papers. Microfilm edition, State Historical Society of Wisconsin.
Van Kleeck, Mary. Papers. Sophia Smith Collection, Smith College.
Vorse, Mary Heaton. Papers. Archives of Labor and Urban Affairs, Walter Reuther Library, Wayne State University.
Vorse, Mary Heaton. Reminiscences. Oral History Collection, Columbia University.
Walling, Anna Strunsky. Papers. Manuscripts and Archives, Yale University Library.
Walling, Anna Strunsky. Papers. Microfilm edition, Tamiment Institute Library, New York University.
Ware, Caroline. Papers. Franklin D. Roosevelt Library.

Books, Articles, and Other Publications

Adickes, Sandra. *To Be Young Was Very Heaven: Women in New York before the First World War.* New York: St. Martin's Press, 1997.
Allen, Oliver E. *The Rise and Fall of Tammany Hall.* Reading, Mass.: Addison-Wesley, 1993.
Appleton's Dictionary of Greater New York. New York: D. Appleton, 1905.
Arens, Egmont. *The Little Book of Greenwich Village.* New York: Washington Square Book Shop, 1918.
Armstrong, Hamilton Fish. *Those Days.* New York: Harper & Row, 1963.
Asbury, Herbert. *The Gangs of New York: An Informal History of the Underworld.* New York: Alfred A. Knopf, 1929.
Baker, Paul R. *Stanny: The Gilded Life of Stanford White.* New York: Free Press, 1989.
Barbuto, Domenica Maria. " 'The Matrix of Understanding': The Life and Work of Mary Kingbury Simkhovitch." Ph.D. diss., State University of New York at Stony Brook, 1992.
Barnes, Djuna. *Greenwich Village as It Is.* New York: Phoenix Bookshop, 1978.
Barry, Alyce, ed. *Djuna Barnes: New York.* Los Angeles: Sun and Moon Press, 1989.
Bartholomew, Ralph I. *Souvenir Book of Greenwich Village.* New York: F. K. Ferenz, 1920.
Bayor, Ronald H., and Timothy J. Meagher, eds. *The New York Irish.* Baltimore: Johns Hopkins University Press, 1996.
Beard, Rick, and Leslie Cohen Berlowitz, eds. *Greenwich Village: Culture and Counterculture.* New Brunswick, N.J.: Rutgers University Press, 1993.
Berman, Avis. *Rebels on Eighth Street: Juliana Force and the Whitney Museum of American Art.* New York: Atheneum, 1990.
Binder, Frederick M., and David M. Reimers. *All the Nations under Heaven: An Ethnic and Racial History of New York City.* New York: Columbia University Press, 1995.

Blaugrund, Annette. "The Tenth Street Studio Building: A Roster, 1857–1895." *American Art Journal* 14 (Spring 1982): 64–71.

Boyer, Paul. *Urban Masses and Moral Order in America, 1820–1920.* Cambridge: Harvard University Press, 1978.

Boylan, James. *Revolutionary Lives: Anna Strunsky and William English Walling.* Amherst: University of Massachusetts Press, 1998.

Brandt, Lilian. *The Charity Organization Society of the City of New York, 1882–1907.* New York: B. H. Tyrrell, 1907.

Brown, Mary Elizabeth. *From Italian Villages to Greenwich Village: Our Lady of Pompei, 1892–1992.* Staten Island, N.Y.: Center for Migration Studies, 1992.

Brown, Mary Elizabeth. "A Case Study of the Italian Layman and Parish Life at Our Lady of Pompei, Greenwich Village, New York City." In *Italian Americans and Their Public and Private Life: Proceedings of the 24th Annual Conference of the American Italian Historical Association, New Haven, CT, November 14–16, 1991,* ed. Frank J. Cavaioli, Angela Danzi, and Salvatore J. LaGumina, 94–102. New York: American Italian Historical Association, 1993.

Brown, Mary Elizabeth. "Italian Immigrant Catholic Clergy and an Exception to the Rule: The Reverend Antonio Demo, Our Lady of Pompei, Greenwich Village, 1899–1933." *Church History* 22 (Mar. 1993): 41–59.

Brown, Milton W. *The Story of the Armory Show.* Rev. ed. New York: Abbeville Press, 1988.

Bruére, Martha Bensley. "The Triangle Fire." *Life and Labor* 1 (May 1911): 137–41.

Bryn Mawr Class of 1907. *Carola Woerishoffer: Her Life and Work.* 1912. Reprint, New York: Arno Press, 1974.

Buhle, Mari Jo. *Women and American Socialism, 1870–1920.* Urbana: University of Illinois Press, 1981.

Burrows, Edwin G., and Mike Wallace. *Gotham: A History of New York City to 1898.* New York: Oxford University Press, 1999.

Callahan, Nelson J., ed. *Diary of Richard L. Burtsell, Priest of New York: The Early Years, 1865–1868.* New York: Arno Press, 1998.

Carson, Mina. *Settlement Folk: Social Thought and the American Settlement Movement, 1885–1930.* Chicago: University of Chicago Press, 1990.

Cartwright, Otho G. *Boyhood and Lawlessness.* New York: Survey Associates, 1914.

Chambers, Clarke. *Paul U. Kellogg and the Survey: Voices for Social Welfare and Social Justice.* Minneapolis: University of Minnesota Press, 1971.

Chapin, Anna Alice. *Greenwich Village.* New York: Dodd, Mead, 1917.

Chauncey, George, Jr. *Gay New York: Gender, Urban Culture, and the Making of the Gay Male World, 1890–1910.* New York: Basic Books, 1994.

Churchill, Allen. *The Improper Bohemians: A Re-creation of Greenwich Village in Its Heyday.* New York: E. P. Dutton, 1959.

Clark, Sue Ainslie, and Edith Wyatt. "Women Laundry Workers in New York." *McClure's Magazine* 36 (Feb. 1911): 401–14.

Cohalan, Florence D. *A Popular History of the Archdiocese of New York.* Yonkers, N.Y.: U.S. Catholic Historical Society, 1983.

Collier, John. *From Every Zenith.* Denver: Sage Books, 1963.

Cook, Blanche Wiesen, ed. *Crystal Eastman on Women and Revolution.* New York: Oxford University Press, 1978.

Crane, Stephen. "Stephen Crane in Minetta Lane." In *Stephen Crane: Tales, Sketches, and Reports,* ed. Fredson Bowers, 400–404. Charlottesville: University Press of Virginia, 1973.

Cross, Robert D. *The Emergence of Liberal Catholicism in America.* Cambridge: Harvard University Press, 1958.

Crunden, Robert M. *American Salons: Encounters with European Modernism, 1885–1917.* New York: Oxford University Press 1993.

Curran, Henry H. *Pillar to Post.* New York: Charles Scribner's Sons, 1941.

Czitrom, Daniel. "Underworlds and Underdogs: Tim Sullivan and Metropolitan Politics in New York, 1889–1913." *Journal of American History* 78 (Sept. 1991): 536–558.

Davis, Allen F. *Spearheads for Reform: The Social Settlements and the Progressive Movement, 1890–1914.* New York: Oxford University Press, 1967.

De Forest, Emily Johnston. *John Johnston of New York, Merchant.* New York: Privately printed, 1909.

De Forest, Robert W., and Lawrence Veiller, eds. *The Tenement House Problem: Including the Report of the New York State Tenement House Commission of 1900.* 2 vols. New York: Macmillan, 1903.

Dell, Floyd. *Love in Greenwich Village.* New York: George H. Doran, 1926.

Di Giovanni, Stephen Michael. "Michael Augustine Corrigan and the Italian Immigrants: The Relationship between the Church and the Italians in the Archdiocese of New York, 1885–1902," Ph.D. diss., Gregorian Pontifical University, Rome, 1983.

Dijkstra, Bram. *Idols of Perversity: Fantasies of Feminine Evil in Fin-de-Siècle Culture.* New York: Oxford University Press, 1986.

"Disillusioned by 'Bohemia'?" *The Literary Digest* 53 (Sept. 16, 1916): 688–93.

Drachman, Virginia G. *Urban Lawyers and the Origins of Professional Identity in America.* Ann Arbor: University of Michigan Press, 1993.

Du Plessis, Rachel Blau, and Ann Snitow, eds. *The Feminist Memoir Project: Voices from Women's Liberation.* New York: Three Rivers Press, 1998.

Dye, Nancy Schrom. *As Sisters and as Equals: Feminism, the Labor Movement, and the Women's Trade Union League of New York.* Columbia: University of Missouri Press, 1980.

Early, Frances H. *A World without War: How U.S. Feminists and Pacifists Resisted World War I.* Syracuse: Syracuse University Press, 1997.

Eastman, Crystal. "A Year's Work-Accidents and Their Costs." *Charities and Commons* 21 (Mar. 6, 1909): 1143–74.

Eastman, Crystal. "Work-Accidents and Employer's Liability." *Survey* 24 (Sept. 3, 1910): 788–94.

Eastman, Max. *Enjoyment of Living.* New York: Harper & Brothers, 1948.

Eckhaus, Phyllis. "Restless Women: The Pioneering Alumnae of New York University School of Law," *New York University Law Review* 66 (Dec. 1991): 1996–2013.

Erenberg, Lewis A. *Steppin' Out: New York Nightlife and the Transformation of American Culture, 1890–1930.* Westport, Conn.: Greenwood Press, 1981.

Felt, Jeremy P. *Hostages of Fortune: Child Labor Reform in New York State.* Syracuse: Syracuse University Press, 1965.

Fields, Anne, ed. *Letters of Sarah Orne Jewett.* Boston: Houghton Mifflin, 1911.

Fifth Avenue Association, New York. *Fifty Years on Fifth.* New York: International Press, 1957.

Filler, Louis. *Voice of Democracy, A Critical Biography of David Graham Phillips: Journalist, Novelist, Progressive.* University Park: Pennsylvania State University Press, 1978.

Finegold, Kenneth. *Experts and Politicians: Reform Challenges to Machine Politics in New York, Cleveland, and Chicago.* Princeton: Princeton University Press, 1995.

Fishbein, Leslie. *Rebels in Bohemia: The Radicals of "The Masses," 1911–1917.* Chapel Hill: University of North Carolina Press, 1982.

Fisher, Robert B. "The People's Institute of New York City, 1897–1934: Culture, Progressive Democracy, and the People." Ph.D. diss., New York University, 1974.

Folsom, Franklin. *Impatient Armies of the Poor: The Story of Collective Action of the Unemployed, 1800–1942.* Niwot: University Press of Colorado, 1991.

Foner, Philip S. *Women and the American Labor Movement.* New York: Monthly Review Press, 1980.

Ford, James L. *Bohemia Invaded, and Other Stories.* New York: F. A. Stokes, 1895.

Ford, James L. *Forty-odd Years in the Literary Shop.* New York: E. P. Dutton, 1921.

Fowler, Gene. *Beau James: The Life and Times of Jimmy Walker.* New York: Viking Press, 1949.

Fried, Albert. *The Rise and Fall of the Jewish Gangster in America.* Rev. ed. New York: Columbia University Press, 1993.

Friedman, B. H. *Gertrude Vanderbilt Whitney.* Garden City, N.Y.: Doubleday, 1978.

Gardner, Charles W. *The Doctor and the Devil; or, the Midnight Adventures of Dr. Parkhurst.* 1894. Reprint, New York: Vanguard Press, 1931.

Garrison, Dee. *Mary Heaton Vorse: The Life of an American Insurgent.* Philadelphia: Temple University Press, 1989.

Garrison, Dee, ed. *Rebel Pen: The Writings of Mary Heaton Vorse.* New York: Monthly Review Press, 1985.

Gilfoyle, Timothy J. *City of Eros: New York City, Prostitution, and the Commercialization of Sex, 1790–1920.* New York: W. W. Norton, 1992.

Glackens, Ira. *William Glackens and the Ashcan Group: The Emergence of Realism in American Art.* New York: Crown, 1957.

Glaspell, Susan. *The Road to the Temple.* New York: F. A. Stokes, 1941.

Glassberg, David. *American Historical Pageantry: The Uses of Tradition in the Early Twentieth Century.* Chapel Hill: University of North Carolina Press, 1990.

Golin, Steve. *The Fragile Bridge: Paterson Silk Strike of 1913.* Philadelphia: Temple University Press, 1988.

Green, Martin. *New York 1913: The Armory Show and Paterson Strike Pageant*. New York: Macmillan, 1988.

Greene, Victor R. *American Immigrant Leaders, 1800–1910: Marginality and Identity*. Baltimore: Johns Hopkins University Press, 1987.

"Greenwich Village." *The Dial* 57 (Oct. 1, 1914): 239–41.

Greenwich Village Improvement Society. "Report of the Greenwich Village Improvement Society." Typescript. 22 pp. New York, November 1914. Copy in stacks of New York Public Library.

Gribetz, Louis J., and Joseph Kane. *Jimmie Walker: The Story of a Personality*. New York: Dial Press, 1932.

Grundy, J. Owen. "Greenwich Village-Washington Square." Scrapbook. N.d. Copy in stacks of New York Public Library.

Hapgood, Hutchins. *Types from City Streets*. New York: Funk & Wagnalls, 1910.

Hapgood, Hutchins. *A Victorian in the Modern World*. New York: Harcourt, Brace and World, 1939.

Havel, Hippolyte. "The Spirit of the Village." *Bruno's Weekly* 1 (Aug. 14, 1915): 34–35.

Hayden, Dolores. *The Grand Domestic Revolution: A History of Feminist Designs for American Homes, Neighborhoods and Cities*. Cambridge: MIT Press, 1981.

Heller, Adele, and Lois Rudnick, eds. *1915, The Cultural Moment: The New Politics, the New Woman, the New Psychology, the New Art, and the New Theatre in America*. New Brunswick, N.J.: Rutgers University Press, 1991.

Henderson, Thomas M. *Tammany Hall and the New Immigrants: The Progressive Years*. New York: Arno Press, 1976.

"The Henri Hurrah." *American Art News* 5 (Mar. 23, 1907): 4.

Herzfeld, Elsa. *A West Side Rookery*. New York: Greenwich House, 1906.

Hijiya, James A. "Four Ways of Looking at a Philanthropist: A Study of Robert Weeks de Forest." *Proceedings of the American Philosophical Society* 124 (Dec. 17, 1980): 404–18.

Hills, Patricia. "John Sloan's Images of Working-Class Women: A Case Study of the Roles and Interrelationships of Politics, Personality, and Patrons in the Development of Sloan's Art, 1905–1916." *Prospects: The Annual of American Culture Studies* 5 (1980): 157–96.

Holmes, John Haynes. "Tannenbaum in the Large." *Survey* 32 (Apr. 25, 1914): 94–95.

Holtzman, Filia. "A Mission that Failed: Gor'kij in America." *Slavic and East European Journal* 6 (Fall 1962): 227–37.

Hopper, Ernest Jasper. "A Northern Negro Group." M.A. thesis, Columbia University, 1912.

Horn, Max. *The Intercollegiate Socialist Society, 1905–1921: Origins of the Modern American Student Movement*. Boulder, Colo.: Westview Press, 1979.

Howells, William Dean. *A Hazard of New Fortunes*. 1890. Reprint, with an introduction by Van Wyck Brooks, New York: Bantam Books, 1960.

Humphery, Robert E. *Children of Fantasy: The First Rebels of Greenwich Village*. New York: John Wiley & Sons, 1978.

Hyde, Henry N., and Emerson G. Taylor, eds. *Quindecennial Record, Class of Eighteen Hundred and Ninety-five, Yale College*. New Haven: Tuttle, Morehouse, and Taylor, 1911.

Irvine, Alexander. *From the Bottom Up*. New York: Doubleday, 1909.

Jackson, Anthony. *A Place Called Home: A History of Low-Cost Housing in Manhattan*. Cambridge: MIT Press, 1976.

Jackson, Kenneth T., ed. *The Encyclopedia of New York City*. New Haven: Yale University Press, 1995.

James, Henry. *The American Scene*. 1907. Reprint, with an introduction and notes by Leon Edel, Bloomington: Indiana University Press, 1968.

Janvier, Thomas A. "Greenwich Village." *Harper's Magazine* 87 (Aug. 1893): 339–57.

Janvier, Thomas A. *In Old New York*. New York: Harper & Brothers, 1894.

Jenison, Madge C. "The Church and the Social Unrest." *Outlook* 89 (May 16, 1908): 114.

John, Arthur. *The Best Years of the Century: Richard Watson Gilder, "Scribner's Monthly" and the "Century Magazine," 1870–1909*. Urbana: University of Illinois Press, 1981.

Jones, Margaret C. *Heretics and Hellraisers: Women Contributors to "The Masses," 1911–1918*. Austin: University of Texas Press, 1991.

Kammen, Michael G. "Richard Watson Gilder and the New York Tenement House Commission of 1894." *Bulletin of the New York Public Library* 66 (June 1962): 364–82.

Keefer, Truman Frederick. *Ernest Poole*. New York: Twayne, 1966.

Kellogg, Charles Flint. *NAACP: A History of the National Association for the Advancement of Colored People*. Baltimore: Johns Hopkins University Press, 1967.

Kennedy, James W. *The Unknown Worshipper*. New York: Morehouse-Barlow, 1964.

Kisch, Arnold I. *The Romantic Ghost of Greenwich Village: Guido Bruno in His Garret*. Frankfurt: Peter Lang, 1976.

Kneeland, George J. *Commercialized Prostitution in New York City*. 4th ed., 1917. Reprint, Montclair, N.J.: Patterson Smith, 1969.

Kurland, Gerald. *Seth Low: The Reformer in an Urban Industrial Age*. New York: Twayne, 1971.

Lasch, Christopher. *The New Radicalism in America, 1889–1963: The Intellectual as a Social Type*. New York: Alfred A. Knopf, 1965.

Lawson, Ronald, ed. *The Tenant Movement in New York City, 1904–1984*. New Brunswick, N.J.: Rutgers University Press, 1986.

Lessard, Suzanne. *The Architect of Desire: Beauty and Danger in the Stanford White Family*. New York: Dial Press, 1996.

Lomax, Lucille Genevieve. "A Social History of the Negro Population in the Section of New York City Known as Greenwich Village." M.A. thesis, Columbia University, 1930.

Loughery, John. *John Sloan: Painter and Rebel*. New York: Henry Holt, 1995.

Lubove, Roy. *The Progressives and the Slums: Tenement House Reform in New York City, 1890–1917*. Pittsburgh: University of Pittsburgh Press, 1962.

Luhan, Mabel Dodge. *Movers and Shakers.* 1936. Reprint, with an introduction by Lois Palken Rudnick, Albuquerque: University of New Mexico Press, 1985.

Makielski, S. J., Jr. *The Politics of Zoning: The New York Experience.* New York: Columbia University Press, 1966.

Martin, George. *Madam Secretary: Frances Perkins.* Boston: Houghton Mifflin, 1976.

Maurice, Arthur Bartlett. *New York in Fiction.* 1900. Reprint, Port Washington, N.Y.: Ira J. Friedman, 1969.

Maurice, Arthur Bartlett. *The New York of the Novelists.* New York: Dodd, Mead, 1916.

May, Henry F. *The End of American Innocence: A Study of the First Years of Our Own Times, 1912–1917.* New York: Alfred A. Knopf, 1959.

May, Lary. *Screening Out the Past: The Birth of Mass Culture and the Motion Picture Industry.* New York: Oxford University Press, 1980.

McCarthy, Kathleen D. *Women's Culture: American Philanthropy and Art, 1830–1930.* Chicago: University of Chicago Press, 1991.

McFarland, Gerald W. *Mugwumps, Morals and Politics, 1884–1920.* Amherst: University of Massachusetts Press, 1975.

McGerr, Michael. "Political Style and Women's Power, 1830–1930." *Journal of American History* 77 (Dec. 1990): 864–85.

Miller, Terry. *Greenwich Village and How It Got That Way.* New York: Crown, 1990.

Milroy, Elizabeth. *Painters of a New Century: The Eight and American Art.* Milwaukee: Milwaukee Art Museum, 1991.

More, Louise Bolard. *Wage-Earners' Budgets: A Study of Standards and Costs of Living in New York City.* New York: Henry Holt, 1907.

Morello, Karen Berger. *The Invisible Bar: The Woman Lawyers in America, 1638 to the Present.* New York: Random House, 1986.

Morrison, Joan, and Charlotte Fox Zubusky, eds. *American Mosaic: The Immigrant Experience in the Words of Those Who Lived It.* New York: E. P. Dutton, 1980.

Mott, Frank Luther. *A History of American Magazines.* Vol. 4, *1885–1905.* Cambridge: Harvard University Press, 1957.

Mumford, Kevin J. *Interzones: Black/White Sex Districts in Chicago and New York in the Early Twentieth Century.* New York: Columbia University Press, 1997.

Muncy, Robyn. *Creating a Female Dominion in American Reform, 1890–1935.* New York: Oxford University Press, 1991.

Nassau, Mabel Louise. *Old Age Poverty in Greenwich Village.* New York: Fleming H. Revell, 1915.

New York Assembly, *Report of the Special Committee of the Assembly Appointed to Investigate the Public Offices and Departments of the City of New York and the Counties Therein Included.* 5 vols. Albany: J. B. Lyon, 1900.

New York City Committee of Fourteen. *The Social Evil in New York City.* New York: Andrew H. Kellogg, 1910.

New York City Landmarks Preservation Commission. *Greenwich Village Historic*

District Designation Report. 2 vols. New York: Landmarks Preservation Commission, 1969.

Oberdeck, Kathryn J. *The Evangelist and the Impresario: Religion, Entertainment, and Cultural Politics in America, 1884–1914.* Baltimore: Johns Hopkins University Press, 1999.

Ogburn, William F. "The Richmond Negro in New York City: His Social Mind as Seen in His Pleasures." M.A. thesis, Columbia University, 1909.

Ohmann, Richard. *Selling Culture: Magazines, Markets, and Class at the Turn of the Century.* London: Verso, 1996.

Ovington, Mary White. *Half a Man: The Status of the Negro in New York.* New York: Longmans, Green, 1911.

Ovington, Mary White. *The Walls Came Tumbling Down.* New York: Harcourt, Brace, 1947.

Park, Robert E., and Herbert A. Miller. *Old World Traits Transplanted.* New York: Harper & Brothers, 1921.

Parry, Albert. *Garrets and Pretenders: A History of Bohemianism in America.* New York: Covici-Friede, 1933.

Paul, Seymour. "A Group of Virginia Negroes in New York City." M.A. thesis, Columbia University, 1912.

Peiss, Kathy. *Cheap Amusements: Working Women and Leisure in Turn-of-the-Century New York.* Philadelphia: Temple University Press, 1986.

Pepe, Vincent "Real Estate Progress in Our Community." *Greenwich Village Spectator* 1 (Sept. 1917): 4–7.

Perlman, Bennard B. *The Immortal Eight: American Painting from Eakins to the Armory Show, 1870–1913.* New York: Exposition Press, 1962.

Perlman, Bennard B. *Robert Henri: His Life and Art.* New York: Dover, 1991.

Perlman, Bennard B., ed. *Revolutionaries of Realism: The Letters of John Sloan and Robert Henri.* Princeton: Princeton University Press, 1997.

Peters, Charles F. "When New York Dines A La Bohe'me." *The Bohemian* 8 (July 1907): 77–85.

Phillips, David Graham. *The Great God Success.* New York: Grosset & Dunlap, 1901.

Plunz, Richard. *A History of Housing in New York City: Dwelling Type and Social Change in the American Metropolis.* New York: Columbia University Press, 1990.

Poole, Ernest. *The Bridge: My Own Story.* New York: Macmillan, 1940.

———. "Maxim Gorki in New York," *Slavonic and East Europe Review* 12 (May 1944): 79–80.

———. "My Street," *Century Magazine* 99 (June 1912): 187–92.

Powell, Adam Clayton, Sr. *Against the Tide: An Autobiography.* New York: R. R. Smith, 1938.

Powell, Adam Clayton, Jr. *Adam by Adam.* New York: Dial Press, 1971.

Ratner, Sidney. *New Light on the Great American Fortunes.* New York: Augustus M. Kelley, 1953.

Reed, Henry Hope, Jr. "Discover New York." *New York Herald Tribune,* Oct. 7, 1962, Today's Living section.

Renshaw, Patrick. "Rose of the World: The Pastor-Stokes Marriage and the American Left." *New York History* 62 (Oct. 1981): 415–38.

Reynolds, James B. "The Settlement and Municipal Reform." In *Proceedings of the National Conference of Charities and Correction*, ed. Isabel Barrows, 138–42 Boston: George M. Ellis, 1896.

Reynolds, Robert D., Jr. "The Millionaire Socialists: J. G. Phelphs Stokes and His Circle of Friends." Ph.D. diss., University of South Carolina, 1974.

Richwine, Keith N. "The Liberal Club: Bohemia and the Resurgence in Greenwich Village, 1912–1918." Ph.D. diss., University of Pennsylvania, 1968.

Riis, Jacob. *How the Other Half Lives*. 1890. Reprint, edited with an introduction by David Leviathon, New York: Bedford Books, 1996.

Ringenbach, Paul T. *Tramps and Reformers, 1873–1916: The Discovery of Unemployment in New York*. Westport, Conn.: Greenwood Press, 1973.

Ritchie, Donald A. "The Gary Committee: Businessmen, Progressives, and Unemployment in New York City, 1914–1915," *New-York Historical Society Quarterly* 57 (Oct. 1973): 327–35.

Rosenzweig, Roy, and Elizabeth Blackmar. *The Park and the People: A History of Central Park*. Ithaca: Cornell University Press, 1992.

Rudnick, Lois Palken. *Mabel Dodge Luhan: New Woman, New Worlds*. Albuquerque: University of New Mexico Press, 1984.

St. John, Bruce, ed. *John Sloan's New York Scene, from the Diaries, Notes and Correspondence, 1906–1913*. New York: Harper & Row, 1965.

Salvetti, Patrizia. "Una parrocchia italiana di New York e i suoi fedeli: Nostra Signora di Pompei, 1892–1984." *Studi emigrazione* 21 (March 1984): 43–64.

Sanborn Fire Insurance Company, *Sanborn Fire Insurance Maps: New York*. 1895, 1904. Microfilm ed. Teaneck, N.J.: Chadwyck-Healy, 1983.

Sanjek, Roger. *The Future of Us All: Race and Neighborhood Politics in New York City*. Ithaca: Cornell University Press, 1998.

Sante, Luc. *Low Life: Lives and Snares of Old New York*. New York: Farrar, Straus, Giroux, 1991.

Scherzer, Kenneth A. *The Unbounded Community: Neighborhood Life and Social Structure in New York City, 1830–1875*. Durham: Duke University Press, 1992.

Schwarz, Judith. *Radical Feminists of Heterodoxy: Greenwich Village, 1912–1940*. Norwich, Ver.: New Victoria Publishers, 1986.

Scott, David. *John Sloan*. New York: Watson-Guptill, 1975.

Seigel, Jerrold. *Bohemian Paris: Culture, Politics, and the Boundaries of Bourgeois Life*. New York: Viking Press, 1986.

Seller, Maxine Schwartz, ed. *Immigrant Women*. Philadelphia: Temple University Press, 1981.

Sergeant, Elizabeth Shepley. "Toilers of the Tenements: Where the Beautiful Things of the Great Shops Are Made." *McClure's Magazine* 35 (July 1910): 231–48.

Sergeant, Elizabeth Shepley. *Willa Cather: A Memoir*. 1953. Reprint, Lincoln: University of Nebraska Press, 1963.

Sermolino, Maria. *Papa's Table d'Hôte*. Philadelphia: Lippincott, 1952.

Shinn, Anne O'Hagan. "Where Barrow Street and Bleecker Meet." *Survey* 39 (Dec. 1, 1917): 245–47.

Simkhovitch, Mary Kingsbury. *Here Is God's Plenty: Reflections on American Social Advance.* New York: Harper & Brothers, 1949.

Simkhovitch, Mary Kingsbury. *Neighborhood: My Story of Greenwich House.* New York: W. W. Norton, 1938.

Sochen, June. *The New Woman: Feminism in Greenwich Village, 1910–1920.* New York: Quadrangle Books, 1972.

Stansell, Christine. *American Moderns: Bohemian New York and the Creation of a New Century.* New York: Henry Holt, 2000.

Stein, Leon. *The Triangle Fire.* Philadelphia: Lippincott, 1962.

Tax, Meredith. *The Rising of the Women: Feminist Solidarity and Class Conflict, 1880–1917.* New York: Monthly Review Press, 1980.

Tomasi, Silvano. *Piety and Power: The Role of Italian Parishes in the New York Metropolitan Area.* Staten Island, N.Y.: Center for Migration Studies, 1975.

Tomkins, Calvin. *Merchants and Masterpieces: The Story of the Metropolitan Museum of Art.* Rev. ed. New York: Henry Holt, 1989.

Tricarico, Donald. *The Italians of Greenwich Village: The Social Structure and Transformation of an Ethnic Community.* Staten Island, N.Y.: Center for Migration Studies, 1984.

Trimberger, Ellen Kay. "Feminism, Men and Modern Love." In *Powers of Desire: The Politics of Sexuality,* ed. Ann Snitow, Christine Stansell, and Sharon Thompson, 131–52. New York: Monthly Review Press.

Trimberger, Ellen Kay, ed. *Intimate Warriors: Portraits of a Modern Marriage, 1899–1944.* New York: Feminist Press, 1991.

Tripp, Anne Huber. *The I.W.W. and the Paterson Silk Strike of 1913.* Urbana: University of Illinois Press, 1987.

Trotter, Joe William, Jr., ed. *The Great Migration in Historical Perspective: New Dimensions of Race, Class, and Gender.* Bloomington: Indiana University Press, 1991.

U.S. Census: New York. 1880, 1900, 1910, 1920. Microfilm edition, Washington, D.C.: National Archives, 1974, 1978, 1982, 1991.

Van Kleeck, Mary. *Artificial Flower Makers.* New York: Survey Associates, 1913.

Vorse, Mary Heaton, "Picture Show Audiences." *The Outlook* 98 (June 24, 1911): 441–47.

Vorse, Mary Heaton. *A Footnote to Folly: The Reminiscences of Mary Heaton Vorse.* New York: Farrar & Rinehart, 1935.

Walling, Anna Strunsky. "David Graham Phillips, the Last Years of His Life." *Saturday Evening Post* 184 (Oct. 21, 1911): 19–20.

Walling, Anna Strunsky, et al. *William English Walling: A Symposium.* New York: Stackpole Sons, 1938.

Walsh, George. *Gentleman Jimmy Walker.* New York: Praeger, 1974.

Ware, Caroline F. *Greenwich Village, 1920–1930: A Comment on American Civilization in the Post-War Years.* Boston: Houghton Mifflin, 1935.

Waterman, Willoughby. *Prostitution and Its Repression in New York City, 1900–1931.* New York: Columbia University Press, 1932.

Watson, Steven. *Strange Bedfellows: The First American Avant-Garde.* New York: Abbeville Press, 1992.

Wertheim, Arthur Frank. *The New York Little Renaissance, 1908–1917.* New York: New York University Press, 1976.

Wesser, Robert F. *A Response to Progressivism: The Democratic Party and New York Politics, 1902–1918.* New York: New York University Press, 1986.

Whitman, Stephen. *Predestined: A Novel of New York Life.* 1910. Reprint, with an afterward by Alden Whitman, Carbondale: Southern Illinois University Press, 1974.

Winter, Ella, and Granville Hicks, eds. *The Letters of Lincoln Steffens.* 2 vols. New York: Harcourt, Brace, 1938.

Wittenstein, Kate E. "The Heterodoxy Club and American Feminism, 1912–1930." Ph.D. diss., Boston University, 1989.

Woods, Robert A., and Albert J. Kennedy, eds. *Handbook of Settlements.* New York: Russell Sage Foundation, 1911.

Zurier, Rebecca. *Art for "The Masses": A Radical Magazine and Its Graphics, 1911–1917.* Philadelphia: Temple University Press, 1988.

Zurier, Rebecca, Robert W. Snyder, and Virginia M. Mecklenburg, *Metropolitan Lives.* New York: W. W. Norton, 1995.

INDEX

References to streets are for New York City, not Greenwich Village only. All streets are in alphabetical, not numerical, order. Numerals in *italics* indicate illustrations; (map)s and (photo)s are identified as such.

GERALD W. McFARLAND received his B.A. from the University of California, Berkeley, and his M.A. and Ph.D. from Columbia University. He has taught at the University of Massachusetts Amherst, where he is Professor of History, since 1964. He is the author of three previous books: *Mugwumps, Morals, and Politics, 1884–1920* (1975); *A Scattered People: An American Family Moves West* (1985); and *The "Counterfeit" Man: The True Story of the Boorn-Colvin Murder Case* (1991).